The Chauffeur

From Federal Prison To Celebrity Chauffeur

A True-Life Tale About Second Chances
By Raymond Torres

Book design by Raymond Torres

Editing by David McKee

Cover photos by Sharry Flaherty

This book is dedicated to my mom Oralia, my sister Debrah, my brother Marcus, my good friend Alex Cardenas -- who has been like a brother to me -- and to my adult children Ray Junior, Alexis, and Serina. It is also dedicated to those who have passed on, such as my father Robert "Beto" Torres, my beloved Antoinette Woods, my friends Scott Potter and Juan "Gonzo" Gonzalez. I hope to see you all in Heaven someday.

1 Timothy 6: 9-10 NLT

"But people who long to be rich fall into temptation and are trapped by many foolish and harmful desires that plunge them into ruin and destruction. For the love of money is the root of all kinds of evil. And some people, craving money, have wandered from the true faith and pierced themselves with many sorrows."

Man is given only one life, live it wisely.

Contents

Preface

I don't believe people are born criminals, gangsters, drug traffickers, or killers. I believe it all starts off at home with parental and environmental influences that later develop into choices one makes in life and which eventually mold a person into who he or she becomes. Everyone has a choice in life to do what is right or wrong and the direction a person chooses has either consequences or rewards. I hope this book will be a deterrent to those who are living a criminal lifestyle. I pray that those who read this book will be encouraged to live a crime-free life of honesty, integrity and purpose.

CHAPTER 1 Troubled Youth

I was born Sept. 22, 1968, at General Hospital in Los Angeles, California, to Robert Beto Torres, a man of Mexican and Portuguese descent who was employed as a roofer, and to Oralia Petra Marquez, of Spanish, Mexican, German and French descent. My mother worked various jobs as a waitress and as a caretaker at a convalescent home. She eventually became my father's secretary, helping him run a small roofing company.

One of my earliest memories as a child was when I was four years old; my sister Debrah and I, who was 11 months older than me, were sitting in an inflatable boat in an apartment swimming pool where we lived. I was rocking the boat back and forth when I fell over into the water. As I descended to the bottom of the pool, I remember looking up at the clear, blue sky. Everything seemed to be peaceful and moving in slow motion; for some reason I wasn't afraid. Suddenly I saw a man dash down a flight of stairs from the second balcony of the apartment complex, and, like an angel sent from above, he dove into the pool, snatching me from the jaws of death. The man was Dale Thomson, our next-door neighbor, who carried me out of the water. I wondered why God spared me. Maybe he had different plans for my life.

The memories of my grandmother Marquez were of a loving woman. She had big, blue eyes and was light in skin color. Grandma Marquez would feed my sister and me blue Cream-O-Wheat. She would tell us if we ate the Cream-O-Wheat our eyes would turn blue like hers. Grandma would often have my sister and I kneel at her bedside to pray to a collage of images of Jesus and Catholic saints. It seemed as if we prayed with Grandma for hours at a time.

As the years went by, my family moved from place to place. I went to more schools than I can remember: Cyril Wengert in Las Vegas,

Cabrillo Elementary in San Pedro, California, and Roosevelt Elementary in Lawndale. Growing up as a youth my family didn't have much money. I remember eating cereal with water because we had no milk. Another time my sister and I were eating sugar cubes and we spilled sugar all over the kitchen floor. The sugar attracted ants, who got into the box of Raisin Bran. My sister and I were hungry, so my Mom held the box of cereal over the stove and she turned on the burner, thinking the heat would draw the ants out of the box. After a few minutes Mom told us that the ants were gone, so we would eat the Raisin Bran. I refused to eat the cereal when I saw the little burnt balls of what used to be ants.

At about age six, I was skating in the back yard at my Aunt Virginia and Uncle Joe's house in Compton. I went to walk up the small steps to enter the back door of the house when I rolled forward and cracked my head on the pavement. It left a knot on the left side of my forehead. I went into the house crying so hard that I could hardly breathe. My mom took a look at my head and she told me that I would be all right. My parents never took me to the hospital. I'm sure it was because they didn't have the money to pay the medical bill.

There were many disappointments, especially when it came to my father. I don't recall my mother or my father ever using the word "love" when I was growing up. I never received a heartfelt hug from my father or words of encouragement. When my parents were together there were no set meal times and very few family gatherings. My father and my mother argued regularly, sometimes about my father's plate of food being too cold or about misspelled words in the roofing contracts that my mother would type. My parents never offered to help with schoolwork, perhaps because they were high school dropouts themselves. My parents never explained to me why I couldn't go places with friends. Most of the time the answer was simply "No."

I'M WATCHING YOU, POPS

As I got older, I would go to work with my father. After work my father -- on a few occasions -- would visit the home of a woman while I waited in the truck or at a burger stand up the street. I never mentioned it to my mom. Every so often, my father would visit his sister Doreen in El Monte, California. Once, I told my father that I wanted a bike just like the one that was lying in Doreen's neighbor's front lawn. My father had been drinking, so later that night he picked up the bike and placed it in the bed of his truck. My heart sank when he did that. My mother yelled at my father, telling him to put the bike back and he did. "Sorry, son," were his words. He wasn't sorry for stealing the bike but because mom didn't let him take it.

During a time when my parents were separated, my sister and I lived with our mother and our baby-sitter, Gloria. My mother was dating Manuel, who resembled Erik Estrada from the TV series *CHiPs*. Many people said that my father also resembled Estrada. I never had an issue with Manuel until the day I wanted to go to the store with my mother. I was no older than seven at the time. Manuel wouldn't let me go with her, so when I ran after my mother, he snatched me by my shirt and flung me across the room. I hit a wall so hard that it knocked the wind out of me.

There were some good times. My father would take our family to Shakey's Pizza Parlor or we would visit my paternal grandmother in El Monte. I enjoyed spending time with my cousins but it wasn't often enough. When my father finished a roofing job and had been drinking, he would hand out money to us kids. But my mother would get upset and take the money back. Occasionally my father took me to work out with him at the Sea Side Boxing Gym in Long Beach, California. My father was a huge boxing fan. I was told that he once sparred with professional boxer Alexis Argüello. I also heard that Argüello busted up Pop's ribs real good.

By age 11, my family settled down in Gardena, California. At the time, I was influenced by gangs; my cousin Joey Lauro was from a gang in Compton and my cousin Larry Cruz was rolling with La Ramba in San Pedro. My father had been a member of the El Monte Flores gang in his younger days.

A friend of mine hooked me up with a weekend job with one of the vendors at the Roadium Swap on West Redondo Beach Boulevard, in

Torrance. With the money I earned, I was able to buy clothes. Though my mother was against the clothes I wore, I continued buying them anyway. At school, I got along with most kids except for one or two bullies. A bully named Eric Garner pushed me for no reason. I wanted to punch him in the face, but I didn't because I was intimidated by his size. Eric was older and had a reputation for beating up other kids.

My friend Steve McCormack found out about what happened and was angered. He met me after school and made me go with him to look for Eric. When we found him, Steve said it was my turn to give Eric a whipping. Steve, who was much bigger, warned Eric if he swung back he would get a beating. Steve ordered me to hit Eric. If I didn't, Steve would have laid hands on me for not doing as he said, so I hit Eric in the stomach. Eric grunted and folded over. Steve ordered me to hit him again, this time harder and in the face. I felt bad hitting Eric, especially in the face. I just stood there looking at Steve. I knew he had a heavy hand just from playing around with him, so I did what I had to do. I let loose five times, hitting Eric in the face, the body and back to the face. Eric folded to the ground in a fetal position. Steve stood over Eric and warned him, "You better think about who you're messing with before you decided to bully someone." After that day Eric never bothered me again.

My first experience with drugs was when I found a large, clear, plastic bag that belonged to my mother and father. The bag contained rolling papers and six smaller, rolled-up sandwich bags stuffed with weed. I took some of the weed from the bags and rolled three joints with a rolling machine that I also found in their stash. It took me a few tries to get the hang of it. I took the joints to school and shared them with friends. When I inhaled my toke, I nearly coughed my lungs out. After the high kicked in, my eyes felt heavy and my body movements seemed sluggish.

During my days at Roosevelt Elementary, my grades were bad. For some reason I just couldn't stay focused in school. I remember being in a special education class with this kid named LaMotte Hayes. He and I had to listen to cassette tapes for our school work, but LaMotte would bring his tape of Le Chic and we would listen to the song "Freak Out" over our headphones.

My last day at Roosevelt was when I got into it with this black kid. He came at me crazily and I pulled out a large pair of toenail clippers that came with a small knife. I chased him down the hall, but he was just a few steps quicker than I. Somehow the school principal found out about the incident and my mother was called. As it turned out, I was going to the wrong school. Where I lived was in the zone of Mark Twain Elementary. The principal from Roosevelt told my mom that I had to register there. He also told her about the knife incident. When she confronted me about it, I denied the whole thing.

Mark Twain was a culture shock for me. It was more of a school for white surfer types. Roosevelt had a few whites but it was made up of mostly Mexicans or Latinos and African-Americans, with some Asians. I knew I didn't fit in at Mark Twain. During one of my first days at the new school, a white girl came up to me and she asked if I was a "spic." Others would walk past me and make comments like "Wetback."

The funny thing was that I didn't speak much Spanish. I was a third-generation Latino; the only time my parents spoke Spanish was when they didn't want us kids to know what they were talking about. There were Latinos who went to Mark Twain, but they were what I called "Coconuts": brown on the outside but white inside. None of the guys called me names --- it was the girls and I didn't want to hit a girl.

One summer, my sister talked me into letting her pick out my clothes. She brought Levi's, Vans tennis shoes, Tiger shirts and Ocean Pacific-style clothing. I had no choice but to wear them. I was tired of people making fun of my *cholo* [lower-class] clothes.

When I returned to school, girls noticed my new style. They were the same girls who had called me names. Now they complimented me on how much better I looked; I liked the attention. One of my new friends was Ronnie Johnson. He asked me if I knew how to play baseball. I told him that I played a little, but in reality I wasn't good at it. I signed

6

up anyway and, when we played, Ronnie found out that I wasn't good at all. I wanted my father to show me how to play the sport but he was too busy working. I was disappointed that my parents didn't show up at the games to support me. I always hoped that my father or family would show to watch me play baseball, but if they saw my performance they might have been disappointed. Our team, the Red Sox, ended up winning the nationals but it wasn't from any of my efforts.

GETTING HIGHER

The first time I smoked hash was during a school play at Mark Twain Elementary. My job was to control the stage lights. There was a 20-minute intermission. A surfer named Ricky Stevens and I had become friends. Ricky and I went to the playground and sat by the swings. Ricky pulled out a wooden pipe and some tinfoil that contained hash. He packed the pipe with the brown dope, then he lit the pipe and took a hit. Ricky passed the pipe to me. I felt super high after the first hit, 10 times higher than I was when I first smoked weed. I couldn't stop smiling and laughing. Ricky and I went back to the school auditorium. One of the teachers took a look at me and asked me if I was OK. I kept laughing, so the teacher sent me outside to get some fresh air. She must have known I was high but never said anything to me about it.

During the summer my hobby was raising show pigeons. My cousins Larry and Joey also raised birds. I think that's where I got my passion for the animals. I had rollers, fantails, top notches, feather foots, homing birds, king pigeons and suicide birds. They were named "suicide birds" because they would fly high in the sky and tumble until they hit a car, rooftop or the street.

I continued to work with my father at his roofing company. After work, my father and his crew hung out in the front yard of our house on Compton Boulevard. They would drink beer and eat chicharonez with Tabasco and lemon juice while listening to Art Laboe oldies over a radio. My father would have me fetch everyone beers from the fridge. I wanted to know what beer tasted like, so I took one of the Coors cans and I went outside to my pigeon coop. I popped open the can and I took a swig. I quickly spat out the beer. I thought it had the most disgusting taste. I didn't understand how someone could drink that stuff.

The summer before I was to start junior high school, I got into physical fitness. At home, our garage was made into a gym; we had weights, a boxing ring, a speed bag, a heavy bag, a timing bag and mirrors. Whenever I was mad at my parents for not letting me go somewhere, I would take it out on the heavy bag. There were times when my father arranged for me to fight bigger kids in the neighborhood; we would put the gloves on and go toe-to-toe in the boxing ring. Sometimes my father and I would spar with each other. Those were some of the good times that I spent with my father.

While attending Rogers Junior High School, I became popular with the girls. I was still a little shy but I was making friends. One of my electives was drama. I wanted to work in the movie industry, so I decided to take up acting. There was a girl in my class named Tammy Morrison; she was popular amongst the other students. I found out that Tammy signed up for the same drama class I was in because she had a crush on me. Later in the school year, students were campaigning for their favorite candidates as prince and princess for the seventh graders' school dance. When the dance came around I learned that Tammy and I were nominated for prince and princess. Tammy must have put in a lot of effort to make sure that we were crowned prince and princess, because when the names of the winners were announced, ours were called. We slow-danced together and it was one of the best times I had at school. Tammy and I became good friends.

A kid named Hector Munoz lived a few houses away from mine and his dad grew weed plants in the backyard of their home. Months later, the plants were like mini trees. One night, I decided to climb onto a wall that surrounded the property. The plants were within reach of the wall, so I cut about two feet off the top of one. I stuffed it into a grocery bag and stashed the weed in my pigeon coop.

My father's work crew was made up of Mexican immigrants and South Side homies fresh out of prison. Jesse Sanchez was one of my father's workers from Lomita. He had a scar just like Tony Montana from *Scarface*. I pulled Jesse aside and asked him to follow me to my pigeon coop. When we arrived, I showed him the bag of weed. Then I asked Jesse how much he would give me for it. Jesse offered me $30 and I took it. It was my first taste of fast money.

DEVASTATED

I came home from school one day to find my mother and my father in a heated argument. It was about my father's cheating. My mother yelled, "Tell them! Why don't you tell them?" They had argued in the past but this was different. My mother shouted that she and my father had never married, and that she was moving out. I felt as if my heart was ripped out of my chest. My mother got her own apartment; she later met a man named Javier Banuelos and moved in with him. My sister and I moved in with Javier, too. He treated us well but he wanted me to wear dress shoes and slacks. My mother and I would argue about it sometimes and most of the time I got my way.

Javier was a repairman for an apartment complex in downtown Los Angeles; he would take me to work with him so I could earn money. Javier had hired a black man off the streets as a laborer. After a day's work, the man wanted to get paid but Javier was taking his time. The black man pulled a knife out and put it to Javier's throat, demanding his money. I stood watching as he told Javier that his child needed milk and diapers. Javier paid him on the spot.

I don't know what else Javier was involved in, but while staying at his house, my sister, my cousin Gina Lauro and I were in the den, sitting on a couch near a window when a vehicle drove through an alley and someone fired bullets into the house. Gina and I were sitting next to each other. When a bullet went through the window I was looking at Gina. The bullet came so close to hitting her that I literally saw the hair on the top of her head move. After the incident, my mother made me and my sister stay at my father's house. Soon after, my mother left Javier and ended up moving back in with my father. Days later, a drunken Javier drove his truck onto the front lawn of my father's house with the stereo blasting. About an hour later, he drove off. After that incident, my father bought a handgun. He hid the gun in a floor panel in the hallway directly outside of my bedroom. I knew that Javier loved my mother but my mother was still in love with my father. I was happy that she was back at home.

Our family was back to normal … as normal as a dysfunctional family could be. When my parents told my sister and I that we were moving to Las Vegas again, my life went into a tailspin. I had made new friends in school but now I had to leave them all behind. I hated my parents for the life they gave me. I felt they didn't understand me. There was no sense of love coming from them. There was no one I could talk to when I went through the problems that any kid went through. I felt alone most of my adolescent years and that my birth was regarded as a mistake by my parents.

There were times when I would sit in my room furious and in tears. I would question God to why he allowed me to be born. I questioned why he would give me such unloving parents. I had a lot of hate toward my father, who was very demanding. I was so tired of being provoked and yelled at, I wanted to end my life; I took my father's gun and sat in the hallway closet of our home. I was alone. I remember putting the gun to my head and tightening my finger on the trigger. As I did, a clear voice inside of me told me, "Stop." I dropped the gun and just sat there, alone and sobbing.

LAS VEGAS, 1983

I was 15 years old in 1983, when we arrived in Las Vegas. The new house was well-kept and the neighborhood was quiet but I didn't want to be there. My parents were gone most of the time and I wanted to get back to California. I decided to find a way. I left the house and walked for miles until I reached a highway. Once on the highway, I hitchhiked toward California. I didn't get far before a highway patrol car stopped me. The officer got out of the vehicle and he asked me where I was going. When I told him California, he placed handcuffs on me, then he put me in the front seat of the patrol car and drove me to juvenile hall. My mother was in tears when she and Debrah came to get me from jail.

Someone at the police department suggested to my mother that we attend family counseling. Of course my father didn't take part. At one of the sessions, a female counselor asked me how I was feeling. She asked me to express my feelings by drawing a picture. I don't remember what I drew but I was very angry. It had continued to build up inside of me. I was bothered that my father never attended any of the sessions nor did he ever mention anything about me attempting to hitchhike to Los Angeles.

There were times when I would visit our next-door neighbor, Mr. Bill Edward, a retired airman. Bill would mow his front lawn every weekend. He was a kind and friendly man who always greeted me when he saw me. Bill seemed to have the perfect life: a beautiful home, nice car and a beautiful wife. He would invite me over for iced tea and we would talk for hours. I shared with him my feelings toward my parents. The most memorable words that he said to me were, "Ray, you are going to be successful in life. I know this because you have a gift. You communicate well with people and you have a likable personality, and that's going to open doors for you."

MY FIRST STRIP CLUB

When summertime came around, I worked with my father at his roofing company. After work, my father and his work crew would usually stop at a bar for drinks. Sometimes I would have to wait in the truck because I was underage. Most times I would fall asleep waiting for my father. On one occasion, my father took me and his crew to a place called the Crazy Horse. It was a topless bar on Paradise Road, just off the Las Vegas Strip. The Crazy Horse was a 21-and-older strip club. I was 16 years old at the time. When my father's truck pulled into the Crazy Horse parking lot, Pops gave me his hat and sunglasses, and my cousin Larry gave me his driver's license in case I was carded at the door. Cousin Larry looked nothing like me; he had light brown hair and green eyes.

My father took a piece of tar oil from the roofing kettle that was hitched to his truck and, with one of his fingers, he brushed it onto my mustache to make it look thicker. My father told me that he and the workers were going into the club first. I was instructed to wait 10 minutes, then go inside.

When I arrived at the door there was a huge bouncer. He asked me for identification. I pulled out my wallet and handed him the driver's license. The bouncer grinned as if knowing that it wasn't me in the photo, but he let me into the club anyway. My father seemed surprised to see me. Maybe he figured they wouldn't let me in. I sat at the bar and he ordered me a beer. He then instructed me to tell the dancers that it was my birthday, so I went along with it.

My father whispered something to one of the strippers. The next thing I knew, the Latina dancer approached me, saying, "Hello, birthday boy." She went on to do a dance routine before me and, when the music stopped, the dancer gave me a kiss on my cheek, wishing me a happy birthday. I handed the dancer a fistful of dollar bills that my father had given me for tip money. The stripper then moved on to the next guy. After a few drinks, I was feeling buzzed from the alcohol. I stepped off the stool to go use the restroom. When I started to walk my balance was off. I felt like I was walking on a slanted hill. My father must have seen this, because when I returned to the stool he told me to slow down on the drinking. The next day I woke up with my first hangover.

PETTY THEFT

During the summertime, when my father traveled to Los Angeles to work, I usually went with him. We stayed at my Aunt Rachel Cruz's house in San Pedro; she was my father's sister; my cousins Larry, Regina and Rene lived there also. The last trip my father and I made to Vegas was to pick up my mother, my sister Debrah, my newborn brother Marcus and my dog Lobo for our move back to L.A.

When we arrived in Los Angeles, we stayed at a motel in Gardena until we found a house. During the day I went to work with my father. He often gave me money so I could buy lunch for the work crew at a local fast food spot. On this particular day, my father sent me on a food run to Jack in the Box. When I arrived, I noticed there was a

Gemco store across the street. I was a big *Star Wars* fan and I knew that Gemco sold *Star Wars* action figures. I put off buying lunch and I decided to walk to Gemco.

When I entered the store, I strolled down aisles looking at all the *Star Wars* action figures. I opened the packages of six action figures that I did not have in my collection and I hid the empty wrappers behind other toys. I then stuffed the action figures into my pants pockets. When I attempted to exit the store an undercover security guard stopped me and led me by my arm to a back room. The security officer instructed me to empty my pockets. I was forced to remove the six action figures. I had money with me, so I offered to pay for the goods.

The security guard ignored my request and asked me where my parents were. I told the officer that my parents and I were staying at a motel in Gardena and didn't have a phone. I said my father was on a job site. The security guard looked frustrated. He then walked me out of the store and told me not to come back. I couldn't believe he was letting me go. I went straight to Jack in the Box, then returned to the job as if nothing had happened.

My family and I ended up moving to San Pedro. Our house was on 1st Street and Bandini Street, near a Mexican fast-food place called the Enchilada House. The new school year was about to begin in a few weeks. I don't recall why my parents didn't buy me school clothes but it was embarrassing to have to go to school, especially with the clothes that I wore the year before. One of my shoes had a hole near my big toe -- and it was the only pair of shoes I owned.

A friend of mine named Frankie Montoya schooled me on how he got his shoes from Payless for free, so I tried it. I walked into Payless store on Gaffey Street acting like I was looking around for shoes to buy. I found the shoes and the size that I needed; they were black corduroy slip-ons known as Coasters. I took off one of my old shoes and I traded it with one of the new ones.

When I was about to trade the second shoe, I noticed a woman who worked at the store looking at me suspiciously. I thought she saw me so I headed toward the exit door. The woman' stopped me and asked to see the bottom of my shoes. I showed her the bottom of the old one. She then asked to see the other shoe. I lifted the bottom of the second shoe as if to show her, then I dashed out the door. I ran as fast and as far as I could. I was scared but I happened to make it home without getting caught. When it was all over I was happy that I got away and that I didn't have to wear shoes with holes to school. I had dodged another bullet.

BAD ATTITUDE

When I attended Dana Junior High School, I had a bad attitude. During the first month, I badmouthed Ricky Rivas, who played football for Dana. Ricky gave me a look that I didn't like and I asked him what he was looking at. It was between classes and the bell had rung, so a staff member told students to get to class. I later got word that Ricky and his boys were looking for me. The next time I ran into Ricky was while I was walking down Western Avenue near Peck Park. I noticed three guys in football uniforms running toward me from a grass field.

When one of the football players took off his helmet, I realized it was Ricky. Three football players were coming at me. There was a slight chance that I might be able to take down one but I was sure I would receive a beating by the other two. Suddenly, I heard a man yelling from the field, telling Ricky and the other football players to get back to practice. That someone was their football coach. He pulled Ricky and the other players away and probably saved me a beating.

I later got transferred from Dana Junior High to Dodson Junior High because (again) my address was part of Dodson's school zone. I attended, but I was only going through the motions. My mind wasn't in it. I didn't attend the graduation ceremony at the end of the year because my grades and my attendance did not meet graduation requirements; I was surprised that I actually passed to the next grade.

Having graduated from Dodson in spite of myself, I moved on to San Pedro High. My father would drop me off in front of the school in his old work truck, filled with roofing materials and a smoking tar kettle in tow. It seemed as if my father was trying to embarrass me on purpose -- but that was the least of my worries. Not only had the black cloud of enemies followed me from my past, I had created new ones. I crossed out the name Pete Santos that was written on a girl's Pee Chee folder. I did not like Pete for some reason; maybe it was because he had beef with a guy that I hung out with. What I didn't realize was that when I crossed out Pete's name I also crossed out the gang that he ran with. Now Pete and his gang wanted to get at me.

At the end of a school day I was walking toward one of the exits when I noticed a big crowd standing in front of the building. I heard people commenting that there was going to be a fight. Unbeknownst to me, I was the one who would be fighting. It was to be a one-on-one fight with me and Willie, one of Pete's homeboys. Willie and I met down the street from the school. We squared off toe-to-toe and I got the best of him, putting Willie on his back. Willie and his boys got mad and planned to rush me. The person who saved me was a guy named Rudy Torres. Rudy went to the same school as I did. We were not related but we had the same last name. Rudy was a big, stocky guy who stopped Pete and his boys from jumping me.

TRUANCY

When I returned to San Pedro High, I learned that Pete had Samoan friends waiting for me after school. I decided not to attend any longer. On a school day, I took a bus to visit a girl named Lydia Morales who lived in Gardena. On the way home, I was waiting at a bus stop and who do you think pulled up in front of me in his work truck? Yep, it was my father. He stopped at a red light right in front of me. When my father saw me standing at the bus stop, he yelled at me to get in the truck. I was expecting a beating but nothing came of it. All he said was, "If you're not going to school then you're going to work." So I went back to work with my father; it didn't take long for us to get into it with each other, so I quit. Like two elks, my father and I were always butting horns.

My father kicked me out of the house again. It happened to be raining. I had nowhere to go, so I slept in the doghouse that was in our back yard. Lobo didn't seem to mind. He was happy to be cuddled next to me. There were other times when I had to sleep in cars. Those were some of the coldest nights, especially living near the coast. Sometimes I would go to sleep hungry. I hated my father with a passion. It seemed as if he was intentionally provoking me.

My family received a notice saying that the home we were renting on Bandini Street was being sold. My parents and I, along with Debrah and Marcus moved to a house near the beach, on Meyler near Paseo Del Mar. I enrolled in Angel's Gate Continuation School. Getting an education was not appealing to me, so instead of going to school I decided to go for a joyride when my parents were out of town. I took the keys to my father's 1968 Ford Ranchero and drove to Angel's Gate to see a girl named Lisa Hernandez. Just my luck, the school dean was standing in front of the school when I drove past. He spotted me right away, for he knew me very well. When the dean called me over, I pressed the gas pedal and sped out of there. My parents later got a call from the dean telling them what took place. I denied the whole thing but I was still suspended for a few days.

There were times my sister and I were hungry, so we would take money from my father's safe. Most of the time he wouldn't lock it and, if he did, Debrah always found a way to open it. My father was tired of us taking money, so he no longer let us in the house. There was a guest house in the back yard that was separated from the main house. That's where we slept. It had no shower or restroom. If I wanted to shower in the morning, I had to use the water hose. When my parents left the house, Debrah and I would break in through one of the windows, and would take food from the refrigerator or look for money so we could buy something at the local mini-market.

I ended up getting kicked out of school for missing too many days. I knew I had to get a job, so while I was with my family I applied to Chuck E. Cheese Pizza, in Torrance. To my surprise I was hired a week later. One of the RTD bus drivers would see me regularly and we would talk during the bus ride to work. He gave me advice about my father -- that was until he found out that I would tear a dollar in half, roll it up and put one half of the bill in the fare box on the way to work and then I would put the other half of the dollar in the box on the ride home.

During one of the last times I worked at Chuck E. Cheese, I was asked to work overtime late into the night. By the end of my shift, the buses had stopped running. I had to walk home, which was about a half-hour drive away. On my way home, I walked through Torrance on a residential street that was a known gang neighborhood. I ran into a group of gang members who were standing at a corner bumping music and drinking beer. I made sure that they didn't see me, because if they did, chances were that I would be in trouble.

Once I was out of their neighborhood, I felt somewhat at ease. It seemed as if I walked for hours; my feet hurt, not to mention I was already tired from working overtime. I searched for something to steal: a bike, a skateboard, skates, anything that would get me home sooner. I was about a 20-minute walk from my house when I spotted a moped parked in an alley. I hopped on it and pedaled it down the street. When I was far enough from where I had stolen it, I hotwired the ignition. I then drove off, but for some reason I decided to make a U-turn away from my house so I could stop by to see my friends Brian and Ben Maldonado, the twin brothers that lived behind my old house on 1st Street.

I picked up Ben and we went for a joyride. I drove down a residential street near the area where I had stolen the moped. Suddenly a car followed close behind us; the passenger yelled for me to pull over. It was the owner of the moped. I told Ben that we would jump off the moped and run when we got near San Pedro High School. As we approached the school, I slowed down and told Ben to jump. A moment later I leaped off, too. I then dashed down the street but when I looked back, I saw Ben on the ground next to the moped.

Two white guys rushed out of the car that was following us; both were bigger than Ben and I. One tackled Ben and the other chased me. I had a lead on him, so I cut a corner and then jumped into a bush to hide. The big guy ran past me. I sat in the bush, trying to control my breathing so the guy wouldn't hear me. Suddenly, I heard someone walking toward me; whoever it was, he was winded because I could hear his heavy breathing. After a few moments the sound faded. I waited for what seemed like an hour and when I felt it was safe I poked my head out of the bush.

There was no sign of the big guy, so I decided to dash for it; when I arrived home I went into the garage, where I slept at the time and laid down on a patio lounge chair that I used for a bed. I was hoping that everything that happened that night was a dream, and that I would wake up the next morning and all would be normal.

I had finally dozed off to sleep when I was awakened to the sound of a loud crash against the garage door. It sounded as if someone threw a rock at it. My mother's voice followed. "Ray! Get your butt up! Your friend Ben ratted you out! Your dad is going to take you to the police department." I was certain that I was going to get a whipping from my father. I got into his truck expecting, something to come my way, but my father didn't say a word. He just drove until we arrived at the Harbor Division police station.

When I walked into the police station, the owner of the moped and his big friend were sitting in the lobby. My father and I approached an officer at the front desk; I explained why I was there. The officer told me to wait and a few minutes later a Latino man arrived, introducing himself as Detective Gomez. The detective escorted me into a hallway; as I walked past a holding tank I saw Ben. He looked directly at me then he put his head down in shame.

Detective Gomez and I entered an interrogation room and sat. Gomez then asked me why I took the moped. I told the officer the truth: I was tired from walking a long way from work and wanted to get home. He then asked me how I learned how to hot-wire the bike. I answered I didn't know how to hot-wire. I had messed around with installing car stereos in the past, so I knew that the red wire was positive and the black wire was negative. I also knew that I had to bypass the ignition by disconnecting the red wire and connecting it to the red starter wire. After questioning me, Gomez brought me before the owner of the moped to ask if he wanted to press charges. He said, "No." I thanked the guy and was released to my father. Ben was also let go. On the way home, my father didn't say a word nor did he bring up the incident any time afterward.

Debrah and my parents had their differences, so she ended up leaving home. And I was eventually kicked out of the house again. I didn't have any place to go, so Brian and Ben's sister Dee allowed me to stay at her apartment under the condition that I got a job. I was no longer working at Chuck E. Cheese; I had been fired for missing too many days. I did manage to land a job at Taco Bell, near the Tasman Sea Hotel where my sister worked as a receptionist. It was a one-bedroom apartment with Brian, Dee, her three kids and me living there at once. I slept on the floor but it was better than sleeping out in the cold. After work I stopped by to visit my sister; she told me that my parents dropped off all my belongings in front of one of the hotel rooms. She added that my parents were moving to Las Vegas without me. I felt abandoned. I was 16 years old and crushed to my core knowing that my parents would leave me on the streets with no place to go.

I ran the streets at night with my friend Frankie Montoya. The night I will never forget was when we were walking down Gaffey Boulevard, getting ready to cross the street and saw a car approaching. I wanted to cross the street before the car passed me so I ran before it and, as I looked at the vehicle, I saw my mother, my father and Marcus. My mother looked directly at me. I stopped to stare at the tan Cadillac, thinking they were going to pull over, but they kept driving down the boulevard. My own flesh and blood didn't bother to come back for me. I didn't understand how my parents could be so heartless. It felt as if a knife was pushed through my heart. I began to walk through life angry at the world. I picked fights if someone looked at me the wrong way.

I was becoming a heartless monster. Ben, Brian and I walked by a house where a kid my age was standing out front. The kid was cool enough to offer to smoke a joint with us but instead of taking the kid up on it, I cracked him in the face and took the joint for no reason.

A few weeks, later my cousin Gina Lauro came by Dee's apartment while I was there. Gina told me that my mother was trying to contact me and that my parents wanted me to go to Las Vegas. At first I didn't want to go; I didn't want anything to do with my parents but a part of me wanted to be with family. I also knew that Dee was probably getting tired of me living in the cramped, one-bedroom apartment.

LAS VEGAS-BOUND

I decided to call my mom. She told me that my father wanted me to work on some roofing jobs in Las Vegas. She added that my father wanted to know if Brian and Ben would come along, because work was busy in Vegas. Brian and I took a Greyhound to Las Vegas. When we arrived, we stayed at my parents' home. But after a few weeks, Brian's mother called and said she wanted him back home, so he returned to California.

My plan was to work with my father and save money so I could buy a truck while I studied to get my driver's license. I calculated how much money I would need to buy the vehicle. When I was paid it wasn't as much as I expected. My father deducted money for food, rent and washing my clothes. I was angry that he would do such a thing but I couldn't do anything about it. I held my tongue and continued to work. While on a job site with my father we got into it again. He made me walk home in the hot, summer heat. I walked for hours; when I was a few blocks away from the house my father drove by in his truck, wearing a big grin as if to taunt me.

It seemed as if my father was always trying to test me, to see if I would snap. I eventually got tired of the way he treated me so I quit working for him. I wanted to get away from him badly but had no place to go.

I looked into joining the Army but I didn't have a high school diploma. I then went looking for a job at the Culinary Union. The union was like a temp agency. After I obtained my health card and my sheriff's card, the union sent me to the Castaways casino, where I worked for a few days. Then I received a permanent job at Circus Circus buffet as a busboy. I ended up getting fired from the Circus Circus for showing up late too many times. I then landed another job at the Las Vegas Hilton as a room service busboy.

On my days off, I would hang out at Circus Circus, visiting the gift shop near the west entrance of the hotel. The shop carried a variety of *Star Wars* masks, magic tricks, pranks and photos. The photos were of movie stars such as Humphrey Bogart, James Cagney and Edward G. Robinson. I later found out that mobster Anthony Spilotro owned the gift shop. Anthony "The Ant" Spilotro was an enforcer for the Chicago mob in Las Vegas during the Seventies and Eighties.

I was fascinated by gangsters. I would see men who I thought were mobsters walking through the casinos wearing pressed suits, gold watches and flashing rolls of cash; I was attracted to the lifestyle. Las Vegas was a town built by Mafiosos like Bugsy Siegel and Meyer Lansky. I would walk down the Strip, amazed at the bright lights, the hotels and the casinos. I told myself that I would own a casino someday.

At home in the real world I had chores. My brother Rob was staying with us. My father told me to clean the front yard. I did as he said and when I was done my father instructed me to clean his roofing kettle. It didn't make sense to me to clean a kettle. It had some tar splatter but was clean compared to other kettles that I saw. I'm sure I said something slick to my father because he made me clean the yard a second time. I gave him a dirty look. His next words were, "Do you think you can whip me? You couldn't whip me if I had no arms and no legs." My father gave me the meanest stare and said, "Go ahead, I'll let you take the first swing!"

My body moved toward him as if it had a mind of its own. I wanted to crack him in the mouth for all the pain he caused in my life. Rob must have sensed it, because he stepped in front of me and told me to cool it. I knew my father could have easily whipped me. He had grown up in the streets of El Monte and sparred in some of the roughest boxing gyms in Los Angeles but I was to the point that I just didn't care. My brother pulled me away but my dad kept talking, "I made you, I brought you into this world and I have a .38 Special that says I can take you out." Those words echoed through my mind for many years to come.

INFLUENCES

I first met Antonio Marcos at Circus Circus; Marcos lived in Vegas but he was from Wilmington, California. When I met Antonio's mom, Charlotte Marcos, I thought she was such a loving woman. Anybody would want to have her as a mother. Charlotte allowed me to stay at her house anytime I wanted. She also treated me as if I were her own son. Antonio had a dark side; he introduced me to *primos* (a weed-and-cocaine cigarette). Antonio was also known for smoking crack and hanging out with hookers. On one occasion, Antonio invited me to a brothel in Pahrump called The Chicken Ranch. The place was about an hour-and-a-half drive west of Las Vegas, down a long dirt road called Homestead.

The Chevy Suburban we drove pulled into the parking lot of the Chicken Ranch; the brothel was constructed of trailers that were connected in a maze. Antonio and I approached a fence where he pressed a buzzer; a moment later, a security gate popped open and we entered the property. We continued up a ramp to a second door, where we were buzzed in again. The interior of the brothel was reminiscent of the 1920s, with red silk wallpaper, old-style furniture and a plush bar. Antonio and I sat in a lounge area where menus were displayed on a table. An elderly Madam checked our IDs to verify that we were 18 years of age.

About 15 minutes later, six women filed into the room, all dressed in seductive lingerie. Antonio and I were given a choice of who we wanted to spend the evening with. After a moment, I chose Felicia, who looked to be of Italian-American descent. Felicia walked me to a hallway that led into a bedroom, so we could discuss the price. I told Felicia that Antonio was paying the bill. Felicia left the room to collect the money from Antonio and when she returned instructed me to strip down while she slipped on a pair of latex gloves. When I got down to my birthday suit, Felicia called me over to a magnifying glass with a light. I'm guessing that she was checking for any visible STDs. For an

18-year-old kid it was embarrassing. It felt more like I was in a doctor's office getting a physical. After Felicia conducted her services, I showered, got dressed and met up with Antonio in the lounge. We then left the Chicken Ranch and headed back to Las Vegas.

Back at home, my father kicked me out of the house again. Rob dropped me off at a weekly motel on Utah Avenue and Casino Center Drive, just off the Las Vegas Strip. The motel looked more like a crazy home for drug addicts, drunks and the insane. I had no other place to go; Antonio had gone to California so I had to stay in the weekly.

I got word that Brian and Ben were planning to take a bus back to Vegas. I was still working at the Las Vegas Hilton but I called in sick for work the day they arrived so I could hang out with them. The twins stayed with me at the one-room weekly. We walked the Strip the night they arrived and partied into the morning. It was afternoon the next day when I awoke to the sound of someone knocking on the hotel-room door. It was my co-worker from the Hilton, Mauricio Styles. He had come by to tell me that I got fired for calling in sick. I was barely making ends meet but now with no job I had no money coming in at all.

Rob came to stay with me at the weekly because my father had kicked him out of the house too. Brian and Ben took a bus back to California; I'm guessing they were tired of going hungry at night. Rob and I ended up getting booted out of the weekly because we couldn't pay the rent. We slept in his old, aqua-blue Ford Ranchero. Luckily, Debrah, her boyfriend George Florencio and a friend named David "Cubie" Betancourt had recently moved to Las Vegas. They came from California because my father needed laborers to help on roofing jobs. George and Debrah were waiting to move into the Camelot apartments on Maryland Parkway. Debrah told Rob and me that we could stay with them when they got the keys to the apartment. Rob and I slept in his car at the Camelot parking lot until the apartment was ready.

After moving in I was happy to have a roof over my head but I didn't have much food to eat. I would buy bags of potatoes with what money I scraped up. Debrah was pregnant at the time, so she and George traveled back and forth from Vegas to California for doctor's appointments. With the Vegas summer heat, the hard labor and my father's demanding ways, George quickly got tired of working for him. After my sister had baby Georgie, she and Big George decided to move back to Wilmington with George's parents. Knowing that I had no place to go, George's father was kind enough to let me stay at his house. Rob also returned to California, to live with his mother in Baldwin Park.

Wilmington was also known as the Heart of the Los Angeles Harbor. It was a predominately Latino and African-American neighborhood. The first week I arrived at George's house, his sisters Pat and Rose had a house party. The night of the party I was introduced to the fellas in the neighborhood; I was also introduced to Sherm Stick (PCP) by Tony, Rose's boyfriend. Tony Ruiz was smoking the cigarette dipped in Sherm and when he passed it around I took a hit. After smoking the joint I felt numb to the world.

The next day I woke up in the back of a van with no clue where I was. About 20 minutes later, Tony and his friend Craig Villa walked out of a unit in the projects. When they got into the van, Craig headed toward Pacific Coast Highway. It was then that I realized that we were in the Harbor City projects. Harbor City gang members were known rivals to Wilmington gang members, so just living in Wilmington and being caught in Harbor City could cost a person his life. When I realized that I put myself in a risky situation I made sure it was the last time I smoked Sherm. I didn't like the high anyway. But the parties continued on Mar Vista block, along with the drinking and drug use.

CAR JACKERS

I hung out on Mar Vista block with David "Cubie" Betancourt, Alex Cardenas, George Florencio and Lee Guzman; we often plotted how to make money. One of us geniuses came up with the idea of robbing someone for their car and Dayton rims. Dayton rims and tires could be sold on the street for a quick $1,000; to a broke kid like me that was a lot of money. Craig Villa, along with Alex, Andy Rubio, Cubie, George and I, went for a ride to South Gate. We drove down Firestone,

24

looking for a car with Dayton rims. It was a bad night for us; we couldn't find anyone. Craig decided to stop at a liquor store. That's when Cubie hopped out of the van and pointed a shotgun at an old Mexican man who was making a call at a phone booth. Cubie demanded his wallet and the man quickly complied. Cubie had what he wanted and we drove off in the van, looking for other victims.

Someone definitely had called the cops on us because we were soon being followed by a sheriff's police car. Moments later, a helicopter was heard circling over us, its spotlight shining on the van. Red lights flashed from the police car and a voice on a bullhorn ordered us to pull over. Craig drove the van into the driveway of a residential home. Police cars stopped, blocking the van. With at least half a dozen guns pointed at us, sheriffs ordered us out of the van. One by one, Alex, George, Craig and Andy crawled out of the van's driver-side window.

When it was my turn, I crawled out the van window with my hands up. I was then ordered by an officer to lie face-down in the street. As I laid on the blacktop a cop rushed over to press his shoe against my back, pointing a shotgun at my head. He warned me that if I moved he would blow my head off. When Cubie exited the van, I heard a sheriff say, "There goes the missing link." Someone had reported a black male robbery suspect. We were all Latinos; but Cubie was dark and he could have been easily mistaken for a black man. The sheriffs retrieved shotguns from the back of Craig's van.

The fellas and I were handcuffed and placed in the back seats of police cars. We later arrived at a South Gate police station. Andy, Craig and I were placed in a holding cell. It was made out of metal walls and had four bunk beds and a toilet. As I laid on the bunk, I thought about what big trouble I was in. I was 18 years old and heading to the big house. I prayed to God, asking Him to get me out of this mess. I promised God that if He got me out of the jam, I would do right with my life.

The next day, sheriffs came to get Cubie out of his cell. When Cubie returned, he told us that he was being charged with violating his probation and would be going back to jail. Alex, Cubie and George were taken to juvenile hall because they were underage. Then the sheriffs came for Craig. He was the oldest of the group, and he had taken ownership for the van and the guns that were found. The charges were later dropped on the rest of us because witnesses would not testify. When I was released from the South Gate jail, my cousin Joey Lauro from Compton stood waiting for me by his car. He had a mean look on his face. I couldn't help but laugh. When Joey saw that he flew off the handle, asking me if I thought it was all a joke. I brushed it off as if it were nothing. Maybe I just didn't care what he had to say.

MAKE IT OR BREAK IT

Because of the crack cocaine flood of the mid-1980s there was money flowing through Wilmington; the Dana Strand Housing Projects on Wilmington Boulevard were a goldmine. On just about any given day I would see kids 12 to 16 years old wearing $100 sneakers, new clothes, thick gold chains, gold bracelets and gold rings. Most of the kids selling drugs rode new bikes, mopeds and mini motorcycles. One of the local kids had a low-rider car with hydraulic lifts, custom paint and Dayton rims, and he wasn't even old enough to drive.

I often stopped by the Villa Don's apartments on Wilmington Boulevard, where some of the neighborhood fellas, blacks, Samoans and Latinos sold crack. I was looking for Tino Rubio, a Mexican kid who hung out there. I knew that Tino was always with another kid named Ricardo "Negro" Uribe. As I approached Negro's bedroom window I heard Tino's voice coming from inside the room. I peeked into a window that was slightly opened; I was surprised to see Negro and Tino counting stacks of cash that were laid out on top of a bed. These guys were 12, maybe 14 years old. Drug dealers were role models in the neighborhood. Every kid wanted to be like them. The drug dealers had fancy cars, money, new clothes and were well known in the neighborhood ... not to mention that many girls in the neighborhood were attracted to the lifestyle.

I didn't mind trading a poor life in for ghetto fame, fortune and females. I was broke and had nothing to lose. It was about survival. I told myself "Make it or break it. Either I make it big in the drug business and live a good life or I break it and go to prison." Either way it was a win-win situation for me; if I went to prison a least I would have a roof over my head and three daily meals, and a cot to sleep on. I felt being in prison was better than sleeping on the cold streets.

I decided to roll the dice. I borrowed $20 from a girl named Rene Mesina who lived up the block from me. I told Rene that I would pay her back in a few days with interest. After I got the money, I went to the Villa Don's apartments and I bought a double-up $20 rock from a drug dealer named Nicolas. I took the crack home and cut it into four $10 pieces. Then I hit the streets. I stood on Hawaiian Avenue behind the Dana Strand projects, where many drug users drove past looking to buy dope. I sold all four pieces of crack within a half-hour. Then I returned to Nicolas to buy a double-up $40 rock; I sold it just as quickly. I paid Rene back the $20 I borrowed, with interest, and I continued to double my money with the sales from crack until I had enough to buy an ounce of crack cocaine.

When I made a $1,000 profit, I folded the money in half and wrapped a rubber band around it, and placed it in a shoebox. When the shoebox was full, I started another one. I was bringing in dollars, fives, tens, twenties, fifties and hundreds. I put enough money away until I could buy a quarter-kilo of cocaine, which was nine ounces at a price of about $4,500.

When I decided to sell drugs, I told myself that I wouldn't do it for long. My plan was to buy a car, new clothes and save $5,000 cash. I planned to get out of the drug business once I reached my goals. My goals changed once I got the car, the new clothes and the $5,000 cash. Making money was too easy and my appetite grew. I kept setting new goals and, once I achieved them, I continued to raise the bar. I had enough sense to know that I needed to show income if I planned to buy things that I wanted in life. I had no formal education but I managed to get a job as a graveyard security guard for Hyundai at Terminal Island. I lasted three months before being fired for falling asleep in one of the cars I was hired to guard. I went back to selling drugs full-time.

DRUG DEAL GONE BAD

Many of the fellas in the Harbor Area were in the drug business, and if they weren't they knew someone who was. George, *aka* "Na Nu-Na Nu," Aldaco had an uncle, "El Tio" who was in the business. George was tagged with the name "Na-Nu" because his voice sounded like Mork's from the 1978 TV show *Mork and Mindy*. Na-Nu called me to ask if I wanted to be a backup gun in a 10-to-30-kilo cocaine deal that he was going to do. I was to earn $2,000. I told Na-Nu I would do it. He was the one who set everything up. A runner named Miguel who worked for El Tio, Na-Nu, and I were to meet the buyers, Harold and June, at a gas station in Hawthorne. June was a black man who Na-Nu met in Scottsdale Town Homes, a low-income housing area located in Carson, California. Harold was June's partner; I didn't know anything about either except that one of the men bought coke from Na-Nu in the past.

Harold drove a tan van with the windows covered by curtains. The cocaine exchange was to take place at Alondra Park, in Lawndale. Miguel drove a white Chevy truck while Na-Nu and I rode in his red Nissan pickup. Both trucks followed the van that June and Harold rode in. The three vehicles pulled into the parking lot of Alondra Park. Harold remained behind the wheel of the van while June got out of the vehicle. Na-Nu and I stepped out of the Nissan and positioned ourselves where we could closely watch June, Harold and the van. June approached Na-Nu and the two exchanged small talk with each other as Miguel walked to the passenger side of Harold's van.

June wore brown dress slacks, a dress shirt, dark designer sunglasses and carried a rolled-up newspaper under his arm. I had the feeling that June was packing a gun. I glanced over at Miguel, who was conducting business at the van with Harold. Harold opened a suitcase full of money that sat in the front seat of the van. Miguel quickly counted the stacks of cash, then left the van and headed to his truck, where he grabbed a duffel bag that contained three kilos of cocaine. June wanted to buy 10 kilos at first but Miguel decided to sell him three for the time being. The rest of the kilos would be exchanged later.

I kept my eyes on June as he continued to talk with Na-Nu. June glanced over at me every so often. I adjusted the compact 9 mm pistol that was tucked in the waist of my pants to make sure I had easy access in case I needed it. I shifted my eyes back and forth from June to Miguel, who was headed to Harold's van, with duffel bag in hand. Harold handed Miguel a briefcase filled with money as Miguel handed Herald the duffel bag filled with coke. When June saw the handoff, he casually headed to the van where he entered the passenger seat.

Miguel walked to his truck, where he opened the suitcase to double-check the money. He found that each stack contained $1 bills in between two $100 bills. It was made to look as if the stacks were all stacks of hundreds. The van quickly sped out of the parking space in reverse, then raced forward through the lot. Miguel yelled at Na-Nu, "They burned us!" I grabbed my gun to shoot at the van but an elderly man walking his dog crossed my line of fire. I saw that there were many people around in the park, so I put the gun away. Miguel yelled, "Chase them!" Na-Nu and I hopped into the Nissan, and we followed Miguel's truck as it chased the van.

The van headed down Redondo Beach Boulevard against traffic. It then cut over an island where it drove onto the right side of the road with the flow of traffic. That's when we lost them. Na-Nu kept saying he was in big trouble. The kilos belonged to El Tio. Na-Nu was worried that El Tio would think he had something to do with stealing the kilos. Na-Nu was the one who set the deal up but Na-Nu had no idea that Harold and June would rob him.

When Na-Nu dropped me off at my house he told me to hide out for a few days until he straightened things out with El Tio. I didn't think I needed to hide out. Na-Nu's uncle didn't know me and I didn't have anything to do with the kilos being stolen. Word got back to me that El Tio came looking for Na-Nu in Scottsdale, where Na-Nu lived with his parents. Na-Nu's uncle rolled into Scottsdale with three cars full of Mexican henchmen. I don't know if El Tio was actually going to do anything to his nephew but the threat was real. I later learned that El Tio had a meeting with his brother; I'm guessing they came to an agreement on how the kilos would be paid back, because Na-Nu never came up missing and neither did I.

DODGING BULLETS

I continued my drug dealings and as my money stacks grew so did my desire for toys. I bought a 1976 Monte Carlo; I put spoke rims on it, new paint, a custom interior and a bumping (i.e., very, very loud) stereo system. It wasn't the nicest-looking car in the neighborhood but I was working my way to the top. I was at home when Serena Sanchez, a girl who lived in a house on the next block, called me to come over and visit. Jacob Slater and I hopped into my Monte Carlo, and headed to Serena's house.

Serena came out and sat in the front seat of the Monte Carlo. We drank beer as we listened to music over the car stereo. I suddenly had a strong urge to urinate. I got out of my car and I rushed to a bush in the next door neighbor's yard where I relieved myself. Before I finished, a green Chevy Impala screeched around a corner and shotgun blasts rang out. I ducked for cover as I reached for the gun that I usually kept in my front pocket; it wasn't there. I realized that I had left my weapon in my car.

When the shotgun blasts stopped, I looked down the block to see if the shooters were still around. The green Chevy was nowhere in sight. I rushed to my car to see if Serena and Jacob were all right; I noticed two shotgun holes in the driver's side of my car door. I looked inside the car but Serena and Jacob were gone. I then walked around to the passenger side of the Monte Carlo where Serena and Jacob were hiding. No one was hit. After I regained my composure I sat in the driver's seat to see if the shotgun slugs would have hit me had I been in the car at the time of the shooting. The two slugs would have entered the left side of my body and exited my right side had I been sitting in the driver's seat two minutes earlier. The Monte Carlo was now marked, so I knew I had to sell it.

I NEED A JOB

Though I was making good money selling drugs, I knew it was wise to have a regular job. I saw an ad in a newspaper for an apprentice welder position at a metal company in Rancho Dominguez. My new boss Jerry Tanner offered to pay for welding school if I agreed to attend, so I accepted the offer. I worked, attended school and sold drugs at night. After a long day at work and at school I usually got home beat, but I always found the energy to go to the projects or to the Villa Don's Apartments to sell dope.

Money motivated me, especially when I brought home at least a couple of hundred dollars a night. At times, I walked home from the projects after a few hours of selling drugs with my pockets stuffed with cash. I worried that someone would follow me home and try to rob me. I knew that I needed to protect myself while I sold drugs. I bought a Raven .25-caliber handgun from a weapons connection. It was small enough to hide in my jacket pocket and if cops were chasing me it was easy enough to toss. I'd rather be caught by the police with a gun than be caught by jackers or rival gang members without one. I earned good money selling drugs while I held a job. So after I sold the Monte Carlo, I bought a new S-10 Blazer. It was two tones in color, root-beer brown and light brown. I went all out and bought Dayton rims and low-profile tires. I hooked up the sound system to where the bass could be heard a block away. I dressed it with a brown phantom top and a Dayton rim bumper kit; I figured it was time to treat myself.

After months, I didn't have the drive to be a welder any longer. I earned more money in one night selling drugs than I did working a week with the metal company, plus the hours at work were long and tiresome. When I gave the news to Jerry that I was quitting, I could tell he was upset; I didn't blame him. Jerry had put in so much time and effort sending me to school, and teaching me the trade but welding just didn't interest me.

SHOTS FIRED

Death seemed to be pursuing me. I let Angel Montes, a kid I grew up with, borrow my Blazer because he wanted to cruise Hollywood Boulevard. In return, Angel lent me his Corvette for the night. Ralph Cerna, one of the fellas from the neighborhood had asked if I could drop off a girl he was seeing in San Pedro. I agreed to take her home and Ralph went along. When I pulled into the alley where the girl wanted to be dropped off, I noticed the Corvette had a flat tire. Worse, we were in rival gang territory. I called Angel on his cell phone, asking him to meet up so he could bring a spare tire. As we waited for Angel, a white Oldsmobile Cutlass drove through the alley and the driver mean-mugged Ralph and me. I was certain the guy in the Cutlass was gang-related. Angel showed up a short time later in the Blazer. He drove Ralph and me back to the neighborhood so we could get a spare tire and a jack. I knew we would have to go back to San Pedro with backup in case any rival gang members were waiting for us when we returned.

We left Wilmington three vehicles deep: my Blazer, Na-Nu's Nissan and another truck. When my Blazer pulled into the alley near Santa Cruz Street where the Corvette was parked, three men opened fire on us. When I heard bullets hit the metal of my Blazer, I slammed the truck in reverse and raced out of the alley. Na-Nu and the third truck scrambled to get out of my way. When my Blazer bounced out of the alley and into the street, I shifted the gear into drive and floored it; the Blazer sped off, the other two trucks following close behind.

Ralph, who sat in the front seat of the Blazer, noticed that my forehead was bleeding. I looked in the rearview mirror. I was hit by buckshot. The wound wasn't bad enough that I needed medical attention. It looked more like a wound from a BB pellet. When we all arrived at the neighborhood, I learned that I was the only one who was hit. After I made a few phone calls, I found out that one of the shooters was Danny Pena, the boyfriend of a girl I dated. Getting shot wasn't something I took lightly. I made plans to get even.

I parked my gold Buick Regal near Danny's house for four days, watching and waiting for him to slip just once, but he never showed. I figured he had been staying somewhere else. A few weeks later, I received a call from a girl who told me that Danny would be at a house in San Pedro later that night. It was my chance to get back at the person who shot at me. I picked up two triggermen, Mr. Black and Mr. Brown, then loaded the trunk of my gold Buick Regal with guns and ammo. I made sure to lock the trunk and I hid the key under the dashboard in case we were pulled over by cops.

The cops would have to break the lock to open the trunk, which would give me an illegal-search-and-seizure defense if I was arrested. Mr. Black, Mr. Brown and I headed to San Pedro on a mission. Mr. Brown drove the Regal while I rode shotgun. Mr. Black was in the back seat. We arrived near the street where I was told Danny would be and circled the area a few times. Suddenly a police car pulled behind us, lights flashing. Mr. Brown pulled the car over. One of the cops approached Mr. Brown and asked who the vehicle belonged to. Mr. Brown told the officer that it was mine. The cop then asked Mr. Brown what we were doing in the area. Mr. Brown explained to the officer that we were going to a house party. The cop gave us a look-over without searching the car. Then he warned us to go home because there had been a recent shooting in the area. That was a sign as clear as day for me. I decided to put off getting my revenge, at least for the time being.

LAPD'S CRASH UNIT

Gang violence was high in the late 1980s. The Bloods against the Crips, Wilmas against San Pedro, against Long Beach, against Harbor City, against Gardena, even Westside Wilmas (the side I lived on) against Eastside Wilmas. Drive-by shootings were constant; they brought added police presence to the neighborhood. When the cops were out on the streets in numbers it was hard for drug dealers to make money. Though I knew cops were out in force I continued sneaking around to make drug sales.

I had received a page on my beeper from a heavy-set black kid known as Kool-Aid who bought dope from me. When I called Kool-Aid I told him I would meet him at a certain time in the Dana Strand Projects. When I arrived at the projects I drove my yellow Dodge Colt into the first circle. I walked through the projects to the third circle, near Wilmington Boulevard, with a small sack of dope in my jacket pocket. There was Kool-Aid. I handed him the dope sack and, as I did, a late-model Chevy Impala swooped into the parking lot. I noticed the car but I wasn't sure if it was cops. Not taking any chances, I tossed the dope that I held in my hand into my mouth. The car came to a stop near Kool-Aid and I.

When the two men jumped out of the Impala I recognized one of the officers as a member of the LAPD CRASH [Community Resources Against Street Hoodlums] Unit. I chewed the crack that I had in my mouth to get rid of any evidence and, as I did, I ran in the opposite direction. When I spat the dope out of my mouth, it landed in some dirt. I only made it a few yards when one of the officers rushed me and slammed me onto the hood of a car. He ordered me not to move as he searched my pockets. Both cops then searched the ground for dope but they found nothing. Kool-Aid's stomach was so big that his skin overlapped and that's where Kool-Aid hid his dope, under the fat of his stomach roll, where the cops usually never searched. They didn't find a thing and, boy, they were upset that they had to let us go.

The cops weren't the only ones a drug dealer had to look out for. The neighborhood haters were the worst. I learned it firsthand when I ran into a Samoan named Amosa "Coco" Niu. He was also a drug dealer who sold drugs on the street corners. When Coco saw me driving down Wilmington Boulevard in my Chevy Blazer he waved me over. He asked if I could give him a ride home. As we drove down Wilmington Boulevard, a motorcycle cop got behind me, flashing his red lights. I figured I was stopped because the stereo in my Blazer was bumping too loud. The officer asked for my driver's license, insurance and registration. Just as I thought, the officer wrote me a ticket for loud music; I was then let go. A few minutes later, I dropped Coco off at his house.

As I drove off, I reached into the ashtray for a chap stick but I also found five crack rocks. I looked down at the carpet and I saw more rocks scattered on the passenger side. There was no doubt in my mind that Coco planted the dope in my Blazer. I had recently washed the vehicle and vacuumed the carpet myself. The dope was not there before Coco got into the Blazer. Coco was confirmed as a hater. In the drug business there were very few people a person could trust. There was always someone out to get what another man had.

THE STREETS ARE TALKING

I had just left Alex Cardenas' house in Carson. As I drove past the Scottsdale Townhouse security gate, a sheriff's car pulled me over. It was as if they were waiting for me. Two officers got out of their vehicle to approach me. One of them ordered me to step out of the Blazer and put my hands on the hood of his patrol car. The officer searched me while his partner searched my Blazer. As the officer searched me, he said, "The streets are talking, and they're saying you are a drug dealer." I kept silent as the officers continued their search.

When one of the officers ran my name, I learned that I had a warrant; it was a warrant for loud music. I had so many tickets for loud music that I must have forgotten about it. I told the officers that if I was a drug dealer I would have had the money to pay for the ticket and not let it turn into an arrest warrant. The officers allowed me to make a phone call so I could have someone pick up the Blazer. I called George Florencio and, when he arrived, I told him to go to my room and get some money out of my shoebox so I could pay for the warrant. George left in my Blazer. Meanwhile I was taken to the sheriff's station in Carson. I was placed in a holding cell; hours had gone by and still George had not arrived. I was taken out of the cell to be chained and cuffed. Then I was loaded onto a bus that was headed to the Los Angeles County Jail.

When I arrived at the jail I was 18 years old, weighed 165 pounds and was scared. It was my first time in County and I didn't know what to expect. Getting processed into the jail took hours; a group of about 30 new arrivals were placed in a holding tank. Sheriffs ordered us to remove all our clothes; we were then ordered to open our mouth, lift up our tongue, lift our scrotum sack, bend over, cough and lift the bottom of our feet. After the body search was complete we were ordered to get dressed. Every holding tank we were placed in had a different process. One was for medical documentation, one was for a shower, one to be issued clothes and a bed roll, and another categorized us for housing placement. If an inmate went to the wrong housing unit it could be deadly.

The gangs were separated from other gangs: north and south, Blacks, Latinos, Whites, Asians, Mexicans, gays, transvestites; sheriffs had a place for all of them. Each holding tank had a toilet but if a person needed to use it he'd be out of luck. Inmates slept on the floor so close to the toilet that a person couldn't sit on it if they needed and the toilets were so filthy with urine and feces that anyone in their right mind wouldn't want to use it. In addition there wasn't any toilet paper. The options weren't good.

I was happy when I made it to a four-man cell, even though six men were housed in each cell because of the overcrowding. There were two Southsiders, Sleepy and Termite, a White and two Mexican nationals known as Pisas. Sleepy hit me up when I arrived in the cell. He asked me where I was from. I told him that I was from Wilmington. He then asked if I knew a Wilmero named Huero (not real name). I told him I wasn't sure. Sleepy lifted his shirt to show me a recent stab wound. He said Huero touched him up. I asked why. His response was, "I messed up. I had it coming." Sleepy changed the subject and I didn't ask any more questions.

One of the things I noticed in the dorm was the position of the televisions. They were mounted above the toilets so when a person used the bathroom he would be looking at a dorm full of inmates who would be watching the TVs. I knew the TVs were set up that way to make an inmate's stay uncomfortable. It was my first county jail time, so I didn't know how things were run; I made sure to stay out of the way. Violence was common in the county jail but the only beating I saw was by a Southsider who was bothered by another Latino because he kept scratching his groin area. The Southsider rushed over to beat the Latino as he yelled, "You are going to give everyone crabs, you idiot!" The Latino ran to an exit door, yelling for the cops to help him, but not before he received a beating. A sheriff heard the yelling, so when he arrived he snatched the Latino out of the unit. I'm guessing they moved him to a different floor, because the Latino never returned.

I heard my name called as I watched TV. A Sheriff told me to roll up my belongings for release. Processing out of County took as long as processing in. I sat in a holding tank, waiting as inmates arrived as others were released. The holding tank door opened and a new group of inmates entered. A white kid about my age caught my attention. He looked as if he had been through Hell and back. The guy had a lost gaze and tears rolled down his face. I asked the kid if he was OK. The guy mumbled that he needed to talk to someone. He went on to say that he was raped by two black men who were his cellmates. He cried as he explained how he screamed for help all night, but no one came to help him. He said the blacks held a razor blade to his throat as they took turns raping him. He went on to say that he didn't know who to tell and he was worried that he may have contracted AIDS. I felt bad for the guy. The whites who were loners and not gang affiliated had it the worst in prison. Some had their shoes taken, some had their food or radio taken and others had their manhood taken.

BACK ON THE STREETS

When I got back to Wilmington, I went to the projects to catch up on making money. I arrived at the third circle when I noticed a familiar brown BMW sitting in the parking lot. Dan Cohen, the owner of the BMW, was in the driver's seat receiving a beating by Tino and two drug addicts. Tino was one of the nickel-and-dime drug dealers from the neighborhood. One of the addicts held a knife to Dan's throat as the other one delivered blows to Dan's face. When I walked up to the BMW, Dan was covering his face to deflect the blows while Tino searched Dan's pockets.

Immediately I knew what was going on; Dan owed Tino money for drugs that Tino gave him on credit. When Dan came into the projects to buy more dope from another drug dealer, Tino caught Dan and beat him in an attempt to get the money Dan owed. I'm guessing Tino offered the drug addicts a little dope if they held Dan while Tino searched Dan's pockets for money. I arrived just in time to stop things from going too far. Both Dan and Tino owed me money. I told Tino that I would clear his debt with me if he cleared Dan's debt. Tino owed me more money than Dan owed him, so he reluctantly agreed.

I got into the BMW with Dan and I told him to drive out of the projects. He was clearly shook up but he managed to drive. Dan expressed how thankful he was that I came to rescue him. He asked if there was anything he could do for me. When I stopped Tino and the drug addicts from beating Dan I sincerely felt bad that Dan was getting the life pounded out of him but I also looked at it as an opportunity. I told Dan that I needed a job; I knew that his Italian girlfriend's father owned a fish company in San Pedro. I also knew that Dan worked there. When I asked, Dan was more than happy to get me a job at the fish company. I started by unloading boats of tuna, mackerel, squid, sardines and anchovies. There were a few Latinos working there but most of the workers were Yugoslavs, Italians and Sicilians. All the workers were older than I, probably in their forties and fifties, and they all treated me pretty well.

After I got my foot in the door at the fish company, I collected two checks; my regular pay and the pay from three of my coworkers who bought coke from me. I also continued to sell dope in the projects and had customers paging me at all hours of the day. With money rolling in, I bought everything a kid my age could want; an IROC-Z, new clothes, gold jewelry -- and I saved a few stacks of cash.

But I still wanted more. My new goals were to save enough money for a legitimate business and to buy a house. I knew that being in the drug business wouldn't last forever. I wanted to rise above a street-level pusher. I was hungry to make money and the right people took notice. My reputation was good enough with my drug suppliers that they trusted me. One of my connections fronted me coke and I returned the money as soon as I was sold out. I began to feel as if I was finally becoming a "somebody."

THE SPOT'S GETTING HOT

Success, street fame, power and respect came with the drug business but with it also came enemies, jealousy and haters. Someone in the neighborhood was talking and it could have been anyone. Wilmington was small and everybody knew each other's business. Whoever was doing the talking gave my name to police at Harbor Division. I regularly got pulled over by cops, who always searched my car. Police patrol cars regularly stopped in front of my house flashing their spotlight into the living-room window. Also, the neighborhood was hot with gang violence, home-invasion robberies and with drug deals gone wrong. CRASH Unit was targeting anyone who looked to be gang related; Wilmington became a war zone.

I knew it was time for me to move out of town when I received a call from Tommy Clark. He worked at a tire shop and often bought coke from me. The last time Tommy came by my house, he picked-up his supply of dope. The next day he called me with a worried tone in his voice, telling me that his boss warned him to stay away from a known drug dealer's home that Tommy had recently visited. Tommy's boss told him that police were watching that house. Tommy explained to me that the only house he went to that night was mine. Tommy's boss knew his movements because the tire shop serviced police cars for Harbor Division. It was one of Harbor Division's officers who warned Tommy's boss.

I knew if I stayed in the neighborhood I would end up in prison or dead. I made phone calls to people I knew in Las Vegas who I thought might be able to help me set up shop in Sin City. I packed my Chevy Blazer and black IROC-Z with all my worldly belongings, and headed out to Las Vegas with Alex Cardenas, one of the few people I trusted.

CHAPTER 2 Viva Las Vegas

I t was 1986 when I drove into glittering Las Vegas. The bright lights, the fast pace and the hustle ... I was lured in by all of it. I could smell money in the air. Las Vegas was a goldmine and I wanted a piece. I envisioned how I would own a casino someday, just like Bugsy Siegel.

My parents and I were "on" in our off-and-on-again relationship. Alex and I stayed at my parents' house on Desert Inn and Sandhill; we didn't actually stay *in* the house but in a storage shed that was converted into a room. Things were different this time; I had money, two cars and a load of cocaine to sell. Alex and I worked with my father at his small roofing company. At the same time, I was making connections to move cocaine into the market. I knew a few people in town that had moved from Los Angeles, so I contacted them about unloading product. My father would look at me suspiciously because I often left the job site to make phone calls. Whenever my pager went off, it was usually a drug sale.

I paid a visit to Antonio Marcos when I arrived in Las Vegas. I knew Antonio used drugs in the past and was sure he had customers who bought the product. Antonio had let me stay at his mother's house, in the past, when my parents kicked me out and that meant a lot to me. Antonio introduced me to some street-level buyers and right away coke money poured in.

I was networking on the streets when I received a page from my mother. She had been looking through the suitcase that I left in the storage house, and she found nine ounces of cocaine that I stashed in hollowed-out Coke and W-D40 cans. She threatened to flush my stash down the toilet if I didn't get it out of her house right away. Ounces of coke were selling for a thousand dollars in Vegas at the time, so if she had flushed it, it would have been nine thousand dollars literally down the toilet. My parents didn't want me at their house after they found my dope, so Alex and I set up shop at a Motel 6 on Boulder Highway. We stayed at the motel for a few weeks until we rented an apartment on Sahara Avenue and Maryland Parkway.

Antonio began to show he had potential to make money. He was eager to move coke and every time I supplied him with product he sold out with no problem. Antonio didn't own his own car, so I let him use the company car, a 1980 Oldsmobile, so he could make deliveries. Antonio later asked if I could lend him money to buy an El Camino from a used-car lot on Boulder Highway. Antonio made me money, so I decided to buy it for him on the condition that I would be paid back.

Antonio and I were at a restaurant having a meeting when he began to reminisce about the neighborhood where we grew up. I mentioned to Antonio that I messed with a chick named Sandra. Antonio curiously asked me if it was Sandra Green, who lived in the projects. When I told Antonio it was, his facial expression changed. Then he said, "Sandra is my girlfriend." I honestly didn't know that, I told Antonio. Sandra never said she was dating anyone. Antonio was clearly bothered. He never talked about it again but his attitude toward me changed.

YOUNG AND FOOLISH

I was an 18-year-old, flashy kid who drove around Las Vegas like I owned it. Maybe I watched too many gangster movies. I had an IROC-Z with tinted windows and Dayton wire rims. I wore gold chains, gold rings, two pagers, and I carried a roll of cash in my pants pocket and a pistol everywhere I went.

Alex and I were out on the town in the IROC-Z; I drove down East Tropicana Avenue to a convenience store to meet Antonio and another drug dealer named Rico Figueroa. Antonio and Rico were in a newly fixed-up and gold-painted El Camino with gold-and-chrome Dayton rims. I pulled up with the IROC-Z's music blasting. I must have stood out like a sore thumb because a Las Vegas Metro police car rolled into

41

the parking lot with flashing lights and stopped behind my car. A moment later a second police car joined it. The two officers got out of their vehicle; one approached my side of the car while the other officer neared the passenger side. The officer who stood before me looked like he was recently out of the military. He sported a flattop haircut, bulging biceps and he had a drill-sergeant attitude.

The cop wanted to know what I was doing in the parking lot. I told him that I came to buy something to drink from the store. The drill sergeant cop didn't seem convinced, so he ordered Alex and me out of the car and conducted a search while the other officer stood watching. I had a gun stashed under the back seat but the cop never found it. What the officer did find was a "Special Agent" badge that was in my glove box. When Drill Sergeant found it, he escorted me away from Alex, Antonio and Rico so they wouldn't hear our conversation. He then asked me what was going on, as though I was an undercover agent posing as a drug dealer. I explained that the badge belonged to a friend who worked for a security company. My friend left the badge in my car as a joke when I gave him a ride.

I still had California license plates on my car. I told the officer that I had only been in town a few weeks. He asked me who my employer was; I told him I worked for my father's roofing company. The officer showed me an insurance policy with a Las Vegas address. The policy had my name on it and it showed I had been living in Vegas for at least six months. Drill Sergeant Cop was so mad that I wasn't being truthful that he handcuffed me and put me in the front seat of his patrol car. Then he drove me to a dark desert road near the airport. He stopped the car in a secluded area and asked me again what I was doing in the store parking lot, insinuating that a drug transaction was going to take place. I told the officer there was nothing going on. The officer boldly asked me where the drug houses were in Las Vegas. I responded that I was not a drug dealer so I didn't know about any drug houses.

The cop then asked me if I had insurance. I asked the officer what he meant by that. "If something were to happen to you, do you have insurance to cover your medical expenses?" I told him, "No." "So if I were to break your legs, the taxpayers would have to pay your medical expenses?" I sat quietly as the cop continued, "If I see you in Vegas again, I will take you out to the desert and I will break your legs. Do you understand me?" "Yes," I answered. The officer drove me back to where Alex, Antonio and Rico were waiting. I was then uncuffed and we were all released. A week later, I sold the IROC-Z to George "Na-Nu" Aldaco. I went to a car dealership and bought a new Buick Century with cash. I also went to the DMV to get a valid Nevada driver's license. If I was to conduct illegal business in Las Vegas I had to be legal in every possible way.

BRINGING IN OUTSIDERS

When Antonio came to me broke, he was humble and hungry to make money. But when money poured in, Antonio got cocky and he thought he could run things. As soon as I saw the change in Antonio's attitude, I decided to cut ties with him. He no longer had access to the drugs I supplied him in the past. Later, word got back to me that he was bringing street-level drug pushers from Los Angeles to sell their coke in Las Vegas. When I expressed my disapproval, Antonio and I got into an argument. During our phone conversation, Antonio threatened to whip me. He said after he whipped me he was going to whip my partner, big Alex, and anyone who was with me.

Antonio and I agreed to meet at Sunset Park so we could settle things. I sat in the parking with Alex when Antonio arrived in his El Camino with Luis Ortega, another of the fellas from Wilmington who came to Vegas to sell cocaine. Antonio and I met in the middle of the park; we agreed to take a walk in an open field where we would go at it. I was walking a few feet ahead of Antonio when he lunged at me with a cheap shot. I ducked but Antonio managed to graze the side of my head with his fist.

Immediately I swung at Antonio, connecting a blow to his face and then one to his body. Antonio attempted to hold me, so I lifted his light frame off the ground and slammed him on his back. When Antonio hit the ground, he yelled as he pulled back his right arm. Antonio grunted, "My hand is broken." It was clear that he was finished fighting. Alex then walked out from behind a bush where he had watched the fight.

"You said you would whip me? It's my turn," said Alex. Antonio walked away, attempting to keep his distance from Alex. "I will fight you when my hand heals," he said. Antonio quickly got into his car, with twigs in his hair and dirt on his clothes. The El Camino then sped off.

Months after the fight with Antonio, he sent word that he wanted to buy cocaine from me. I didn't trust him, so I let him know that I wasn't interested. Sometime later, an explosion went off under my car as it sat parked near the townhouse where I lived. I learned about the explosion when cops knocked at my door to question me about it. An officer asked if I had any enemies. Being in the drug business I was sure that I made enemies but told the police that I had none. I wasn't sure if the explosion was meant for me. I thought it might have been kids in the neighborhood playing with firecrackers. But in case it was meant for me, I made sure that I always carried two firearms and made it a rule to move to different homes frequently.

I ran into Luis Ortega, in Wilmington, the same Luis that Antonio brought to Vegas. He wanted to know what I did to anger Antonio, because he talked about taking me out. I was told that Antonio planned to have someone knock at the door of my home and when I answered I would be sprayed with lead. The conversation Luis spoke of occurred about the time that explosion went off under my car. It's strange how the truth comes out eventually.

KTE

The more money I made, the bigger the toys I wanted. I bought a late-model red Corvette. Then I took it to Vegas Vettes on Industrial, next to the Crazy Horse Too gentleman's club and had the owner Vinny put on a Testarossa body kit, front spoiler, wrap-around tail and side rocker panels. Then I took the car to California and had All Star Auto Accessories in Long Beach put low-profile tires with Lorenzo rims, a bumping sound system and, for the finishing touch, a Nardi Italy classic Mahogany steering wheel. I was a 19-year-old kid driving around in this sleek sports car, living my dreams.

I was also stacking money, making plans to buy a business and a home. I gave my parents a sealed manila envelope filled with $25,000 to hold for a down payment on my first house; I was sure that my money would be safe with them. A few months later, big Alex commented that my parents had been spending a lot of money. They moved into a different home, bought property in Pahrump and a new van. It was not a coincidence that my parents spent money buying new things. When I asked my mother for the manila envelope filled with $25,000, she told me that her and my father didn't have the money. I was furious. After everything my parents put me through, I still reached out to them for acceptance and felt as if they spit in my face. If I couldn't trust my own mother and my own father then who could I trust?

I was so enraged that I warned my mother that she and my father were lucky they were family, because if they weren't I'd put a bullet in the back of their heads. They eventually paid me back, but it took months and it was nickel and dime; they gave me a car that I didn't want, gave me furniture that I didn't need and gave me their credit cards to ring up. It wasn't the same as having $25,000 in cash but what could I do? I had to let it go.

My plan was to open a business and get out of the drug game eventually. The first business that I bought into was a fiberglass-molding shop that was located in a warehouse behind Crazy Horse Too. The business made body kits, spoilers, tails and panels for Corvettes, similar to what I had on my car. I knew nothing about running a business. I depended on my new partner, Pops, to make sure things ran smoothly. It didn't take long for me to realize that the management and the investment were both bad.

WEDDING BELLS

When my girlfriend Camille Currans' mother Connie learned that Camille was pregnant, she continually asked me when we were going to get married. I told Connie that Camille and I would get married soon. That's all it took. The next thing I knew, Connie was making wedding arrangements. It was set for May 20, 1989, at a church in

Long Beach. The reception was to be held at the Holiday Inn. My best man was to be Alex Cardenas.

May 11, 1989, nine days before my wedding. Alex and I were at home in Las Vegas when he received a phone call from his sister Lourdes. By the look on Alex's face and the tone of his voice I knew something was wrong. The phone went dead on the other end. Alex tried calling back but the line was busy. Alex then told me that his sister had been shot, and the shooters were Jesse "Jay-Rock" Morrison and Michael Berry. Immediately, Alex and I caught a flight to Los Angeles. When we arrived in L.A., we drove to the hospital where his sister was being held in Intensive Care. Alex's family and close friends were there, along with detectives.

I learned that Jesse Morrison, Michael and Shawn Berry, and a young kid named Nathan had come into the house demanding money. Jesse shot and killed Alex's brother Cesar. Alex's sister, Lourdes was shot next, hit by bullets in her face and breast as she held her four-month-old daughter. The people responsible for the shootings were African Americans that Alex and I knew. I wasn't raised to be racist but after Cesar's death my feelings toward black people changed. I began to dislike them. It wasn't the color of their skin and it wasn't all black people that I disliked. But it was the ones who were in the drug game who seemed to be the most scandalous and ruthless animals.

Alex and I knew the Berry family very well. Shawn Berry was our age and he lived across the street from Alex's home. Shawn hung out with Alex and me at times. Michael resembled rapper Ice-T. He was in and out of prison, and showed up at his mother's house from time to time. I recall one occasion when I arrived at Alex's house in Carson. When I pulled my Corvette into the driveway, Cesar told me that Alex was next door at Shawn's house. I drove to Shawn's home. Michael was outside, washing his Cadillac. When I pulled up, he looked at my Corvette with envy. He then turned to me and said, "When Jay-Rock gets out of prison, we're going to jack you." I looked Michael in his eyes, then lifted my shirt to show him the 9 mm handgun tucked in the waistband of my pants. "Don't you have the balls to do it yourself," I asked. Michael laughed it off.

46

At the hospital, Alex and I were approached by a man who introduced himself as Detective Richard Simmons. He advised us to let the police do their job and made it clear that if anything happened to any of the Berry or the Morrison family members, Alex and I would be the primary suspects. I was filled with so much rage it didn't matter what the detective said. If it was up to me the shooters would pay with their lives.

Nine days later I got married but it wasn't easy. On top of the tragedy that happened to Alex's family, my parents didn't show to my wedding. It was another disappointment but something I was now accustomed. Thinking about what had happened to Alex's family consumed me with anger toward those responsible. One side of me contemplated how I would take revenge on the Berry and the Morrison families but another side of me knew the families had nothing to do with what Michael, Shawn, Nathan, and Jesse had done. Michael's mother was a churchgoing woman. After I thought things through, I didn't wish any harm on the Berry or Morrison families but I felt Michael, Shawn, Nathan, and Jesse should pay with their lives. If an opportunity had presented itself I would not have thought twice about pulling the trigger. I later received word that Michael Berry and Jesse Morrison surrendered to Rockville, Maryland, police on March 27, 1990, a day after an "America's Most Wanted" segment detailed a manhunt for the two. Michael, Jesse, Shawn, and Nathan were locked away. I still wanted revenge but, I also knew karma would visit them someday.

After Camille and I were married, she moved in with me on Green Valley Parkway in Green Valley, Nevada. Trouble brewed early on in our marriage. I enjoyed the married life but still wanted to run wild.

MY 21ST BIRTHDAY

For my 21st birthday, I walked into Crazy Horse Too with a few friends and a pocket full of cash. I sat at the bar in front of Skip, the bartender who usually chased me out of the club for not being of age. I looked straight into Skip's eyes and asked him, "Aren't you going to say something?" Skip responded, "Nope." "Why not?" Skip replied,

"Because the way you walked in here like you owned the place. That tells me you must be 21 now." As I grinned I said, "You're damn right I'm 21!" I slapped my driver's license onto the bar top and told Skip, "Get drinks for all my friends." The club scene was new to me and I enjoyed the nightlife. The fellas and I visited the latest hot spots in Vegas: Tramps, Shark Club, Mets, The Palladium and Botany's. A door opened up to a whole new world for me and I was going to explore it.

KTE

My son, Raymond Ernest Torres Junior, was born Oct. 21, 1989, in Las Vegas. When I first held Ray Junior in my arms, I remember staring at him and being one of the happiest moments of my life. A few months later, Camille and I moved into a house near Desert Inn and Pecos Road. The birth of my son slowed me down for a time; I quit drinking and began working out.

But it wasn't long before I began to party again. Camille and I argued about the smallest issues and it continued to escalate. Our relationship began to crumble. Every so often, I would send Camille to her mother's home in Bakersfield, California where Connie had moved. When my wife was out of town all I did was make money and party. Crazy Horse Too became one of my hangouts. I was there so much that the management began to take notice of me. A beefed-up bouncer named Moe McKenna, weighing about 300 pounds and with no neck, approached me one day to warn me that I better not be selling drugs in his club. Moe informed me that cops frequented the place. I assured Moe that I would never sell drugs in the club and that I respected the place. Moe and I later became friends.

KTE

I was at my parents' house on Desert Inn and Sandhill Road, washing my Corvette in the front yard when a beat-up, red, 1976 Monte Carlo pulled up across the street. The car let out a huge cloud of black smoke as the engine died right on the spot. Out of the car stepped Antonio Marcos, unshaven and smoking a Camel cigarette; he looked a mess.

He was with a young Latin woman and a child. When he approached me, he gave me a sad story about how badly he was doing. He needed to make money to support the girl and the kid. Antonio nearly begged me to help him get on his feet. It was a totally different Antonio from the loudmouth that I fought at Sunset Park.

I knew better than to trust him and I was familiar with the notion, "Shame on you for betraying someone who helped you." and "Shame on me for helping a known betrayer a second time." I was also familiar with the notion, "Keep your friends close and your enemies closer." I gave Antonio a small sack of dope and cut him loose, not expecting to see him again. He came back within a few days to pay me the money from the coke I gave him on credit. I gave Antonio another sack and he did the same, time after time. I saw that Antonio was hungry to make money again. If he was going to be a hustling machine, then I was going to run the machine until it couldn't run any more.

Antonio's appetite for baller status increased. He was attempting to rise to the top with the rest of us who hung out together. Antonio dated high-maintenance women and began to dine at some of the fancy Italian restaurants that I frequented. On a few occasions Antonio invited me and some of my associates to dine with him. I was all for celebrating making money but Antonio was moving too fast and it bothered me because it impaired his work performance -- and that affected the money flowing back to me.

I drove a Corvette and most of the fellas in my circle drove high-end cars. Antonio went out and bought a red Corvette similar to mine. Being in the drug business was getting to Antonio's head. He purposely hit on dancers who dated known drug dealers. He visited a local strip club and told one dancer to give a certain drug dealer a message: "Tell him, Antonio is running things in Vegas." He often told people we were brothers and then started a beef with them. The problem was that Antonio's bark was bigger than his bite and I was the one who had to clean up his messes.

I was at a popular Las Vegas nightclub with a few friends; we were all sitting at a table near a huge window with a view of the main entrance.

One of the fellas noticed Antonio's Corvette pull up at valet parking. Antonio strolled into the club, wearing a new suit. He was also accompanied by one of my old friends, Mauricio Styles. This was the first time I saw Antonio wear a suit. Antonio not only owed me money, he owed other people money. Antonio and Mauricio walked to a table across the room. Through the night I watched Antonio toss cash around like it was confetti. Antonio noticed me and the fellas from across the room. He casually walked to my table and introduced Mauricio as one of his "Boys." Mauricio and I were friends before Antonio came into the picture. I gave Mauricio a look that said, "Oh, you are his boy?" Mauricio must have read the look on my face or maybe he was offended by Antonio's words, because the next thing he did was grab Antonio by his suit jacket and say in a threatening tone, "I don't work for you and you don't pay me to protect you! So don't ever call me your boy!" Antonio looked surprised. "All right," he said. I had a smile from ear to ear; it let Mauricio know he was right for straightening out Antonio.

On the outside Antonio looked like a baller but behind closed doors he was digging himself into a deep pit of debt. I began to receive complaints that Antonio wasn't calling customers back when they wanted to buy product. Scotty "Rock" Potter, Antonio's roommate, also complained that Antonio would crush the bricks of cocaine that I fronted him till they were powder, then cut the cocaine with B12, a vitamin supplement. Other complaints followed. Antonio cut the coke in an attempt to make up for the money he spent on his lavish lifestyle. He was living beyond his means with other people's money. To make matters worse, Antonio began to get high on my supply. All the signs were there; he slept all day, the money he owed me kept coming up short and he was cutting the cocaine. Antonio's rise to the top took a nose dive and he descended at full speed.

The father of Julie Hermann, a chick Antonio dated, called me to inform me that Antonio was bragging about money he kept in a safe at his mother's house. Antonio told Julie's father that he wanted to invest the money into his seafood business. Julie's father thought that Antonio was just bragging, so he called me to ask if I wanted to invest in importing seafood to Las Vegas. I declined the offer but I was thankful for the call. I kept one of my safes at the home of Antonio's mother and I knew Antonio had been bragging to Julie's father about the money I had. The call from Julie's father was a sign that Antonio was about to do something foolish. I knew Antonio was getting desperate and I knew he was counting the money I kept at his mom's house as his. I arrived at Mrs. Marcos' house and went into the garage to remove all the money from the safe. Antonio was already cut off from any involvement in my drug dealings. I knew it was a mistake to bring him into the business a second time but what was done was done. I sat back, waiting for Antonio to strike.

Antonio owed me money and his payments were overdue. I went to Antonio's house unannounced with one of my partners, Mark Romero. We took anything of value: a bag full of cocaine cut with B12, a '64 Chevy, even his Shar Pei dog. When Julie found out that her dog was missing, she called the cops. The cops came by my house to warn me that if I didn't return the dog I would be charged with kidnapping. I thought it was crazy that I could be charged with kidnapping a dog. I told the cops that I didn't know anything about the dog being missing. I later had someone drop it off in Julie's yard, not because I was worried about going to jail, but because the dog kept pissing, crying and tearing up the place where he was being kept. I had bigger things to deal with than dog sitting.

I received a phone call from Antonio's mother. Mrs. Marcos asked me if I had taken the safe out of her garage, because she hadn't seen it where it was kept. I told her that I did not take the safe but not to worry about it. I arranged for Antonio to meet me at his mother's house to confront him about the missing safe. Antonio said that his ex-girlfriend Sandra was in town with a few guy friends and he blamed them for taking the safe. I knew Antonio was lying through his teeth. If it wasn't for his mother being there at the time, I would have done something to him. Sandra was the mother of Antonio's daughter, Susanna. Antonio must have wanted me to do harm to Sandra. There was no other reason for him to blame Sandra. She was the girl in California that I messed with back in the day, not knowing that she and Antonio were dating. I thought to myself, "What kind of sick person would do that to the mother of his child?" Antonio was a snake to the

51

core but I let him slither away. I did it for his mother. I didn't want Mother Marcos worrying or being brokenhearted over harm to her son. I was a businessman and knew that it was impossible for a dead man to pay his debt. Antonio was in deep water and he was accumulating more enemies on top of those he already had.

Antonio went into hiding. No one had heard from him for months. I then received a phone call from him, telling me that he had the money he owed me. I agreed to meet up and chose the place. I packed two guns and brought Cisco, a triggerman, as backup. When Antonio showed up at the meeting spot, Cisco was there to pat him down for weapons. Antonio looked surprised that I had him searched; he then removed a stack of hundreds from a small paper bag that he carried. It was $15,000. Antonio told me that he left some sucker waiting at a bar. The guy wanted to buy three kilos of cocaine at $20,000 each. Antonio told him he had connections. Instead of getting the kilos for the guy, Antonio decided to keep the money but, most important, he wanted to pay me. Antonio went on to tell me that he planned to do it just like I did it. He wanted to buy a kilo of cocaine, break it down and sell it by grams and ounces. Antonio asked me if I could help him get some product. I told him that I couldn't help him. I wanted nothing to do with Antonio. He went his way and I went mine.

I took a trip to California and, when I arrived in Wilmington, I got word that Antonio was in town looking to buy at least one kilo of cocaine. I was also told that he bought two cars, a '65 Chevy Impala and a Riviera. He was spending the money he stole as fast as he stole it. Jodi, the cousin of Julie – Antonio's girlfriend at the time -- somehow got my phone number. Jodi called me to tell me that her boyfriend Edward gave Antonio $60,000 so he could buy kilos of cocaine. Antonio said he was picking up the goods from me but hadn't been heard from. Antonio was up to his dirty tricks and again I was left to clean up the mess.

I met up with Jodi and Edward, who told me that Edward's father and a friend of his put up the $60,000 so they could buy three kilos. Antonio had told Edward that he had a connection who could get whatever he needed and it happened to be me. I told Edward that I didn't have anything to do with Antonio or the money he stole. I explained that Antonio owed me money; he had recently called me to pay me and that was the last I heard of him. Edward was angered and had every right to be. Edward asked me if I owned a safe that had been stolen. That got my attention. "Why," I asked. Edward told me that he was with Antonio when he put a medium-sized black safe into the back of his pickup truck. Antonio took the safe to the desert, where he sledgehammered it for hours until it cracked open. I asked Edward what he found inside the safe. Edward said, "Nothing. It was empty." "Yup, that was my safe." I apologized to Edward for his loss and told him I didn't know where Antonio is. I figured eventually one of Antonio's enemies was going to catch up to him.

A BUSINESS INVESTMENT

Driving to meet an associate about a business proposition, I was rear-ended by another vehicle. I later settled with the insurance company and received a large paycheck. It was clean money, so I bought into an auto-body shop called Bodies Unlimited. My new partners were Andy Pardo and Fernando Fallacara, two guys from Argentina. I owned one third of Bodies Unlimited. The company later branched out into buying cars at auctions. Las Vegas was a lucrative market for high-end cars, so I was always scouting for exotic cars in which to invest. During a drive through Hermosa Beach, California I saw a red Porsche 911 Slantnose Cabriolet at a used-car lot on Pacific Coast Highway. It wasn't a new Porsche nor was it a factory Slantnose but it was a beautiful one.

The only salesperson on the lot walked over to me and introduced himself as Stan Harvey. "How much for the red Porsche," I asked. Stan told me the owner was asking $30,000. When I took the car for a spin, I liked it so much that I offered Stan $25,000 cash. Stan explained that the owner left the car at the lot on consignment. Stan said he would call the owner to see if he would accept $25,000. When he returned a short time later, he said the owner accepted the $25,000, cash offer. I told Stan that I would return in a few hours with the money.

I went to Wilmington where I kept the cash, then returned to the dealership with Rick Uribe, a neighborhood friend. When I arrived at the car lot, I told Stan that I had the money. Stan closed down the dealership. He, Rick, and I then entered an office. I handed Stan a brown paper bag that contained $25,000 cash. The money was stacked in thousands. Stan began to sweat profusely as he counted the cash. I could tell the guy was nervous. I asked Stan if he was OK. Stan responded by saying he had never seen so much money in his life. After he verified the count, Stan handed me an official car title. He thanked me with a handshake, then opened the gate and I drove off the lot the proud owner of a Porsche.

I focused on making money through my body shop and through buying cars at auto auctions. I put the red Slantnose Porsche 911 up for sale. Right away I received calls. I arranged to meet with Chris Chaplin, a potential buyer who wanted to test drive the Porsche. Chris was a telemarketer and the girl he was dating was a blond exotic dancer named Tiffany White. She fell in love with the car at first sight and urged Chris to buy it. When Tiffany expressed how much she loved the car, I knew it was sold. Chris paid $32, 000 for the Porsche. A $7,000 dollar profit was not bad for a day's work.

I scouted Porsche 911s from auctions in California and from private owners. I even looked for theft recoveries where the car was stripped of all parts. I then had my guy Estefan Santos in Anaheim replace all the missing parts at a discounted price. Estefan did everything from assemble the wiring harness to welding corner panels to painting the car; and he did it very well. Estefan could put a Porsche 911 back together blindfolded within a few weeks. Once the car was reassembled, I put it on the market for resale. I continued to flip car after car.

While in Hermosa Beach, I took my usual drive down Pacific Coast Highway scouting for Porsche 911s. I decided to stop by and see Stan again. When I pulled into the parking lot, an unfamiliar salesman approached me. He asked if he could help me with anything. I told him that I was looking for Stan. I went on to say that I bought a red Porsche 911 from Stan about four months earlier. The salesman was surprised. "You are the one who bought that car?" "Yes." "Stan took the money and he never came back to work. No one has heard from Stan since."

IN LOVE WITH A STRIPPER

My father called one day to ask if I could help him on a roofing job. I hated roofing but agreed to help anyway. I brought Tino Lopez, who was visiting from California, with me. After work, I stopped by Crazy Horse Too to have a drink. I wore work boots, Levi's pants and a black hooded sweater. When Tino and I walked into the club, I immediately noticed a beautiful woman with big brown eyes, dark curly hair, a pretty smile, nicely trimmed eyebrows and a beautiful body. I was a regular at Crazy Horse Too but I hadn't seen her before. I asked one of my friends if he knew her. "Yeah, that's Antoinette. I went to high school with her," said my friend. When I approached Antoinette to ask her for a dance, she smiled and led me to a table. Antoinette seemed a little shy as she danced before me. She told me it was her first day at the club.

After a few dances, Antoinette asked if it was okay for her to sit with me and talk; I had no problem with that. As Antoinette and I faced each other, I felt a sense of mutual attraction. I offered to buy Antoinette a drink but she didn't want me to waste my money; Antoinette said she would buy me a drink. After talking with her for some time, she told me that her full name was Antoinette DeAnna Woods. Antoinette was Italian and Native American, and had recently gotten out of a relationship. She asked me what type of work I did. I told her that I was part owner of an auto body shop and car dealership. Antoinette didn't seem convinced but we hit it off so well that I gave her my business card before I left the club.

I was at my shop Bodies Unlimited the next day when I heard the office phone ring. My partner Andy answered it. He then turned to me saying a woman was asking if I was part owner of the shop.

Andy then handed me the phone. It was Antoinette. We talked for a few minutes, then I promised her I would be at the club to see her later that night. Before I went I made sure to dress to impress; I put on my best threads and hopped into my black, polished Porsche 911. When I arrived at Crazy Horse, I parked the Porsche near the back entrance. I walked in the club and saw Antoinette near the bar as though she was waiting for me. Antoinette saw me and greeted me with a big hug then complemented me on my clothes. We then moved to a booth where we spent the next hour or so talking with each other.

Antoinette was more interested in getting to know each other than working. I didn't mind talking to her but I knew she was there to make money. Antoinette told me she thought I was lying about owning the body shop. When she first saw me she thought I was a mechanic because of the boots, Levi's pants and zip-up hooded sweater I wore. She said she felt bad that I was spending my hard-earned money on dances. I smiled the whole time Antoinette talked. When she stopped, I grabbed her by the hand and I told her that I want to show her something. She looked puzzled but agreed to go along. I walked her to the back door of the club. She looked into the parking lot and saw my black Porsche 911 Cabriolet.

Antoinette didn't believe the car was mine so I offered to give her a ride home after work and she accepted. On our first date, I took Antoinette to a movie. She wore raggedy tennis shoes that had holes and cut-off Levi's shorts. She would frequently look down at her shoes in an insecure manner. As we stood in line at the snack bar; she said she needed to use the restroom. As Antoinette walked away I heard two girls make fun of Antoinette's shoes and her cut-off shorts. One of the girls said Antoinette looked "tacky." It bothered me that the girls made fun of her. I didn't say anything about the comment when Antoinette returned but the next day I took her on a shopping spree at Fashion Show Mall on the Las Vegas Strip. I bought her new shoes and clothes. Antoinette was so happy that she cried tears of joy. I didn't know Antoinette's financial situation but the signs were there that she wasn't doing well.

Camille and I were separated, and she was pregnant with my daughter Alexis. We agreed to file for divorce after Alexis was born. Camille gave birth to Alexis on March 20, 1991, soon after we finalized the divorce. Antoinette and I spent more time together. Antoinette often wanted me to stop by the club to see her. When I walked into Crazy Horse Too to see Antoinette, she treated me like a king. She would run up to me like a teenaged girl in love, giving me hugs and kisses. If Antoinette was onstage when I arrived at the club, I would make sure to sit stageside. If guys tossed ones, fives, tens or twenties onstage to get Antoinette's attention, I pulled out a roll of hundreds and, one at a time, tossed them onstage at Antoinette's feet. She disapproved of me tossing hundreds around. She thought other customers would be too intimidated to tip anything after seeing all the hundreds. The first time I made it rain, she gave the money back to me when she arrived at my house. Knowing I would get the money back from Antoinette made me want to make it rain hundreds even more.

After Antoinette and I dated for a few months, she asked me what I thought about her doing a photo shoot for *Hustler* magazine. Antoinette's friend was a scout for adult-magazine models. I told Antoinette that I would support her in any decision that she made. Antoinette did the shoot with her friend Melissa. The photos were published in *Hustler*'s February 1991 issue. The centerfold used assumed names, "Rita and Doreen: Brush Strokes." After the magazine was published Antoinette got requests to travel around the world as a featured performer at local strip clubs.

There was so much criminal activity going on in Las Vegas it was like I was in criminal college. I learned about chop shops, credit card fraud, insurance scams, fencing stolen goods and about drugs that I hadn't heard of: methamphetamine, Ecstasy, Valium, LSD and peyote, to name a few. If there was money to be made in Las Vegas, I wanted in on it. I often came across Rolex watches, diamond rings, emerald rings, gold chains and other items of value. I occasionally told Antoinette, jokingly, "You stick with me and you'll be wearing diamonds." In reality, I did drape Antoinette with diamond and emerald rings, emerald earrings and emerald bracelets with a matching necklace. I was making enough money to shower Antoinette with things that she never had and most of the time I didn't pay full price for the goods, so what did I care about spending the money?

MEETING LEANNA

I met Leanna Torres in 1992 through Alonso Diaz, a mutual friend. Leanna was a friend of Vanessa Moreno who dated Alonso. Vanessa and Alonso invited Leanna and I on a double date, with the intention of introducing us to each other. Leanna grew up in San Pedro, California and she was of Puerto Rican descent. Leanna had long, curly hair and beautiful brown eyes. Some people said that Leanna resembled songstress Mariah Carey. After meeting Leanna, we began to date.

I was dating Antoinette Woods and Leanna Torres at the same time. Initially Antoinette didn't know about Leanna and Leanna didn't know about Antoinette; neither knew about the other women I dated. After dating Leanna for some time, she called me to tell me that she was pregnant. Not long after, we stopped seeing each other. I'm sure it was because I dated Antoinette and other women, and because I was being a jerk. Months later, I ran into Leanna while visiting mutual friends in California. I was in Wilmington when I stopped by Victor Flores and Margo Sanchez's apartment to take a shower. When I walked out of the restroom, Leanna was sitting in the kitchen having a conversation with Margo. I could tell Leanna was bothered but I said hello to her anyway. I then gave Leanna money for some of the baby's needs.

Serina Elizabeth Torres was born on March 1, 1993. I wasn't present at the hospital the day my daughter was born; Leanna and I were not talking at the time. Months later while attending a wedding in San Pedro, I ran into Leanna. We began to communicate again. Leanna made plans to baptize Serina. The night before the baptism, I went out and partied with friends. I awoke when Leanna called my cell phone. By the time I arrived at the church, the baptism was over. Leanna was very upset and had reason to be: I began to party often and with more partying came more drug use.

Leanna made plans for us to take Serina to Disneyland; again, I partied the night before and Leanna came looking for me when I didn't show up. When Leanna found my van, she left a nasty note on my windshield. I arrived at her place a few hours late with a hangover. Leanna had the look of death in her eyes. After Leanna's anger subsided, Serina, Leanna and I went to Disneyland, where we enjoyed the day.

The drug business continued to flourish and I continued to travel to California to pick up loads of cocaine. It was always business first and then I partied for a few days. When I arrived in Los Angeles, Tino Lopez called me on my cell phone to invite me over to his place. Tino knew I came to town to pick up loads but he never knew any details. I had already picked up my supply of cocaine from my connection. The coke was kept at a secure home until I was ready to transport the goods to Las Vegas.

I stopped at Tino's place to have a few beers. When I arrived the small group of people were drinking and smoking weed while music played over a stereo. The party went late into the night, and Tino insisted that I stay at his place so I wouldn't be drinking and driving. The next day, when I walked out of Tino's apartment, I noticed the blue minivan that I drove had been broken into. The door panels were ripped off and the back seats were lifted up. I knew whoever broke into the van thought I had a load of cocaine hidden in the vehicle. It was the first time I used the van to pick up a load in California and Tino was the only person who knew the van was at his house. It wasn't hard to figure out who sent someone to ransack the van. That someone was hoping to find the load of cocaine that was headed to Las Vegas. I couldn't blame Tino because I had no proof but I knew eventually the truth would come out.

Months later, I ran into a drunken Tino while I was in Los Angeles. He told me with a guilty look on his face, "I hope you don't think I had anything to do with your car getting broken into. I would never do that to you. I love you man." Tino had given himself away; my suspicions about him were confirmed.

LEANNA VISITS LAS VEGAS

Alonso Diaz called me to let me know he was coming to Las Vegas and he was bringing his girlfriend Vanessa, along with Leanna. When Alonso arrived in town, we stayed at the Aladdin Hotel and Casino. Alonso and I decided to shoot craps while Vanessa and Leanna watched. The mood was set: I was on a winning streak and got cockier than usual.

The chubby Italian dealer at the craps table said something slick to me, so I decided to taunt him. I held the dice to his face and I told him to blow on them for good luck. Every time I rolled the dice, my number hit. I was buzzed from the alcohol and was on a winning streak, plus I had a beautiful woman by my side. The night was perfect until Alonso leaned over and whispered in my ear, "Let's take a stroll to the restroom. I have some coca." I grinned and nodded yes. Vanessa and Leanna stayed behind with the money as Alonso and I took a walk.

When we entered the restroom, Alonso handed me a plastic bag filled with powder cocaine. I peeled a hundred-dollar bill off the stack of cash I had in my pants pocket and rolled it up into a snorting straw. I dipped the straw into the bag of coke and inhaled into each nostril. After the bathroom break, Alonso and I returned to the craps table. Immediately I felt the cocaine drain down my throat and my teeth began to grind. I wasn't able to talk any longer and my breathing got heavy. I had snorted too much coke and when I rolled the dice I began to lose. My winning streak was over.

The Italian dealer had a grin on his face; it was obvious that I was coked up. I felt paranoid, so I asked Leanna to cash in the rest of the chips. When Leanna returned, we decided to go to the hotel room and Alonso and Vanessa went their way.

I was so high on coke that I could barely talk. When I got to the room I sat on a chair and watched TV as I guzzled down beer after beer, trying to bring down my high. Leanna sat on the edge of the bed; there was an uncomfortable silence between us. Leanna finally said, "What's wrong with you? What is it? You don't want to talk to me?" I couldn't answer her. With hand signals I told Leanna to wait for a moment, because I couldn't talk. Leanna looked at me with a puzzled stare. After I downed more beers my high began to wear off. I then explained to Leanna that I snorted coke, and my throat was so numb that I couldn't talk. Leanna laughed as she realized what a fool I was.

THE MAN FROM CHICAGO

Santi Rivelli had a reputation within our circle of friends for putting together inside jobs. Santi was an Italian from Chicago who I met in the late 1980s through mutual friends. Santi specialized in security alarms, cameras, recording devices, debugging equipment and so on. Word on the street was that Santi was associated to the Hole in the Wall Gang; a burglary ring that operated in Las Vegas in the Seventies and Eighties and was run by Chicago mob enforcer Anthony Spilotro. I never asked Santi about his ties with any organizations and he never directly told me that he was connected, but it was mentioned by a few mutual friends occasionally.

One of Santi's moneymakers was robbing self-storage units. Santi would have someone rent a storage unit. Then he would enter the gate using the passcode. The office closed at 5 p.m., but a person renting a unit had access to the premises until 7 p.m. Santi usually brought two guys with him, one to keep watch for any unwanted visitors and the other to take notes of inventory once the unit lock was popped open. Valuables found in units that were broken into were transferred to a unit that was pre-rented by an associate of Santi's. The stolen goods were removed after office hours so employees wouldn't interrupt and were later sold on the black market.

Santi had many friends in Vegas: business owners, street hoods, attorneys, bailiffs and at least one Las Vegas judge. Santi took me to a warehouse where he introduced me to one of his business associates. The warehouse was equipped with jewelry-manufacturing equipment and a huge sifting machine that separated dirt from gold. As Santi walked me through the warehouse he showed me a variety of finished jewelry; he then brought me to a six-foot-tall safe. Santi opened the safe to remove a black satin pouch. He instructed me to hold out one of my hands and when I did he poured about three-dozen large, dark, emerald rocks out of the pouch and into my palm. Santi bragged that I was holding over a million dollars' worth of emeralds in my hand. Santi must have noticed the dollar signs in my eyes, because the next thing he said was, "Don't get any ideas." Hanging around Santi, one never knew what to expect but he always had jobs lined up.

After Antoinette was featured in *Hustler* she was offered to dance at clubs all over the world. She accepted an offer where she was flown to Guam and provided an apartment. Antoinette earned very good money and every two weeks would mail me a few thousand dollars in money orders so I could save it for her. When Antoinette was near the end of her tour I'd take a flight to Guam and we would vacation together, then return to Vegas. The flight from Vegas to Guam was approximately 15 hours. It was the longest I'd been on a plane. When I arrived in Guam, Antoinette was at the airport to greet me. She was so happy to see me that she screamed in excitement when I walked into the terminal. After settling in, Antoinette and I went on a tour of the tropical island, visiting Tamuning, Talofofo Falls, and Coco's Island. We sipped drinks aboard a ship that took us to international waters so gamblers could play in the casino. In the evenings, Antoinette took me to her workplace, Vikings Tavern, where she introduced me to her friends and coworkers. The people from Guam treated me as if I was a local.

IS GOD CALLING ME?

When I arrived back in Las Vegas, it was business as usual. Although I lived a life that was out of control, I still wondered if I would go to Heaven when I died. I wasn't a religious person, but I've always believed in God. I was raised on saying prayers with my grandmother as a child, so I often prayed before I went to bed. In my prayers I asked God to forgive me for my sins but I still held onto the sinful lifestyle.
I was with Tony Alverez, a former producer from Scandalous Records, when we were working on music tracks that I was funding. Tony and I left Rocket Plant Recording Studio in Burbank to grab a bite to eat. While in the drive-through of a fast-food restaurant a homeless woman approached my car begging for change. When she did, I cussed her out

and chased her away. Tony wanted to know why I would do such a thing. I told him that beggars were scammers trying to swindle people out of their money. I explained that I knew at least one beggar named Colonel, who hustled on Las Vegas Boulevard.

Colonel wore raggedy clothes, he was unshaven and he usually disconnected his prosthetic leg when he sat on the Las Vegas Strip begging for money. At the end of the day, Colonel would call me to drop off a sack of cocaine. A friend of mine saw Colonel at a hotel party but Colonel wore his prosthetic leg and he sported new clothes. After I gave Tony my explanation he asked me, "How do you know that lady wasn't an angel?" I wasn't sure if Tony was being serious. Then Tony went on to share a scripture from Hebrews 13:2 NIV, "Do not forget to entertain strangers, for by so doing some people have entertained angels without knowing it." That scripture was food for thought. Tony had asked me to go to church with him but I always made excuses not to. I promised Tony that I would go someday.

Tony often reminded me about going to church. Though I lacked in many areas of my life, I made sure to keep my word when I was able. When I arrived at Tony's house to pick him up, I had the impression that we were going to a recording studio but Tony told me that we were going to church. Tony had me where he wanted and I couldn't get out of it. We arrived at First Church of South Bay, in Torrance. I entered it not knowing what to expect. Tony introduced me to some of the congregation and reintroduced me to his family, who I hadn't seen for some time.

The church service started with worship music. The music was so uplifting that I felt at peace just being there. I don't recall what the message was about but I remember feeling the same way I did when I attended a church service when I was 16 years old for the first time on the east side of Wilmington. While I sat in church I quietly asked Jesus into my life, just like I did when I was a kid. I knew deep in my heart that church was where God wanted me to be and was where I needed to be.

After church service, I dropped Tony off at his house and I headed to my hotel, where the chick I dated that night waited for me. Usually I went to a movie, grabbed something to eat and spent the night with one of the ladies I dated, but something inside of me kept me from wanting to have sex with my date. It was clear to me that God was tugging on my heart.

LIVING MY DREAMS

When I arrived back in Las Vegas I was on a spiritual high but life in Sin City got the best of me. It was back to business. Coca sold as fast as the loads came in. Money was practically falling out of the skies of Las Vegas. The fruits of my labor allowed me to enjoy such things as championship fights at the MGM Grand Garden Arena. I took Ray Junior with me to see Oscar De La Hoya defeat Jorge Paez at the Garden on July 29, 1994. We sat ringside with celebrities and sports figures.

I was living my dreams but the icing on the cake was when I received a phone call from Santi Rivelli, who told me that Martin Scorsese was filming a movie in Las Vegas about Anthony Spilotro called *Casino*. Santi told me that if I wanted to be in the movie I could contact a friend of his named Frank De Luca at a local casting agency. I had mentioned to Santi in the past that I wanted to work in the movie industry.

I took Santi's advice and went to the casting agency. I was hired on the spot as an extra. I played a news photographer in a scene where Joe Pesci, Oscar Goodman, and a few goons walked out of the U.S. courthouse in the Foley Federal Building and onto the sidewalk as the news media pursued them. I wore blue bell-bottom pants and a checkered coat from the Seventies as I snapped photos of Nicky Santoro, Joe Pesci's character in the movie. My hair was combed back and I wore fake sideburns. I was even more pleased when I obtained Screen Actors Guild membership from working on the movie. To be in a Martin Scorsese gangster movie with Robert De Niro and Joe Pesci was an honor even if I was only an extra.

Antoinette called me excitedly, telling me that she wanted me to come to the Crazy Horse right away to meet someone. When I asked who it was, she said it was a surprise. I arrived at the club to meet Antoinette who grabbed me by the hand and led me to Joe Pesci's table. Antoinette introduced me to Pesci as her boyfriend. He shook my hand, then he went on to tell me that I had a beautiful girlfriend. He said she reminded him of Marisa Tomei, his costar in the movie *My Cousin Vinny*. Pesci was a gentleman and he was nice enough to sign "God is good, you be too" and his autograph on a napkin for Antoinette.

A few days later I ran into Pesci again at the Riviera Hotel and Casino, in a nightclub scene where he sat at a back table with actor Frank Vincent as they watch and badmouthed characters Ace Rothstein (De Niro) and Billy Sherbert (Don Rickles), who walked into the club and sat at another table with two showgirls. During a break. I walked over to Pesci, who sat alone. I reintroduced myself and I told him that we met the other night at Crazy Horse Too. Pesci said he remembered me and brought up that Antoinette resembled Marisa Tomei. I wanted to be respectful and not take much of his time, so I kept my conversation short and went on my way. Playing a role in a gangster movie was fun but living the gangster life was a totally different story. I was living my dreams but knew someday I'd pay a price for the illegal things I had done.

GUAM AGAIN

Antoinette made arrangements to travel to Guam so she could make extra money but she was hesitant to leave because she felt that I was going to cheat on her. I convinced Antoinette that I would be good. Most of the time my intentions were not to hurt her. After a few months, I flew to Guam to meet up with Antoinette. The long flight had me jet-lagged. After we settled into our hotel room in Tamuning, we showered and then went out on the town with Antoinette's friends Sherrie and Rudy.

The four of us bar-hopped most of the night and then Rudy offered me some ice. I'm not talking about frozen H20; I'm talking about a pure

65

form of methamphetamine. I had never tried ice but I was drinking and was there to party. When we arrived at Rudy's house he brought out a pipe, a torch and a bag of ice that looked like pieces of clear crystal. When Rudy told me that one gram of ice sold for $1,000 in Guam, I saw dollar signs. That was $28,000 dollars an ounce and, with those prices, profits would be enormous. I thought about the money that could be made, as I took a small hit of ice. The drug made me paranoid and -- after hours of being awake -- I wanted badly to sleep but was unable to for nearly two days. My eyes felt strained and my head ached. It was a drug that I didn't want to mess with again.

When Antoinette and I woke, I went with her to a paid phone service so she could check her messages. One was from a chick named Tina Ramirez, who I dated in Las Vegas. On the message Tina was crying because she found out that I was in Guam with Antoinette. A so-called friend of mine had given Tina Antoinette's beeper number. When Antoinette confronted me about Tina I denied the whole thing. I knew I had messed up. Antoinette and I were on vacation, and we were supposed to be enjoying life. Just when I thought things couldn't get any worse, on May 20, 1994, Antoinette received a call from her mother. Her brother Ricky Woods had overdosed on drugs. Antoinette was devastated. We decided to cut our vacation short and fly back to the States. On the plane home, Antoinette cried her eyes out. I felt so bad for her and finding out about Tina didn't help. After hours of weeping, Antoinette fell asleep.

As I sat next to Antoinette, I stared out the window at the massive ocean. I could see the curvature of the earth from the altitude of the plane. I began to wonder if there was more to life than the life I was living. I made money, dated beautiful women, bought fancy cars and took vacations -- but I wasn't happy with myself. There was something missing in my life. My thoughts shifted and I wondered if we would be found if the plane crashed in the ocean. The chances were that sharks would eat us if we had survived the crash. It made me think about where I would go when I die. Deep inside my soul I knew the answer and didn't like it.

Antoinette's brother's funeral was held in Michigan. Antoinette wanted me to attend but I refused because I knew her family didn't like me and with good reason. After the funeral, Antoinette brought Ricky's ashes back to Las Vegas in an urn and kept them in our spare bedroom closet. Antoinette planned to spread the ashes in a canyon at an ecumenical shrine in Pahrump. We drove down Highway 160. When we arrived at the canyon the sky was clear but there was a slight breeze.

Antoinette stepped out of the car carrying the urn with Ricky's ashes. I followed Antoinette a few yards behind, as she walked onto a bridge made of rope and wood that led to the other side of the canyon. Antoinette stopped halfway on the bridge; I stood not far away as she removed the bag of ashes from the urn. Antoinette paused for a moment as if to say a prayer then she poured the bag of ashes out into the canyon. Out of nowhere, a gust of wind carried Ricky's ashes right at me and hit me in the face. The ashes were all over my face and my clothes. I yelled at Antoinette, "Hey! What are you doing?" When Antoinette turned and saw that I was covered in ashes, she cracked up laughing. "Ricky is still making us laugh even in his death," she said. I guess if it would have happened to someone else I would have been laughing too.

HELP A BROTHER OUT

I received a call from a family member who I will call The Messenger. The Messenger told me that he was in Las Vegas and that we needed to talk. The Messenger was associated with a criminal organization I'll call Mi Gente. When I arrived at the meeting, The Messenger informed me that the higher ups in the Mi Gente organization got word that I was doing very well in Las Vegas and they wanted a monthly payment to help other "Brothers" who were facing legal troubles. I knew what The Messenger was getting at. I had no problem helping family, I told The Messenger, but I did have a problem with someone coming into my backyard, trying to muscle me.

I didn't care how The Messenger was sugarcoating it; he was attempting to tax me on my illegal business in Las Vegas. I let The

Messenger know that I wasn't okay with what he was asking of me. The way I saw it, The Messenger and I were family, and family was off limits to any taxation. I also felt that because I was in Las Vegas, I wasn't bound by the so called "Monthly taxation payments" that Mi Gente charged to those involved in illegal activities in California. I wasn't giving them a dime; I had enough muscle backing me up in Las Vegas if I needed to flex it. To smooth things out, I told The Messenger that I would take care of him one time and one time only, and if he wanted to give his share of "monthly payments" to someone else, then so be it. I gave The Messenger a package of cocaine for him to do as he pleased and told him, "It is more than enough to help your brothers." He seemed content and departed.

A few months later, The Messenger arrived in Las Vegas asking for another payment. The Messenger named a list of benefits I would receive for a small monthly fee. Again I told him that I wasn't paying rent to anyone. I wanted The Messenger to understand that I meant business, so I took him to a stash house where I kept a small arsenal of weapons. I showed The Messenger a sample of what I had: AR15s, an AK47, M16s, a Calico 9 mm and then some. I made it clear to The Messenger that my people had no problem protecting their bread and butter in Las Vegas. "If you are with them, then you are against me. I'll let you pick sides," I told him.

The Messenger stood silent as he stared at the weapons. He then said, "Blood is thicker than water, familia." The Messenger had chosen sides, but that didn't mean there weren't other snakes slithering in the jungle. For extra security, I had audio and video cameras installed all around my house, and guns stashed in every vehicle I drove. I bought bullet-resistant vests and had recording devices installed on my home phones. I wanted to be fully ready for whatever came my way. Taking security precautions was a part of being in the drug business; though there were potential threats, it was still business and pleasure as usual.

DEATH KNOCKING AT THE DOOR

It was another party weekend in Sin City. I was to meet up with friends at the Shark Club, a popular night spot. But first I had to drop off an eight-ball of coke to a girl named Kathy Smith in exchange for 50 Valium. I met up with Kathy and we did the exchange. Then I drove home to change clothes, something more fitting for the nightlife. I left 20 Valium in a stash spot and bagged 30 to take with me out on the town. I wanted to start a buzz early, so I popped two Valium in my mouth and I chased then with a beer before I left the house. I didn't know much about Valium except it was a muscle relaxant and was told by a friend that I couldn't overdose on the pills. When I arrived at the Shark Club, I passed out the Valium to friends like I was handing out candy for Halloween.

As the evening went on, I continued to drink and pop more pills. I remember my body feeling heavy and then the night's events became a blur. I didn't remember leaving the club but I remembered driving my car home. I didn't remember pulling my car into the driveway but I did remember unlocking the door to my house and stumbling into the living room. The last thing I remembered was entering a bedroom and falling forward onto a bed. I was so drugged up that I didn't bother to remove my clothes or my shoes. When I awakened, my sister Debrah told me that I had been asleep for two days. She had kept checking on me to see if I was alive. When I searched my pants pockets I found the empty bag that once contained 30 Valium. I later learned that I could have overdosed from taking it, especially when used with alcohol.

My cocaine use was out of control. There were nights I'd flush eight-balls down the toilet because I was sick of getting high after an all-night snorting binge. I attempted to quit on numerous occasions. It lasted for a few weeks, then I would start using again. Through it all, I told myself that I wasn't hooked and felt that I was able to quit if I wanted.

During an all-night coke fest, I was so high that every few seconds I'd change the TV channels with the remote control, then I would look at the home-surveillance camera monitors. When the sun came up, Ray

Junior, who was four years old at the time, crawled into bed with me. He laid his head on my chest and a moment later asked, "Daddy, why is your heart beating so fast?" I was lost for words. I told my son, "Daddy is tired. That's why my heart is beating fast." My son hopped off the bed repeating the words, "Daddy's tired," as he ran out the room. I knew I had hit rock bottom. If I didn't stop doing drugs my life would end shortly. I was tired of drinking and I was tired of using cocaine. After Ray Junior left my room, I crawled out of bed and I dropped to my knees. I leaned over the top of my bed and I asked God to help me change my life. I pleaded with God, "If you are real, Lord, then change me." But after that night of praying, my life didn't change much and it was business as usual the next day.

Pecas was a Mexican national from Sinaloa, a state where some of the top drug traffickers were born. I had been purchasing product from Pecas long enough to earn his trust. Pecas often sent larger amounts of cocaine to Las Vegas that he gave me on credit. I would sell the cocaine, return the money to Pecas, and wait for the next load to arrive or I would drive to California to pick up the load myself.

I received a call from Pecas about a load that I was to pick up in California. I drove to Long Beach, where I met Pecas, who handed me the keys to a Nissan Sentra. Pecas gave me directions on where I was to pick up the vehicle, then he gave me the number of kilos that were in the vehicle's secret compartment. Pecas instructed me to call him when I arrived in Las Vegas. Before my road trip, I inspected the car to make sure all lights were working; I also checked for current registration, insurance and tags. I then headed to the freeway to Las Vegas.

Four and a half hours later, I arrived at a Vegas safe house. When I unloaded the coke, I found five extra packages with wrappings that were different from the cocaine. I wondered why there were more packages than what Pecas had told me. I thought he was testing me to see if I would tell him about the extra packages. I called Pecas on his cell phone right away to let him know about the extra tickets. "Ticket" was a code word we used for kilo, package or pound. Pecas said he knew about the tickets and he asked me to sell them for him. I agreed to do so and, when I opened a package, I found that it contained methamphetamine. I didn't deal meth but I put the word out that I had a new product for sale. The meth sold just as quickly as the cocaine did, so I decided to add it to my menu.

It was December 1994 and usually when Pecas visited Las Vegas, it was to relax for a few days, collect money and see a show or a championship fight. But this time Pecas came with bad news. He told me that his right-hand-man, Armando Flores had been busted. Pecas was collecting cash to pay for Armando's attorneys. I was told that Armando got popped by the feds while picking up 175 kilos of cocaine at a ranch in Riverside, California. After I gave Pecas the money that I owed him, he headed to Los Angeles. The next time I drove to Long Beach to meet up with Pecas, he seemed paranoid. He kept looking at the sky, saying a helicopter was following him and I also saw one circling the area. Pecas informed me that he was going to Mexico to lay low because things were too hot in California. He said he would contact me when he returned; we then said our goodbyes and Pecas went his way.

GOING-AWAY PARTY

It had been months since I heard from The Messenger. When he contacted me, I was told that high officials from Mi Gente were asking for my help. The Messenger explained to me that a member of Mi Gente, who I will call Mr. Greedy, was making moves to take control of business dealings for his own personal gain. Tension had been rising amongst the group because of Mr. Greedy. A secret meeting was held and a vote was cast. All agreed that the bad seed needed to go. The voting members had a plan to invite Mr. Greedy to Las Vegas for a party and that's when they would make him disappear. The same people who tried to tax me suddenly needed my help. I was asked to have a place in the desert ready where the bad seed would be laid to rest. I couldn't believe I was being asked such a thing. I made it clear to The Messenger that whatever was going on between his people was none of my business and I was cutting all ties with him. The Messenger's last words were, "I respect your decision." We parted ways.

Sometime later, I received threatening phone calls from an unknown member of Mi Gente who wanted in on my Las Vegas drug profits. I also received phone numbers to the FBI office and Secret Witness on my beeper. Somebody wanted me out of the picture.

KTE

Santi Rivelli asked me if I wanted in on his next job and I was all for it. Santi usually called me when his partner-in-crime Matteo Calvi wasn't available. Santi instructed me to have someone rent a unit at the storage place in Green Valley on Sunset Road. Santi said it had no alarm systems for individual units and would be a piece of cake to hit. I had Antoinette rent a storage unit in her name. A person was permitted access through the security gate with a passcode. Once we were on the property, I followed Santi as he picked the locks to each unit. I then opened the unit's door, wrote down the unit number and made a list of inventory that might be valuable so we could return with a truck to load the goods.

The next day while I was at the body shop, I received a phone call from Santi who wanted me to meet him at the storage unit right away and to bring a truck. When I got there, Santi and Matteo were present. Santi told me that he found a unit that contained 20 pieces of artwork and other valuables that belonged to Wayne Newton. Santi, Matteo and I approached the storage unit; Santi popped the lock with a pick set, then rolled the door open. We all grabbed what we could and loaded the goods into a Toyota until the bed was filled. I drove the truck to Santi's home, where we stored the loot. We then returned to the storage facility a few times until the unit was empty.

On our last trip I attempted to exit the security gate but it wouldn't open. It was after the 7 p.m. cutoff time. At 7, the automatic security system kicked in and the gates locked. No one could enter the property nor could anyone exit until the automatic system unlocked at 7 a.m. the next day. We were locked in the facility with a load of Wayne Newton's stolen goods piled in the back of the truck. If the truck was left until morning, someone might know that we hit the units. I had to think fast. I decided to walk along the fence to see if I could find a way out. I noticed a wide gate used for the entrance of RVs, but it had a lock on it. I also saw that the fence had hinges so I retrieved a wrench from my truck and I unscrewed the nuts that held the hinges. I then pulled open the gate wide enough for the Toyota to fit through. I drove off the property and parked it up the street. I walked back to the fence and tightened the hinges, making sure to leave the gate how I found it. I then drove the Toyota to Santi's house, where Matteo, Santi and I unloaded the goods in the garage.

KTE

I continued to buy high-end cars at auctions, so I needed a local guy who did high-end custom work. A client referred me to Aldo Walter who was part owner of a custom motor-and-body shop in Las Vegas. Aldo had many upper-end clients who poured money into their toys. All types of cars rolled into the auto shop, everything from Ferrari to Porsche, Jaguars and antique Corvettes. Aldo was my new go-to guy for sleeking out my auto investments.

I was asked by Santi if I could find a buyer for the 20 pieces of artwork that were stolen from Wayne Newton's storage unit. I knew it wouldn't be easy to fence the artwork and I had to find a buyer from out of the country. One of the persons I contacted to inquire about potential buyers was Aldo Walter. I figured Aldo might know someone interested in the artwork, since he dealt with high-end clients. When I visited Aldo at his body shop, he told me he would arrange a meeting with his client Juan Carlos, to see if he was interested in the artwork. In the meantime, Aldo and I drove to California to research art galleries, so we could get an idea of how much the artwork was worth. It was difficult to determine the true value.

ANTOINETTE GOES TO GUAM

My business dealings continued all the way to Los Angeles. When I was away from Las Vegas for weeks at a time, Antoinette would call me or page me, continually asking me to come home. When I ignored her calls and pages, she would call every hotel in the area where I stayed until she found me. Antoinette had never been to Wilmington but, when I didn't come home for a week she drove there to look for me. Antoinette and I began to drift apart. I knew she was tired of the way I treated her. Antoinette told me she needed to get away from Las Vegas and was moving to Guam. A few days before Antoinette was to leave for Guam, she asked me if I could take her to the airport. I told her I would, but when the time came I didn't show. I decided to let things be. Antoinette and I broke up, and I began dating Leanna Torres again.

KTE

In April 1995, Aldo Walter introduced Alex Cardenas and myself to Juan Carlos at an Italian restaurant in Las Vegas. Juan was a former city manager in California who claimed to have contacts all over the world. We had a meeting to discuss the sale of the artwork. Juan claimed to have people in Spain that might be interested in purchasing the art but it would take a month or so to arrange for the buyer to come to the U.S. At the meeting, all agreed on the minimum asking price of $250,000 for the artwork. Juan Carlos asked if anyone cared who he sold the paintings to. All agreed that Juan could sell them to anyone he chose -- as long as the person had cash. The meeting ended with Juan declaring a toast "to a prosperous year and to making lots of money!"

I visited Juan at his home in Coronado, California from time to time to see how things were progressing with the art buyer. Juan had other business deals. I agreed to go with him to look at a property that he wanted me to purchase with him in Mazatlán, Sinaloa Mexico. It was a five-bedroom house near the beach in a cul-de-sac; it had a security gate and a maid's corridor, with marble floors and fancy fixings. After visiting the property, Juan and I decided to purchase the house from a woman named Silvia Garcia. She was the wife of a man named Ezekiel Garcia who got arrested for smuggling a ship filled with cocaine. Times were hard on Silvia, so she decided to sell the place.

A few weeks after our trip to Mazatlán, Juan contacted me to let me know that he had set up a meeting with potential buyers who were Colombians. Juan wanted me to bring one of the paintings to the meeting so he could show the buyers. I contacted Santi Rivelli to let him know that I needed to take one of the paintings to California. It was like pulling teeth but I finally convinced Santi and Matteo to let me take the artwork.

Juan and I arrived at Fuddruckers in his red Porsche 944. We walked into the restaurant and took a seat at a table. Something didn't feel right with me. I said to Juan, "I have a feeling that cops are watching us." "Relax, you're being paranoid," Juan responded. Juan received a call on his cell phone; it was the Colombians. Juan informed the buyers that we were in the restaurant; a few minutes later two Colombians entered Fuddruckers. Juan introduced me to a short, medium-built man named Lucho Bocanegra and a tall, slim man named Jorge Falcon. Both wore Miami-style clothing and spoke with Spanish accents. Juan and Lucho went to Juan's Porsche to see one of the paintings while Jorge and I remained in the restaurant. Jorge asked me where I was from. "California," I told Jorge. I didn't want to be too specific. After all, I didn't know this guy. Jorge then asked me if I worked for Wayne Newton. The question surprised me; I told Jorge that I'd never met Newton nor did I work for him. After Jorge and I shared small talk, Juan and Lucho came back. The meeting ended with the Colombians saying they would get back to us after they discussed the deal with their people.

ARTWORK

I alerted Santi Rivelli, so I could arrange to pick up the artwork. Santi's partner Matteo was at Santi's house when I arrived. I told Santi that the deal with the Colombians looked promising. I mentioned that the Colombians hired an art expert to appraise the paintings and, after a lot of convincing, Santi and Matteo allowed me to take the artwork. Matteo, Santi and I loaded the precious cargo into my Plymouth van. I then headed to California, where I delivered the artwork to Studio City with Juan's brother for safekeeping. A few days passed and still no deal with the Colombians. I had my regular cocaine business that I needed to attend to so I let Juan know that I was going back to Las Vegas. I told him to call me when the Colombians were ready to do the deal.

When I arrived in Las Vegas without the artwork, Santi and Matteo pressured me to bring the paintings back. Santi felt that I wasn't moving the goods fast enough. I had to convince Santi that the deal was going to go through with the Colombians. I explained to him that it wasn't easy to dump millions in stolen artwork, especially when it belonged to Wayne Newton. I told Santi and Matteo that I was waiting for the phone call so we could make the trade. Santi kept warning me to be careful. The last thing he wanted was Wayne Newton knowing that we were selling his goods.

CHAPTER 3 Robbing Mr. Las Vegas

It was 1995. I had been involved in criminal activity in Las Vegas for nearly 10 years. Constant amounts of cash were coming in from ongoing moneymaking deals; some were legit but most were illegal. I considered myself a one-stop-shop. If a person needed something, it didn't matter what it was. I would do what I could to get it for him.

On May 19, I received the phone call that I was waiting for. Juan Carlos called to let me know that the Colombians agreed upon a deal and that we would make the transaction on May 24th. The artwork was estimated to be worth $1 million to $2 million.

I had to meet again with Santi Rivelli. When I arrived at Santi's house, Matteo was present. I explained to Santi and Matteo that a deal with the Colombians looked like it was going to go down. Santi asked me few questions and gave me the approval to deal with the Colombians. Santi and Matteo were looking forward to their cut. Santi told me to be careful and handed me a small electronic device, saying it was an audio-and-video detector. He instructed me to keep the detector in my front pants pocket. Santi went on to explain that if anyone was recording me at any time, the device would vibrate, letting me know to get out. I told Santi that I would let him know how the deal was coming along.

When I arrived home, I tossed the detector onto my bed. I knew the local cops wouldn't follow me to California and felt untouchable. I didn't believe that I needed the audio-and-video detector, so I left it behind.

The plan was for Alex and me to travel to San Diego to do the deal with the Colombians. His suitcase was packed and ready, but something deep inside of me told me not to let Alex go along. I said it would be better for him to stay behind in Las Vegas in case something went wrong. There was no reason for both of us to risk the possibility of getting busted. Alex looked at me with a blank stare, then he agreed to stay.

I got into my Plymouth Voyager and set off for Los Angeles. It was five days before the artwork deal was going to take place and Leanna asked me if I would take her to pick up her half-brother Felix Marquez, who was being released from a California prison camp. I had already agreed to take Leanna before getting the phone call from Juan about the deal with the Colombians.

I arrived in Wilmington at Leanna's house and the next day I drove her to Yosemite National Park, where we rented a room. In the morning, Leanna and I went to the state prison to pick up Felix and drove him to Wilmington.

On May 23, it was time to head to San Diego. I made a side trip to pick up Victor Mercado. He was a 19-year-old kid from Wilmington who visited Alex and me in Vegas from time to time. He walked out of his house wearing jeans, a black, hooded sweatshirt and carrying a duffel bag filled with clothes. A few days earlier I had told Victor that I was going to pick up some money in San Diego and asked if he wanted to come along as backup.

On the drive to San Diego I was thinking about ways to invest the money I would receive from the deal, either putting it into real estate or a small casino. I had always wanted to open a casino and I was thinking about building one in Pahrump, with limos for VIPs and a helicopter to fly in "whales," as high-rolling players were known. Women would be available for them when they visited this brothel-themed casino. I was also thinking about what kind of new, fully loaded Chevy Suburban SUV I would buy after the deal went through. I was thinking about everything except the risk I was taking.

When I met Juan Carlos, he informed me that the Colombians agreed to trade the artwork for 50 kilos of cocaine and the deal was going to take place the next day. The artwork was dropped off at a house in

Studio City for safekeeping. Victor and I rented a hotel room in San Diego.

The next morning May 24, we had time to spare, because the artwork deal wasn't going to take place until 2 or 3 p.m. So I drove Victor to Tecate, Mexico to visit his uncle and to grab a bite to eat. After a few hours, Victor and I headed back to the U.S. Just before we reached the border there was a police checkpoint: four SUVs with four Mexico federal police officers. One of the officers raised his hand ordering me to stop my vehicle. When I brought the van to a halt, the officer asked Victor and me to get out.

The officer asked if we had any weed, cocaine, crystal meth or heroin in the van. Two other officers searched the vehicle. I knew we didn't have any drugs on us but I did have a .38-caliber handgun and $5,000 in cash stashed in one of the van's secret compartments. The *federales* went over every inch of the van. I knew they were looking for a secret compartment and the agent was close to finding it; he even tapped the panel behind which the compartment was hidden, but he suddenly moved in a different direction. I was very relieved when the agents let us go.

After Victor and I crossed over to the U.S. side, I called Juan. He instructed me to meet him at his office in downtown San Diego. When Victor and I arrived, Juan informed me that he arranged to meet the Colombians at a restaurant in Irvine. Juan and I headed to the stash house in Studio City, where we retrieved the U-Haul boxes that contained the artwork. We loaded them into my van and headed down the San Diego 805 freeway to Irvine with Juan's Chevy leading the way.

After driving past an immigration checkpoint, I lost sight of Juan's van and my cell phone lost signal. I decided to exit the freeway and stop at a gas station so I could call Juan on a pay phone. When I contacted him, he gave me directions to the restaurant where we were to meet Lucho. I drove back onto the freeway and headed toward Newport Beach. When I arrived, I pulled the van into the parking lot of the restaurant. Juan was waiting for me. Our plan was to leave my van with the paintings in the restaurant parking lot, with Victor guarding the precious cargo while Juan and I inspected the 110 pounds of cocaine at a secure location. Juan called numerous times but Lucho did not answer.

After Juan and I had sat at the restaurant for over an hour, Lucho finally arrived. As they talked, I tried to make out what was being said. Juan and Lucho spoke Spanish, and I was not fluent in the language despite being a third-generation Mexican on my father's side and Spanish on my mother's side. Lucho told us that he would have to inspect the artwork before we met with the buyer. Juan and I were instructed to follow Lucho to where the cocaine was kept. As we left the restaurant, Juan instructed me to have Victor follow us in the van with the artwork. I went against my better judgment and agreed to drive my van with the artwork instead of leaving it at the restaurant parking lot with Victor guarding it, as I initially planned.

Juan and I followed Lucho's white pickup truck to a hotel in Irvine. Immediately I felt something was not right about being at the hotel. Juan explained that Lucho's boss had a plane full of cocaine nearby at John Wayne Airport and people at the hotel that were on the payroll, so it was safe to conduct business there. I was skeptical -- but I was also looking forward to the money that I would earn on the cocaine deal. Greed set in and I wanted to get the deal over with.

At the hotel, Lucho shuffled through a stack of Polaroid photos, matching the photos to the artwork in U-Haul boxes in back of the van. I asked, "You want us to take the artwork out of the boxes?" Lucho told me to do it. Something wasn't right with Juan; I could tell that he didn't want Lucho to inspect the artwork but Lucho ignored him until he noticed that we only had 17 pieces, not 20. Juan had held back three of the paintings for himself. That's what he was trying to hide from the Colombians.

Juan was trying to pull a fast one on the Colombians and on me. He wanted to keep three of the paintings for himself, plus he was going to charge the Colombians more coca -- and Juan was asking for a kickback from the Colombians for the artwork sale. What a snake.

Lucho told us to search the van for the three missing paintings, then he tore one of the boxes open. I said, "What are you doing? Be careful you're gonna tear up the paintings." Lucho asked me to calm down and I took one of the Polaroids from him, attempting to match it with a painting.

I didn't understand how Juan thought the Colombians wouldn't know that three of the paintings would be missing when he had promised to deliver 20. The argument with Lucho grew more heated. "You told me that all the paintings would be here, man," said Lucho, to which Juan replied, "Idiot! I told you. No, it's fine like that, stupid."

As they quarreled, a Chevy Impala pulled into the parking lot and parked near my van. Juan saw it and panicked, saying, "Let's get out of here. Someone might call security." Lucho ignored Juan as he continued to search the boxes until he was finally satisfied enough to lead us into the hotel.

When we entered the lobby I noticed people eating at a sushi bar while others sat, going about their business. A man wearing a suit with running shoes caught my attention. This guy had 'undercover cop' written all over his face. Was I being paranoid? Lucho interrupted my thoughts, saying, "I'm going to wait for them to call me. I can't use my cell phone. It's an illegal one. I pay a hundred dollars a month. I can call anywhere and talk as much as I want but I can't accept calls."

Lucho punched a number into a pay phone's keypad. He paged someone, then hung up. I asked him if he wanted me to bring the paintings up. Lucho replied, "No. It would be better to leave them in the van while you look at the coca. We can have some whiskey and relax." Then he received a page on his beeper. He checked the number. "OK, Room 1516."

We took an elevator to the fifteenth floor and walked to Room 1516. When Lucho knocked at the hotel door, a voice with a Spanish accent was heard inside. The door opened and Jorge Falcon, a Colombian wearing Miami attire, was there to greet us. I noticed two large black suitcases on a coffee table. I also noticed two separate doors, one on each side of the room that led to connecting suites.

This was a red flag for me. I've seen this setup on cop shows and movies numerous times. I wondered if there were cops waiting on the other side of those doors. I had met Jorge once before with Juan to discuss the artwork deal but I knew nothing about him. I figured if Juan knew these people then they must be the real deal.

Jorge ordered three Johnny Walker scotches and a beer from room service, then shifted his body to get comfortable in his chair. Lucho walked over and stood next to the two big black suitcases. I asked if all the kilos were the same. Jorge told me I could check them at random if I liked. I zipped open one of the black suitcases and shuffled through the kilos, counting them one at a time. There were 25 in each suitcase - - 50 brick kilos of cocaine.

While I was doing this, Lucho recapped the scene in the parking lot, telling Jorge, "Well, brother, I counted up to 12. And since it's in the parking lot, there were a lot a people." "You checked them out," Jorge chimed in. Juan answered, "There's no problem at all with the paintings," to which Jorge replied, "No, and it had better not be."

I removed a bottle opener from my pants pocket and used the pointed end to cut out a triangle from one of the kilo's wrappings. I then scooped out a small amount of coke and tasted it with my tongue. It was as good as gold.

Meanwhile, Juan was making up wild stories about the art: "Well, look, a guy came from the French Embassy in Mexico and wanted to buy all this artwork, because they're French. And they said, don't sell the artwork to anyone else ... it's because it's a national treasure, man." I decided to sit back and watch Juan fib his way through the deal.

"You said that one of them is worth a million bucks," Jorge asked. "There's about two or three that are around one-and-a-half, two million," Juan replied. Lucho cut in to say that if there were any problem, Jorge knew people who could track us down where we lived. "You know what I mean? I'm taking your word that everything is good. And now Juan has been telling me that he wants to raise the price on the paintings."

Eager to move things along, I suggested I could load the paintings into the Colombians' truck. "I'll take them," Jorge replied, "I have to take them to my people." I suggested that we just pull the van in front of the hotel and load all the coca there.

Juan was looking out a hotel window. "A car arrived over there in the parking lot too," he said. "There's that guy that was around earlier." Jorge tried to brush it off, "Hotels, you know, this time of the day everybody's in and out."

Juan, in the meanwhile, was now trying to sell the Colombians on our 'street cred.' I played along. "We got Vegas and L.A. by the balls," I bragged. "I got a lot of people there, but like you said, it's kind of getting dry because I've been getting calls lately asking me if I got some product for them. In Vegas, it's like everybody watches each other's back. They go to jail, do the time for whatever. They got money when they get out, or someone pays for the lawyer or whatever they need. In California everybody's messed up. Why do you think I moved to Vegas in the first place?"

Juan asks, "Where are the drinks that you guys promised us?" Jorge grabbed the phone and called room service. "Yes, I'm in room 1516 and I ordered some scotch and some ... oh; it's on its way? OK, good. I thought they were making it."

I lifted one of the suitcases off the table and placed it on the carpet. "Take them off of the table and put them on the floor so the waiter won't wonder what we are doing in here," I said.

A knock was heard. Jorge looked through the peephole, then opened the door. A waiter rolled a cart into the room and asked where we wanted it set up. He asked if we would be paying cash and Jorge said he'd just sign for it. Once the waiter was gone, Juan said, "Now we conclude."

"And you thought it was just an empty promise, Juan," Lucho responded, to which Jorge said, "So before we toast, we got a deal then, right?" I replied, "Yeah. It's a done deal." Jorge said, "OK." We all grabbed our drinks and Jorge toasted the score. Everyone guzzled down a drink.

Then I remembered Victor down in the van. "I'm going to make sure he's still out there," I said. "I told him we would be down in a little while. I'm going to go downstairs and pull the van in front of the hotel so we don't have to walk all the way through the parking lot."

Jorge replied, "No way! Let's all go together." I suddenly sensed that something wasn't right. It seemed as if the Colombians didn't want us to leave the room. Were they attempting to rob us of the artwork? Maybe I was being paranoid again. I asked, "What do you want to do then?"

Lucho answered my question with a question, "How are you going to go [out] with all of that coca?" "OK, let's go," I urged. "I have a long drive home!" I lifted one of the suitcases and headed for the door. I groaned, "This weighs a ton!"

Jorge said. "Grab your suitcases Juan and let's go." I seconded the emotion, replying, "*Vamonos*. I don't want Victor to leave without us."

Suddenly, a door from a connecting suite swung open and federal agents rushed into the room pointing firearms and screaming commands. "Police! Don't move! On the ground! I said, on the ground *now!*"

Juan and I were forced to the floor at gunpoint by federal agents. Agents stood over us with their weapons drawn while other officers handcuffed Juan and me. After we were secured, the agents pulled us to our feet and ordered us to sit on a couch. When they left Juan and me alone for a moment, he leaned over and whispered to me. "Tell the cops that we were supposed to pick up $50,000 cash and when we arrived at the room there was fifty kilos."

Two federal agents in street clothes entered the suite; Larry Gordon, an African-American federal agent in a suit accompanied them. The agent stared at me with an upset look. He asked, "Are you stupid or something?" I remained silent, wondering what the agent was talking about. "How do you know that coke wasn't laced with cyanide," he asked.

I didn't bother to answer. Agent Jan C. Sakert, who was of slim build with blonde hair entered the room with Agent Richard Cuthbert. Agent Cuthbert resembled Jeff Bridges so much that I did a double-take, thinking it was really the actor. Sakert placed a laptop computer on the table. He then played a video of Juan and me accepting the cocaine. Everything we'd said and done was recorded. Sakert then turned off the laptop and he read me my Miranda rights. Agent Simeon Green, who looked more like a biker than an agent, also entered the room.

Sakert cut to the chase. "You are in very big trouble. You are looking at 15 to 20 years in prison. Now is the time to help yourself. Once we take you before the judge it will be too late." I sat in silence, playing hardball.

Agent Cuthbert said, "Call your friend who is in the van; tell him to come up to the room." I replied: "Victor doesn't have a cell phone." Cuthbert wasn't buying it. "How were you going to instruct him to bring the paintings up to the room?" I replied, "Victor wasn't supposed to bring the paintings to the room. He doesn't know what's going on up here. He only came for the ride. I told Victor that I was going into the hotel to pick up some money. That's all he knows."

Cuthbert said, "Are there any weapons in the van? I don't want officers to shoot your friend when they arrest him." I replied, "There's a handgun tucked in the back seat but Victor doesn't know that it's there. The gun belongs to me." That admission would come back to hurt me later, but the last thing I wanted was Victor to go to prison for my mess.

Sakert opened my wallet and shuffled through my photos, then asked, "Who's the pretty lady and the kids?" I didn't bother to respond. "Do you think your woman will wait 20 years for you? Because that's how much time you are facing," he said. I figured the DEA agent was attempting to scare me into spilling the beans. I thought I'd probably be looking at five years or so.

Sakert piled on. "Are you going to turn your back on your family?" Cuthbert cut back in. "Where did you get the paintings?" I noticed him taking notes, so I paused to think about the question before I answered. I wanted to get Victor off the hook but I didn't want to implicate anyone in the case. I said, "I got them from some dope head who stole them."

Sakert: "How much coke were you going to give him?"

Me: "Give who?"

Sakert: "The thief."

"I wasn't going to give him any coke," I said. "We were supposed to get cash for the paintings. I didn't know about the coke deal until I got to San Diego."

Agent Green cut in and said, "He's lying!" Sakert was insistent. "How much would you have given the thief if you would have received the coke?" I improvised, "He was some dope fiend. He would have been happy if I gave him three kilos."

"Who were you going to take the cocaine to," Sakert asked. I played along. "I don't know. Coke is like cash. A person could dump that at any street corner in L.A. The coke sells itself."

Cuthbert asked, "Do you know anybody with money?" I thought it was strange that a federal agent asked me such a question. I replied, "If I knew someone with money, I wouldn't be here right now."

Cuthbert couldn't resist rubbing it in. "Hey, man, thanks for the van. We're going to confiscate it." I couldn't help replying, "Make sure you keep making the payments on it; the bank will want their money."

Agent Cuthbert wasn't happy with that. Victor was then escorted into the room by two federal agents. He stood nearby in handcuffs as agents packed up their equipment. After about 10 minutes, six agents escorted Juan, Victor, and myself out of the suite and through a hallway. Cuthbert held me by the handcuffs. The group of us walked through the hotel lobby and outside to the parking lot. We were then placed in the back seat of an unmarked police car. The agents put Victor and me in one vehicle and Juan in another. The police cars then rolled out of the hotel parking lot heading toward downtown Los Angeles.

CHAPTER 4 Metropolitan Detention Center

Unmarked police cars arrived at a gate in front of a white, high-rise building on the corner of Alameda and Alison streets; the building was high security. Agents Sakert and Cuthbert presented their credentials to a guard at the booth. A moment later, a gate opened and the vehicles rolled into a secured underground parking lot of the Metropolitan Detention Center. It was located in downtown Los Angeles, off the Hollywood Freeway 101. It was an administrative facility used to house pretrial inmates.

Once the vehicles were parked, Juan, Victor and I were removed from the police cars. We were then escorted to a steel door where the agents placed their firearms into lock boxes. After the weapons were secured, the steel door popped open and we entered a sally port where there was a second steel door. One of the agents spoke into an intercom and, a moment later, the second door opened. We were strip-searched, then placed in one-man cells; one at a time, we were called out of the cell for fingerprinting, photographing and for filling out processing forms. I was issued federal identification number 03388-112 and told to memorize it.

After we were processed the three of us were taken to an elevator that brought us to Receiving & Discharge, better known as R&D. We were placed in a holding tank that had steel benches, a sink and a toilet. I walked over to a bench and laid down; for some reason I felt physically drained. I needed something to rest my head on. When I searched the cell I saw a roll of toilet paper so I grabbed it and I tucked it under my head. I closed my eyes, attempting to get some sleep and hoping that it would all be a bad dream. Hours later, when I awoke, I was still in the holding cell. I walked to a small window where I looked out into the city night; the only view was of a nearby building. I lay down again and closed my eyes but I couldn't sleep.

After hours of waiting, we were moved to another cell that had a pay phone. When I called Leanna collect to tell her that I had been arrested, for some reason she didn't believe me. I finally convinced her that I was not playing. I told Leanna that I needed her to call Alex to let him know that I had been popped. Leanna assured me that she would make the call. Time seemed to drag on as we waited in the holding tank; inmates were then called out three at a time to be strip-searched and issued pants, underwear, socks and white T-shirts, along with a bedroll which included a pillow, blanket, sheet, pillow case, toothpaste, small toothbrush, comb, a bar of soap and razors.

Walking into the federal system as a first-time offender was like walking onto a battlefield with no weapons. I entered prison as a high-school dropout with only a ninth-grade education. I was street smart and had business smarts that I learned from partners, but being at the mercy of the feds was something different, I did not know what to expect. Juan, Victor, and I were moved to ninth floor's south wing where we each bunked up with another inmate in a two-man cell. The ninth floor was where inmates were housed until they were moved to their assigned unit. I was so tired when I arrived at the cell that I didn't realize my bunk didn't have a mattress. I crawled onto the wooden bunk frame and immediately went to sleep. The next morning I met my cellmate, Art Lopez, who was also Latino. Art had been busted on bank robbery charges; he mostly kept to himself and seemed as if he didn't want to be bothered by anyone.

Nine south had a top and bottom tier and housed about 130 men in two-man cells. Each cell had bunk beds, a wooden desk, a mirror, two small lock boxes, two plastic chairs, a sink, toilet, carpet and a small window with a view of the street below. The unit had a common area with a dining hall and tables; there were three TVs, a pool table, ping-pong and a rack of books. There was also a recreation area where we could play handball and basketball, or use the weight machine. To top things off, the unit came with microwave ovens so inmates could have warm meals.

Breakfast was served at 6 a.m.; cold and hot cereal was usually offered, and sweet rolls with milk and fruit. Lunch was at 11 a.m.; it was usually, chicken, sloppy Joes or spaghetti. Wednesday was hamburger day and fish was served on Fridays; the meals were part of the Bureau of Prisons' nationwide menu. Dinner was at 3:30 p.m. and was similar to the lunch. Besides the meals served three times a day, the detention center had a canteen once a week, so inmates could buy extra food like tuna packs, soups, peanut butter, crackers, hygiene products and rolls of quarters so one could purchase food from the vending machines.

Victor and I had enough food to make our stay at MDC a little more comfortable. As part of the daily routine, officers would lock all inmates in their cell for count time. There were six counts a day: 5 a.m., 9:30 a.m., 4 p.m., 9:30 p.m., midnight and 3 a.m. Each afternoon at 4 p.m. inmates were required to return to their cell for the most important count of the day. This was a stand-up count so guards would know that a real body was in that cell and to make sure that body was breathing. The 4 p.m. count was the only count that was called and reported to Washington, D.C., every day.

Victor and I would often talk when we were away from Juan. We were angry at him for setting us up with the Colombians; Juan should have known that Lucho and Jorge were informants working with the feds. I wanted to do something to Juan, but knew that I needed to hold back my anger because Juan had those three missing paintings. If Victor and I did something to Juan, he would not give up the paintings.

KTE

While I was sleeping, I was awakened to the sound of an officer's keys opening the cell door. The officer carried a paper with a list of names. He called out, "Torres! Get dressed. You have court." I hopped off the top bunk and quickly got dressed. The federal agents who arrested Juan, Victor, and I were waiting for us; they cuffed us, then escorted us out of the MDC to the federal court building. It seemed strange to me that the agents would walk us out in the open where a group of kids were having a field trip. Then I spotted a dark-skinned man with a pot belly who had a camera hanging from his neck. He stood waiting at a corner, looking up at the sky, but when he saw us approaching he

90

began snapping photos of Juan, Victor and I as if he was expecting us. It was as if we were being paraded in front of the federal building for the media photographer.

We entered the court room for our arraignment before Magistrate Judge Charles F. Eick. My attorney, Robert Kirste, was present when I arrived. I was confident, knowing that I had an attorney there to represent me and I mentioned to Kirste that Victor was going to need representation also. Kirste told me he would see what he could do for Victor, but first he wanted us to wait it out so he could learn what evidence the feds had. I stood before Magistrate Eick as he read the charges against me. He asked if I understood what I was being charged with. I stared at the judge in silence with a distant gaze. Victor then leaned over to tell me, "Say 'yes,'" Victor, Juan, and I pled "not guilty" to the charges. When my attorney petitioned the judge for me to be released on bail, Assistant U.S. Attorney Tom Warren argued against it, stating that I traveled to Mexico the day of my arrest and that I was a flight risk because I had ties there. Judge Eick agreed with the prosecution and denied the motion. At the end of the arraignment Kirste told me that he would see me at the detention center in a few weeks.

Sometime after the arraignment, I received an indictment charging me with possession with intent to distribute more than five kilograms of cocaine and conspiracy. After my bail was denied, I told Kirste that I wanted him to keep fighting for my release on bail. After all, Juan's battle for bail had paid off after his older brother, Jesus Carlos, a retired city worker, put his house up for Juan.

Before Juan's release, I instructed him to deliver the three remaining paintings to Las Vegas. I also told Juan to get the house that we bought in Mazatlán ready, because I was going to try for bail again. If I was granted bail, I was planning to run to Mexico. Mr. Warren wasn't wrong about me being a flight risk. Juan assured me that he would deliver the paintings to Vegas and he said he would have the house in Mexico ready for me. The next day a guard called for Juan and he was escorted out of the unit to be released.

Victor and I were out on the recreation deck when Victor was called to a visit by a unit officer. He wasn't expecting anyone. When Victor returned a few hours later he told me that he met a man who said he was a mediator. The man said that he was there to help and that he did not work for the court or the prosecutor. The mediator asked Victor if he knew anything about the case. Victor said that he told the mediator that he did not know anything; he had only come along for the ride. He went on to tell him that he wished that he knew something so he could help himself out.

I told Victor that he did well by not saying anything. A moment later, an officer entered the unit and called me. He escorted me to an elevator. I was taken to a small room that was separated by a metal security cage, where a heavy-set man with a suit and tie sat on the other side of a steel screen. He introduced himself and said that he neither worked for the court nor the U.S. attorney. He told me the same thing that he told Victor: that he was a mediator and he was there to help me. The mediator asked if I had anything to say about the case. I told him that I did not. The man then told me to have a good day and left.

A few weeks later, the unit officer instructed us to roll up our property because we were being moved to a different floor. Victor and I gathered our belongings, then waited near the officer's desk. I was hoping that Victor would be released; his woman had recently given birth to a baby girl. There was no reason for both of us to be locked up if we didn't have to. I'd rather take the blame than have Victor locked up with me.

We followed the officer into an elevator. It stopped at the sixth floor and Victor and three other inmates were instructed to exit. Unsure if Victor and I were going to see each other again, we said our goodbyes. When the elevator door opened again, our group of inmates was told to walk to the unit door at the end of the hall, seven south.

As I stood by waiting for the officer to assign me a cell, I was approached by two Southsiders from 18th Street, Oso and Maton. The latter had a tattoo of the number "1" on the right side of his face and the number "8" on the left side. Oso had thick Old English numbers "1" and "8" tattooed on the front of his neck in black ink. Oso asked me where I was from. "Wilmas, Westside," was my response. Oso and Maton greeted me with a handshake. I then asked Oso if there was anyone from the Wilmas in the unit. At first Oso said, "No." Then, as if he remembered someone, he said, "Yeah, there is a Christiano named Armando Villa who lives on the second tier. That's his cell right there." I looked up and saw Armando through a door window as he looked down at the group of new arrivals. When the officer assigned me a bunk, Oso helped carry my bags to my new living quarters. As he did, he explained to me how things ran on the floor. I learned that any Southside rival neighborhood that I had on the streets I would be running with behind the walls. The prison rules were different than the street rules; in prison Southsiders stuck together.

When I arrived at the cell, I introduced myself to my new cellmate, Victor Hernandez. He was at MDC on drug charges. Then I headed to Armando Villa's cell. As I walked up the stairs to the second tier, Armando saw me. He seemed surprised. Armando and I knew each other from the neighborhood, and we had mutual friends from Sinaloa, Mexico. I had heard that Armando got busted on federal drug charges about six months before my arrest. After talking to Armando and reading about his case in the *Los Angeles Times*, I learned that undercover agents had infiltrated his organization in Mexico. They posed as truckers willing to run drugs to California.

Armando was driving a van that contained 175 kilos of cocaine. That's when the feds swooped on his ranch. Armando told me that he signed a 10-year plea deal and that he was awaiting sentencing.

Armando worked in the detention center's kitchen during the day. I had no job at the time, so I would spend my days at the law library researching my case. At other times I would sit in front of the TV and watch the O.J. Simpson trial, which was taking place right across the street at the Los Angles courthouse.

I was warned by other inmates that at any given moment a fight could erupt. It was 6 a.m. when a guard unlocked my cell door and yelled, "CHOW!" I got up and washed my face. Then I headed to the common area to get my food. I stood in the chow line and when I got my tray, I walked over to sit at a table with other Southsiders who were eating breakfast. There were a couple of whites at the table when I arrived. One of the whites who looked to be a white-collar criminal had made the mistake of reaching over the plate of a Southsider to grab a salt shaker. The Southsider jumped to his feet and cracked the white guy three times in the face with his fists before the man hit the ground; the white inmate didn't know what hit him. I later learned that reaching over someone's plate is a violation. It was disrespectful, especially knowing that there was a possibility that the man's underarm hairs could have fallen into the Southsider's food. The white man had violated another man's space and those who violate the unwritten prison rules pay the penalties.

When I met Whitey O'Connor at MDC, I found out that he happened to know an acquaintance named Sal Penada. He ran with Mi Gente, who controlled a large part of street activity in parts of Los Angeles. I got word that Sal nearly died from an overdose of heroin and that he had turned his life around and became a Christian. When I spoke with Sal over the phone he told me, "You getting arrested may have saved your life." Sal went on to tell me that there were important people talking about visiting me in Vegas before my arrest. I took that information to mean that members of Mi Gente were planning to send people to Vegas to attempt a takeover of my drug business. I responded, "There are two sides to that point of view; by me coming to prison it may have saved other people's lives." Sal wished me well and we said our goodbyes.

LETTER FROM ANTOINETTE

I called Debrah, who told me that Antoinette wanted me to write her. We had broken off our relationship a few weeks before I was arrested, so she decided to move to Guam to work at Vikings Tavern as an exotic dancer. Antoinette didn't like to be called a "stripper." "Dancer" was what she preferred. Her plan was to save money while she went to college.

I was eager to hear from Antoinette. During mail call I would sit waiting excitedly, hoping Antoinette's letter had arrived. Mail was delivered Monday through Friday, except federal holidays. Most inmates were exited to get some type of mail, but there were other inmates who didn't bother to listen for their name to be called because they knew they had nothing coming. As I stood by waiting, I heard the officer call out my name, I yelled, "Pass it back!" The officer handed the letter to an inmate and the inmate handed the letter back to other inmates until it reached me. The letter was from Antoinette and it was sent from Tamuning, Guam. I returned to my cell, sat on my bunk, and opened the envelope. I pulled out the letter dated May 30, 1995. Antoinette had written:

"You do not know what I'm going through. Not being able to talk to you is killing me inside. I talked to your mom and your sister and Leanna. It hurts so bad knowing that you talk to Leanna every day and you're depending on her. I should be there for you, but I can't." She wanted to know if she should take care of my kids, offering to send them $250 now and more money every month, for as long as I was in prison. She said she would come to see me in late August or early September. "You know I'm the only one who will stand by you that long," she concluded.

I was moved to call Antoinette and when she heard my voice she began to cry. We talked about my situation, we talked about our plans, and about being honest with each other. Antoinette told me that she loved me and that all she ever wanted was to be with me. Her words made me realize what a selfish person I had been. I continued to receive letters from her.

On June 12, 1995, she wrote from Guam, "Hearing your voice makes me feel so good. I got another letter today, so that makes three. When I got your first two letters I couldn't believe you wrote me. I can't tell you how much your letters mean to me. I read them over and over. At first I thought you were saying things because of what has happened. You are known to do that. But, talking to you today and reading your letter today -- I can't believe it's you. You wrote in one letter, 'Your cutie is back.' I really think it's true. This is the person I fell in love with."

She said I sounded like I really wanted to change my life and she acknowledged that she also needed change. Although she knew I didn't approve of her dancing, she said she wanted to keep doing it "just for a little while more," in part to save money while I was in jail. "I know what's happened is so upsetting and it hurts," she added. "I'm so sorry that you have to be in there. But, maybe this might be the best thing that could happen. I always told you someday you would realize what you have ... Even though you're away, you're still a very lucky man." She talked about the happy life we could have with my kids once I got out. Then she turned jealous. "It hurts me so much when Leanna tells me how much you love her and all the things you two do together. I want to be the only girl in your life. Sometimes I feel that you love her more than you ever loved me ... I think both of us need God in our lives. I realize I need God more now. I never thought I did before. I'm feeling so much better about myself now that I'm in school." She reiterated that she would try to visit me in August, concluding, "I know you love me Ray. But, you know I need to hear it a lot!"

KTE

Armando usually invited me to church on Sundays and my answer was always no until I found out that inmates from other floors would met at church if they wanted to talk to each other. I sent a message to Victor Mercado, who had been moved to the sixth floor. I told him to meet me at church so we could talk. Armando and I attended church but Victor never showed. Once an inmate arrived at church he could not leave until the service was over. The day I went, outside volunteers had come to share God's message. One of them was a Mexican-American man who told his story how his life had been changed when he came to have a relationship with Jesus. He explained that it wasn't about religion, but about a relationship with the Creator of the world. He talked about what a broken man he was, and how he went through life with no direction and with no purpose before God rescued him.

Though I didn't intend to be at church, I felt that the message was directed to me. I didn't know what was happening to me. My heart was touched by the man's story. His words brought tears to my eyes. Was I the broken man he spoke about? I definitely knew that I needed forgiveness for all the bad things I'd done. I said a silent prayer. I asked God to change my life. I was tired of living a promiscuous lifestyle, of drug use and of illegal activities. Maybe my arrest was what it took for God to get my attention.

I admit that it bothered me when people came to prison and all of a sudden they found God. It seemed as if they were hiding behind the Bible because they were scared or were telling on someone. But I knew there were sincere people who came to prison and wanted to change their lives. Growing up I had so many unanswered questions about life. I wanted to know why I was born to parents who I felt didn't love me. I wanted to know what my purpose in life was. I wanted to know who created humans and animals. I wanted to know where a person went when he or she died. I wanted to know if there was a Heaven and a Hell. I wanted to know who made the rainbow and what it meant. I wanted to know why there was so much destruction and evil on earth.

When Armando told me about a Bible-study course, I was hesitant but then I thought maybe it had the answers to life's questions. I didn't want anyone to know that I was studying the Bible, so I did the courses in my cell when I was alone. Once I completed all my courses, I received a certificate of completion and a book titled, "Twice Pardoned." It was the same book that a real estate agent had given me before my arrest. The agent had told me that something in her heart was telling her to give me the book. The cover had a picture of handcuffs on it; "Twice Pardoned" was a story about a man who was pardoned for his sins and pardoned for his crime by a governor. I wasn't the preacher type nor was I about to push Jesus off on anyone. I wanted to learn about the Scriptures for personal reasons. The more I learned about the Bible the more I enjoyed it, so I made it part of my daily routine.

KTE

I decided to call Leanna. She told me that Victor came by her house after he was released. Victor wanted me to call him. After I hung up the phone, I immediately called Victor collect. He told me that the feds dropped the charges on him. That was great news to me. I was the one who brought Victor into the deal, so I felt I needed to do all I could to get him out. It was a relief to know that Victor was home. I'm sure his wife was just as happy as I was. Victor's release gave me hope that the feds might drop the charges against me.

Later that week, I was told by the unit officer that I had an attorney visit. Robert Kirste was waiting for me. After some small talk, he removed a pen and a pad from his briefcase, and he began to ask me questions about my case. I was hesitant to say anything that might incriminate me or anyone else; I felt that my attorney didn't need to know everything about me. I was going to minimize my role in the case because I never totally trusted attorneys. Kirste told me that he would talk to Victor and get his statement about what happened. He went on to say that he was on his way to visit Tom Warren, who was prosecuting my case. Kirste wanted to see what evidence the feds had on me.

KTE

Being at MDC L.A. was like being on the streets when it came to drugs. There were all types available if a person wanted them, from primos, to crack, heroin and weed. I wasn't interested in any of them. Drug use was the farthest thing from my mind. I found filmmaking and screenwriter magazines at the book cart. I also read magazines like *Newsweek, Money*, the *Wall Street Journal*, and *USA Today*. I didn't read at all when I was on the street, but after reading a few magazines it became something I enjoyed. I read anything that caught my

98

attention. I came across an article about a man in New York who got busted on drug charges and agreed to work with the feds to set up his drug connection. The guy was granted bail and he was released from a detention center while awaiting the outcome of his case. The DEA instructed the man to obtain drugs from his connection with the feds' buy money. When the guy arrived at his connection's house, instead of setting him up he warned the connection that the feds were on to him. Then the informant fled out a back window of the house with the buy money and went on the run. When I read what the New York guy did, I thought it was a good getaway.

After reading the article, I began to entertain the thought of getting out on bail and fleeing to Mexico. I figured I would be safe if I didn't come back to the U.S. If I decided to do so, I knew I wouldn't be able to contact my family because the feds would be watching them. Not knowing the outcome of my future was stressful. I knew there was a possibility that I could be spending decades behind bars.

After Armando signed his plea deal, he was sentenced to 10 years. A month or so later he was transferred to Terminal Island, a federal prison between Long Beach and San Pedro, California. When Armando left MDC, I began looking into education programs. Sitting in prison made me feel that my dreams of working in the movie industry were shattered. That was until I met Brian. I would see Brian sitting at a table alone, writing every day. Being the friendly person that I was, I approached Brian and I asked him what he was working on. Brian told me he was writing a movie script and with those words a lightbulb went on inside my head. I asked Brian what were the best books to order on learning how to write screenplays. Brian referred me to "The Screenwriter's Bible" by David Trottier and Syd Field's book "Screenplay." I asked Debrah to order them for me. She was happy to do it. Once the books arrived, I studied them vigorously. I told myself if I had to do time at least I would have something to show for it -- a stack of movie scripts. So my writing journey began.

I decided to give Juan a call to check whether he was delivering the three paintings to Las Vegas. He told me that he hadn't been to Vegas yet. I asked him what the holdup was. Juan gave the excuse that his oldest son Francisco had been arrested in a methamphetamine bust and was being held at MDC San Diego. Juan also told me that the feds broke into his storage unit and confiscated the documents to the house that we bought together in Mazatlán. Juan complained that he had a lot going on and that he couldn't do much. I understood that to mean that the feds were watching him. He gave me his word that he would go to Vegas when the opportunity came but Juan's word meant nothing to me. And there wasn't a thing I could do about it. Juan was on the streets and I was locked away.

SUICIDE

One thing about being in the federal system was that there were all types of people from all levels of society. I met Bob Stevens at MDC through Speedy, a Southsider from Venice Beach. Bob was in his sixties and he was the owner of a limo company when he got arrested on federal bank robbery charges; Bob claimed that he was set up. According to Bob he rented his limo out to some "Blacks" who robbed a bank and, in the trunk of the limo, police found a ski mask and a gun that authorities said were used in a bank robbery. At least that's the story Bob told me.

Speedy would talk with Bob regularly but I think it was mostly for Speedy to amuse himself. He would give Bob a hard time about his young wife cheating on him while Bob sat in prison. Bob's wife would visit him at MDC along with his two-year-old daughter. By looking at Bob's wife one would assume that she was high maintenance. I would sit and converse with Bob because I felt sorry for the guy.

Bob often talked about taking his own life. He told me that during one of his visits he had mentioned to his wife that he didn't want to live. Bob's wife responded, "Do what you have to do," because she needed the money. Bob had a life insurance policy and his wife didn't seem to have a problem benefiting from it. Bob felt that he had nothing to live for. Other people who knew Bob told me that he tried to electrocute himself by disconnecting the light switch in his cell and attempting to touch the hot wire with the ground wire, but his cellmate walked in and stopped him before he could succeed. I was also told by another inmate that Bob would save his daily issue of prescribed pills; he would also buy pills from other inmates until he thought he had enough to overdose. Bob had taken all the pills but the suicide attempt failed. Every chance I had, I tried to encourage Bob; I would tell him how much his little girl needed him. I could tell that Bob had his mind made up. He was in a deep depression and eventually he was going to end his life.

I had just finished working out when I returned to my cell to grab some clean clothes. As I approached the showers I noticed what looked like water mixed with blood seeping from under one of the shower doors, running into an overflow drain in the walkway. I knocked at the shower door and I asked if the person inside was OK. When no one answered, I opened the door to find Bob lying on his back with both wrists slit. Blood was flowing from his veins and his body was going into convulsions. I quickly shut off the water and dashed to the officer to let him know that Bob was in the shower with massive bleeding. The officer rushed to Bob and then called on his radio for a medic. I stood over Bob, telling him to "Hang in there. Help is on the way." I could tell that Bob had lost a lot of blood. He was pale and his eyes had a distant gaze.

When medics arrived, they wrapped bandages around Bob's wrists. The medics then placed him on a gurney and rolled him out of the unit. Weeks passed and I hadn't heard anything about Bob's condition … that was until I saw him on the news. A story broke about an inmate who had taken a guard's gun at a medical facility and was holding people hostage. It was Bob. The story ended with Bob surrendering. That was the last I heard of him.

I continued to call Juan about delivering the paintings to Las Vegas. Juan would give one excuse after another. He then stopped accepting my phone calls. The last time I tried his phone was disconnected. I was furious; in my mind I was adding up all the times that Juan got over on me. He owed me money that I lent him before our arrest. It was Juan's Colombian contacts that set us up to get busted by the feds. I was sure that I would not see the three paintings that Juan put aside for his own profit. I wanted to send Juan a message, so I decided to write a letter letting him know that I would take real good care of his son Francisco when I came across him in the prison system. Weeks passed and Juan still did not respond to me. It was a letter that I would have reason to regret.

I was in my cell when a corrections officer knocked at the door to tell me that I had a visitor. When I arrived at the visiting room, Robert Kirste looked upset. He told me that Juan Carlos sent my letter to Assistant U.S. Attorney Warren. The news didn't surprise me: Now more than ever, I wanted to physically do something to Juan. Kirste warned me not to write any more letters to Juan. I gave him my word that I would not.

Kirste then explained to me that the sentencing guidelines for conspiracy to possess with intent to distribute 50 kilos of powder cocaine in a Category One felony carried a sentence of 135 to 168 months for a first-time offender. In addition, a 50-kilogram conspiracy charge carried a mandatory minimum of 10 years and the gun charge could add an extra five years to my sentence. Kirste compared a conspiracy to a game of soccer. He said, "All members have their part in the game and they all work together as a team to complete their goal, which is to win the game. It's the same in a drug conspiracy; all members have their part in distributing drugs and all members involved in the drug deal will be charged for the crime, even if they were not present during the transaction. Conspiracy takes place when two or more people make a plan to commit a criminal act. It only takes one action on behalf of one of the conspirators to further the crime for any of the conspirators to be criminally convicted of conspiracy, even if the criminal act was never carried out."

I found it hard to believe that I was facing 19 years in prison. I thought there was no way that the feds could give a 26-year-old man that much time for drugs. In my eyes, the feds were the ones who brought the drugs and now they wanted to charge me for them. It didn't seem right. I told. Kirste that, unless I got a deal for five years, I would be going to trial. He assured me that he would talk to the assistant U.S. attorney to see what he could come up with, then get back to me.

After Kirste's visit, I called Victor and told him how much time I was facing. Victor offered to take the blame for the gun so I would get a lighter sentence. I told Victor that I didn't think it would help because the gun was registered in my name. Victor wanted to try anyway. He said he would meet with Kirste.

I agreed to call Victor back within a few days. I knew I needed to learn about the federal laws involved and any defenses that might be available to me. I decided to spend time in the law library and the first book that I read was the "Federal Sentencing Guidelines Manual." I asked inmates who had been in the system for years for their opinions. An old-timer who had been in federal prison for over 28 years and who worked as the law library clerk advised me not to play games with the feds. He told me that the feds had a 98 percent conviction rate. I searched cases that were similar to mine and I read about downward departures. The big legal words that I didn't understand I had to look up in the dictionary. I read for so many hours that day that my vision began to blur and my brain began to throb from thinking so much, but I was fighting for my life; there was no way I was going to give up.

MASTERS OF THE GAME

Those busted by the feds were said to be in the big leagues: drug traffickers, bankers, judges, murderers, politicians, sports figures, dirty cops, attorneys, computer hackers, telemarketers and Ponzi schemers just to name a few; the feds did not discriminate against any of them.

103

Leonardo Moreno was a 36-year-old millionaire Colombian who got busted on money-laundering charges. Leo's cell was located near mine, so he would stop by and talk to me often. I guess he enjoyed my company but mostly Leo enjoyed sharing pictures of the wealth he acquired during his money-laundering years. He told me stories of how some of his rich Colombian friends were "Masters of the Game," meaning they knew how to make tons of money through drug trafficking and, if caught, how to avoid a long prison sentence.

Leo shared stories with me on how to work the system; he said that his Colombian friends would buy safe houses in the name of a dead person and store kilos of cocaine there, in case one of the members of their organization got busted. The plan was to not only give the feds the name of a (deceased) drug trafficker but to provide actual drugs to validate their story, so they would receive a reduction in their prison sentence for assisting the government in the arrest of people committing other crimes.

Leo told me that he had been fighting his case for over three years but after hearing his stories I wondered if there were other reasons why he had been at MDC so long. Leo told me that he knew Colombians who got busted but had associates on the outside who paid runners to cross the border with loads of drugs. The Colombians who hired them would tip off the feds to the place and the time the runners would be crossing. In exchange for the information, the Colombians got time knocked off their sentence. Leo's rationale was that the Colombians would take care of the families while the runners did time in prison. When I heard the stories, it made me think about Lucho and Jorge, the two Colombians who set me up. It wasn't right what the Colombians did; it was still snitching and I expressed my feelings to Leo. He just smirked and shook his head at me in pity.

He said I was loyal but I was also naive about the reality of the drug business. "Everything you've learned about being loyal is a bunch of *mierda*," Leo said. He referred to the drug business as a game of chess and said, "When you know the game and all the rules, that's when you can master the game and win." There were three types of people in the drug business. There were the ones who got in trouble and would turn in their best friend, their own mother and their grandmother, because they were cowards and did not want to go to prison. Then there were the ones who had the guts, the ones who kept their mouth shut because of their pride, because of what they stood for, because they were taught to be loyal and never snitch. Those were the ones who sat in prison and rotted their life away while another man slept with their wife, enjoyed their money and raised their kids.

"Then there was, the master of the game; the highly sophisticated drug trafficker," Leo said, "the one who had attorneys who knew state and federal laws and they knew how to use the law to their advantage. The master of the game used knowledge to get away with crimes and to move his drug shipments. This was the guy who had a license to commit crimes and, if he was caught, he got slapped on the hand and told, 'Don't do it again;' and he does it again knowing that he always has something to offer the feds as a gift in exchange for a 'get out of prison free' card."

It was hard for me to believe that people were doing the things that Leo described to me, but what did I know? If anything, Leo sure had some entertaining stories. The last time I spoke with him, before he was transferred in the middle of the night, he told me that I would be faced with making two decisions. The first was that I would be asked to betray my partner in crime. The second decision would be to betray my mother, my father, my kids and my girlfriend. Those words continued to ring through my mind for many days to come.

Being locked up in a cell away from the free world can get a man's mind to play tricks on him, especially if a man has kids and a woman waiting for him in the free world. At times I would lie on my bunk with my mind racing as I wondered what my future held. I was 26 years old; a 19-year prison term was like a life sentence to me. Snitching wasn't an option for me but the thought did cross my mind, especially when Juan made me to want to get even with him. Maybe I was breaking weak; maybe I was trying to justify ratting out Juan? I convinced myself that I needed a plan like the ones Leo talked about.

Early in the morning, I was awakened by a corrections officer who told me that I had 15 minutes to get ready for court. After breakfast, I was escorted with other inmates out of the unit and down a hallway to the garage floor where I was placed in a holding cell. I was then strip-searched and instructed to place my burgundy pants and shirt into a mess bag tagged with my name. I was given a khaki shirt and matching pants with a pair of blue slip-on shoes that looked like knockoff Vans.

After I was dressed, I was moved to another cell where I waited. Six marshals arrived, carrying a milk crate containing leg irons, chains and handcuffs. One of the corrections officers opened the cell door and called names from a list held in his hand. When my name was called, I walked over to what was set up like an assembly line; the marshal placed leg irons, a waist chain and handcuffs on me.

Along with other inmates, I was then loaded into a white passenger van with black-tinted windows. Two vans loaded with inmates drove out of the underground parking garage and through a security gate as a chase car followed. The three vehicles made their way onto a freeway. The few months at MDC had me restless; just leaving the detention center was like taking a field trip. When the vans drove down the Santa Ana freeway I took in the scenery as if I were seeing for the first time. A woman waved at me from a passing vehicle; that simple gesture made my day.

When we arrived at Santa Ana federal court house, we stepped onto the pavement and then shuffled through a door to holding cells. I was placed in a cell, and my cuffs and chains were removed, enabling me to move freely. Soon after, two marshals approached the cell to hand inmates a big, juicy burger, soda and fries. It was the best burger I had tasted in a long time. I waited for what seemed like hours as other inmates were called by marshals and taken out of the cell for court.

One of the inmates came back from court relieved that he received a 12-year sentence. I thought to myself how could anyone be happy about getting a 12-year sentence? The feds had people brainwashed to think that 12 years was a deal.

106

One of the marshals opened the cell door as he called my name; when I answered, I was instructed to step into a walkway and place my hands on the bars of the cell. The marshal searched me for weapons, then he cuffed my hands behind my back. I was escorted into a courtroom where other marshals stood guard. I was seated next to Robert Kirste. Juan was seated, without cuffs, next to his brother Jesse, since he was free on bail. I shook like a leaf, not because I was afraid but because the cell I was in had the air conditioner blowing full blast and the courtroom was just as cold. An officer instructed all to rise when an elderly white woman wearing a wig and prescription glasses entered the room. Judge Alicemarie H. Stotler would be presiding over my case. She went over its status, then announced the next court date.

KTE

While sitting at the detention center visiting room with Kirste, I asked him about my bail. He told me that the judge denied my bail and it was useless to keep trying. I was hoping that he had negotiated some kind of plea deal for me but instead he said, "If you agree to plead guilty, the assistant U.S. attorney is willing to drop the gun charge." Without the gun charge I was looking at a sentence of 168 months.

I reminded Kirste that Victor offered to take the blame for the gun if it would get me a lighter sentence. Kirste replied that Victor could not take ownership because the gun was registered in my name. Also, after I was arrested I had told the federal agents that Victor didn't know the gun was in the van. My attempt to clear Victor's name had backfired on me.

It was hard for me to believe that I was looking at so much time for a first-time, nonviolent offense. I told Kirste that 168 months in prison was not a deal. I mentioned to him that a person I knew at the detention center signed a deal for 10 years after being caught with 100 kilos. I told Kirste that I should get 10 years or less since I was busted with only 50 kilos. Kirste responded by saying that I did not know what kind of deal my friend made with the prosecutor to get the 10-year sentence. "There are only two ways to go under the mandatory minimum sentence," said Kirste. "Either you win in trial or you cooperate with the government and they file a 5K.1 Downward Departure motion to the court requesting a reduction in your sentence."

I told him that I had read about the departures in the "Sentencing Guideline Manual." Kirste responded, "So then you know how it works?" I answered, "Yeah, I know how it works; a person gets a reduced sentence if he tells. I also read about the Safety Valve." He went on to say, "If you decide to go that route, the Safety Valve will bring your sentence level down two points and if you are granted the three points for acceptance of responsibility for pleading guilty you would be at a level 33, which carries a 135-to-168-month sentence."

Kirste advised me to hear what the prosecutor had to offer. He said, "It wouldn't hurt to hear him out. You are the one who will be doing the time alone, no one else." I took a moment to think about that. I wanted to know if the feds knew about any of my illegal activities in Las Vegas. I told Kirste that I was willing to hear what the prosecutor had to offer. He informed me that he would set up a meeting with the assistant U.S. attorney.

A few days later, I was called for a visit. When I arrived in the attorney room, Kirste was present with Assistant U.S. Attorney Warren, and DEA agents Jan C. Sakert and Richard Cuthbert. When I sat at the conference table, Warren immediately slid a document to me and he asked me to sign it. The document gave him permission to question me. I asked Warren what kind of deal he was offering me. Warren responded by saying that I needed to sign the consent form. He explained to me that if I had any useful information we would take it from there. After I informed Warren that I was not signing anything, he looked bothered. I then slid the document back to him. The prosecutor wanted to know why I would not sign it. I responded that I did not want to walk out of prison someday and have to worry about getting a bullet in the back of my head. Agent Cuthbert assured me that they would protect me. "No thanks," I said. I got up and walked out of the room. I didn't feel right about the whole situation and about being there.

ANTOINETTE'S FIRST VISIT

I was excited for Antoinette's arrival. She was scheduled to take a flight from Guam to Las Vegas. Then she planned to drive to MDC Los Angeles, where she would visit me. The last time Antoinette and I saw each other was before she moved to Guam.

There are no conjugal visits in the feds. Usually only immediate family could visit, no girlfriends, only spouses and the mother of an inmate's child. I had no children with Antoinette but I was fortunate that my counselor, Mr. Taylor, gave me permission for a special visit. When I arrived in the visiting room, I saw Antoinette sitting at a table. She was beautiful, with her Italian and Native American features. Her dark, curly hair and her brown eyes were so caring. When Antoinette saw me enter the room, tears filled her eyes. As I stepped close to her to give her a hug, Antoinette stood to wrap her arms around me as if she never wanted to let me go.

Antoinette and I were extremely happy to see each other. We sat at a table and she told me how much she loved me. Suddenly Antoinette's attitude changed and I could tell she was upset about something. She told me that the guard who was sitting at the officer's desk asked her who was she, "The wife or the girlfriend?" When I looked over at the officer, he turned away. I was angered, but I didn't want to ruin our time together; I would confront the officer after the visit. Antoinette wanted to know the truth about who was visiting me. The old me would have tried to cover it up but I couldn't do that to her anymore. I told Antoinette that Leanna would bring Serina to see me. She asked me why I hadn't told her that Leanna was visiting.

Antoinette was right. I should have told her. My excuse was that I did not want to hurt Antoinette anymore. I was sure if Antoinette knew that Leanna was visiting me that she would be upset. I felt I had put Antoinette through enough. Antoinette expressed how much it bothered her that Leanna came to visit me. I didn't want to hurt Antoinette anymore, so I agreed to not let Leanna bring Serina to visit me any longer: I would have my mother or my sister bring my daughter instead. Antoinette cried, telling me how much she wanted me home. She said that I was her life and her breath, and that she couldn't live without me.

I tried to cheer Antoinette up. I knew it hurt her that I couldn't be with her when she needed me the most. I genuinely wanted to listen to her and I cared about what she wanted instead of what I wanted. We talked about our past hurts and our future plans. Antoinette would ask me about my past cheating. I owed it to her to be truthful and I told Antoinette, but I didn't volunteer anything she didn't already know. I felt that it was best that way. After visiting, Antoinette left in good spirits.

After the visit I was tired, but still bothered by the officer who asked Antoinette if she was the girlfriend or the wife. It was clear that the officer had gotten involved with my personal life. I asked other inmates for his name and was told it was Officer Martinez. I knew eventually Martinez would end up in Unit 7 South. Weeks later, he happened to be assigned to the same floor on which I was being housed. I confronted Martinez about why he had asked my girl if she was my wife or my girlfriend. He smirked. I responded by telling him to be careful, because it was a long walk to his car and accidents are known to happen. I must have angered Martinez, because his smirk was no longer there. He responded, "Are you threatening me?" I grinned and said, "No, it's not a threat. I'm just giving you a heads-up to be careful." He walked away, looking angry. I saw Martinez at least twice a week when he worked the unit but he didn't bother to say a word to me. Martinez was no longer working the visiting room, so I never had an issue with him after our talk.

The next time Antoinette came to visit, she brought Ray Junior and Alexis. We were enjoying our time together so much the hours that we spent together seemed like minutes. Next thing I knew, a corrections officer approached the table to tell us to say our goodbyes. Visiting time was up. I gave Alexis a hug and a kiss, then turned to Ray Junior and did the same. It was time to tell Antoinette goodbye. She grabbed me and held me tight. I told her that I loved her and gave her a kiss. Antoinette and the kids walked away. A moment later Ray Junior screamed, "No, Daddy! Don't go!" My heart sank. I stopped and I turned to walk back to my five-year-old son; I knelt down before him. I explained to Ray Junior that I had to go to work, so I couldn't go with him. Ray Junior replied, "Let me go with you." The corrections officer approached me again. "Say goodbye to your visitors," he demanded. After saying goodbye for a second time, I sat watching Antoinette and my children leave the visiting room; I knew my son was hurt because I was absent from his life.

I returned to the housing unit and went straight to my cell; I felt sick to my stomach and depression overcame me. When I lay on my bunk I thought about how my kids must have felt without me being in their lives. I then realized that I had to face my situation and my consequences alone. There was no one who could help get me out of the mess I was in.

I continued my research in the law library; I wanted to know if it was worth going to trial and what kind of defense I could use if there was one. I was reminded by the old-timer's advice: don't play games with the feds. He advised me to wait for the best deal and take it. I waited and, as each day went by, I crossed it off my calendar. The best deal I was offered was 168 months and I wasn't about to take that. I kept waiting, but in the meantime I researched the laws of entrapment and sentencing entrapment. After I read a few cases that were similar to mine, I called Kirste at his office and I mentioned the entrapment and sentencing-entrapment defense. He claimed that I was not entrapped and said he would be at the detention center in a few days to see me.

During mail call I received another letter from Antoinette, that ended, *I love you, your soon to be wife Antoinette Woods Torres. Sounds good doesn't it?* Antoinette had always wanted to get married. I asked her to marry me when I got out of prison but Antoinette wanted to get married right away. I felt that she deserved more than a prison wedding. She deserved to be treated like a princess and I wanted to prove that I could be her prince. In her voice and in her letters I felt the pain that I caused her. I wanted to be the man who loved and cherished her. I had a lot of work to do to become the man I needed to be and was willing to give it my all.

I was called to an attorney visit and, when I arrived, Kirste told me that he had something to show me. He removed a videotape from his briefcase and he slid it into a VCR. There, on tape, were Juan and me along with two large suitcases containing 50 kilos of cocaine. The video also showed me bragging that my people had Vegas and L.A. by the balls. There I was, agreeing to trade $2 million worth of artwork for 110 pounds of cocaine and I was toasting to the deal with the Colombians.

Boxer Oscar De La Hoya & Me
before he fought Giorgio
Campanella at MGM Las Vegas,
May 1994.

The Great Boxer Julio Cesar
Chavez & Me at Johnny
Tocco's boxing gym in Las
Vegas, 1994.

Boxer Greg Haugen & Me
at the Shark Club in Las
Vegas, 1993.

Boxing Promoter Don King and Me at the
Chavez VS. Randall II after party, MGM
Las Vegas, 1994.

Antoinette DeAnna Woods and
Me in Guam, 1992.

Me and boxing Promoter
Rock Newman at the Chavez
vs Randall II fight, 1994.

(Left side) Anemones-1898. The original was valued at $176,000. (Right side) Mother and Child Pierre-Aguste Renoir. Paintings similar to the ones stolen from Wayne Newton: *ARCHIVES*

Victor Mercado and Alex Cardenas picking me up for a POV transfer from Camp Atwater, California to Camp Nellis, Nevada, 2003.

Me at Terminal Island Federal Correctional Institution, 2008.

(Bottom Photo) G-Unit, South Yard where I was housed.

116

(Top photo) VIP & Celebrity Chauffeur.
Photo *by Rusty Lane Primeaux*

(Middle photo) With my client Gucci.

(Bottom Photo)
Me with MMA Fighter Randy Couture.

117

With New England Patriots for Super Bowl XLIX. Arizona.

Transported VIPs to the Mayweather VS. Pacquiao fight.

Me & Billionaire Warren Buffett leaving Money Mayweather's gym in Las Vegas.

Me and Top Model Latina Veronica
Montano in Las Vegas for the Latin
Grammys, 2014.

I ran into Wayne Newton A.K.A.
"Mr. Las Vegas". He was nice
enough to take a picture with me.

Me speaking to a group of youths about the harsh realities of making bad choices. Pearson Community Center, Las Vegas.

Former Boxing Referee Richard Steele was a guest speaker for Real Talk.

I received Senatorial Recognition from United States Senator Dean Heller, a Certificate of Commendation from Senator Harry Reid, and a Certificate of Recognition from Las Vegas Councilman Ricki Y. Barlow for my commitment to change the lives of our youth in Southern Nevada.

After getting my passport back, I took a vacation to Cartagena, Colombia with Alex and Victor. The three amigos.

Me and former L.A.P.D. Officer Kelley Clemons.

After looking at the video, I knew I didn't have a chance to win at trial. It was embarrassing to hear that every other word I used was a curse word. My mind felt drained from all the thinking I was doing. I was tired of not knowing what the outcome of my sentence would be and just wanted to get things over. I told Kirste that I was ready to take the best plea deal that he could get me. Kirste said that he needed to present me to the government as a small-time dope dealer who got caught up in something over his head; that was the picture he wanted to paint. Kirste warned me that the feds were going to want to know about my role in the art-for-cocaine deal. He advised me not to volunteer any extra information to the government because it could open a can of worms. I agreed. I was well aware that loose lips sank ships. I was planning on keeping mine closed tight but I also wanted to get the best plea deal I could without implicating anyone else.

A few weeks later, I was at the U.S. Courthouse on North Spring Street when marshals escorted me out of a cell and into a hallway where Sakert and Cuthbert, two of the DEA agents that arrested me, were waiting. They walked me into an elevator, which stopped at one of the top floors. We approached a Plexiglas security booth. One of the agents flashed his credentials at a female secretary who then buzzed us through a security door that led to a room filled with cubicles and doors that led to offices. The federal agents walked me to one of the offices.

When I entered the room, Kirste and Warren were present. I noticed a desktop computer on a table and a world map on the wall. Boxes containing court documents sat in a corner near a wooden desk. Chairs were also positioned throughout the room. Agent Cuthbert asked if I would try to escape if he took my handcuffs off. I asked, "Where am I gonna go?" The same document that was presented to me by Warren at the MDC visiting room was before me again. I was asked to sign it, giving the government permission to question me. I reluctantly signed the paper and the questions began.

I knew I had to be careful. The feds knew that the artwork was stolen from a storage facility by an unknown thief. That's all I knew and I was sticking to my story. Warren wanted to know why I had sent a threatening letter to Juan Carlos. I explained to him that Juan owed me money. I was upset that he didn't send me the funds -- especially when he was out on bail knowing that I needed money for my defense attorney. The prosecutor wanted to know if my father had anything to do with the artwork stolen from Wayne Newton. I replied that my father had nothing to do with it. I was curious why the feds would ask about my father. I later learned that the feds must have thought I was related to Newton's ex-partner, Ed Torres. Torres and Newton owned the Aladdin hotel and casino together back in 1980. Ed Torres was no relation to me, but the feds sure seemed to be stretching for some connection.

They were very interested in knowing about Wayne Newton. I was asked if I worked for him and my answer was no, nor had I ever met him. I was also questioned about Victor. Warren wanted to know what Victor and I were doing in Tecate, Mexico, on the day of our arrest. I was asked if we were taking stolen cars across the border. I explained that Victor and I went to visit his uncle since we had some time to spare before we were to meet the Colombians in Irvine. That was the only reason we were in Mexico -- that and to grab something to eat. Warren made it clear that he wanted a conviction if Juan Carlos decided to go to trial. I later realized that the feds didn't know anything about my activities in Las Vegas. I wanted to keep it that way. The only thing they knew about was the artwork-for-cocaine deal … and it was enough to put me away for a long time.

The plea deal proposed to me, which was offered to many who were busted in the feds, was if I provided the government with substantial assistance into the investigation of my case or any another cases then they would consider filing a 5K1.1 motion to the judge, recommending a reduction in my sentence. The government used the 5K1.1 as an incentive to keep inmates flipping on people who were committing crimes. Tom Warren explained to me that, in order for the judge to accept a plea agreement, I would have to plead guilty. He said the judge was going to ask if I was promised anything in return for my guilty plea and I was to say, "No" because the government was not allowed to promise anything in exchange for a reduced sentence.

Warren went on to say that the judge was the one who decided if a reduction in a sentence should be granted. I would have to show the court that I was sincerely remorseful. I sure didn't want to do 168 months in prison but I wasn't about to rat on anyone. I must have had a reluctant look on my face because Cuthbert suddenly said, "Do you know how many people sitting in prison would love to have the opportunity that we are offering you?" He went on, "We are giving you the chance to be Queen for a Day." I stared at Cuthbert; I was bothered by his words. My understanding of being "Queen for a Day" was that the feds wanted me to be their bitch. The word "Queen" went through my mind. The agent could have used the words "King for a Day." But he didn't. I didn't want to be there any longer, so the meeting ended without me making a commitment.

When the feds pulled me in for a second meeting, I was asked if Alex Cardenas had anything to do with the stolen artwork and my answer was "No." I told the feds that I was the one who received the artwork; Alex had nothing to do with it at all. The feds knew that Alex was my brother-in-law so they asked me if I was covering up for him. My answer remained, "No." I was asked how I knew Aldo Walter. I explained that Aldo regularly worked on my Porsche 911s. Warren then asked, "Who are Matteo Calvi and Santi Rivelli?" I responded, "People I know from Vegas." I was asked if Santi and Matteo had anything to do with the stolen artwork. I commented that they knew about the art deal but were not involved.

I was asked if I knew Juan's son Francisco, who was arrested on federal drug charges. I admitted that I had met Francisco a few times but I did not know of his personal business. Was Juan involved in any known drug dealings? I did not know. I had only known Juan a short time and I was telling the truth. Now the million-dollar question was asked again. I told the feds that the artwork was given to me by a meth-head who robbed storage units. His street name was Dirk; I didn't know his real name. Warren looked upset; he yelled, "Are you sure their names are not Santi Rivelli or Matteo Calvi?" I stared at him. It was obvious that someone was feeding him other information. I answered, "No."

It was clear that the assistant U.S. attorney did not believe my story. Warren said threateningly, "If I find out you are lying, all leniency deals are off." I knew I was playing with fire but continued anyway. Warren asked, "What were you going to do with the cocaine?" "I'm not sure," I answered. "My initial plan was to get cash. The informants were the ones who offered us the cocaine in exchange for the artwork." Warren yelled, "That's not what I want to hear!" I calmly asked, "What do you want me to do? Lie?" He answered, "No! I want the truth!" I then realized that he didn't want my truth: He wanted *his* truth and he wanted convictions. Warren wanted to indict a long list of people in Vegas who had nothing to do with the case but mostly he seemed interested in building a case against Wayne Newton.

When I arrived for the third debriefing, Newton called Warren's office. Warren was on speaker phone with Newton and, from the conversation, I could tell Newton was upset that Warren had insinuated that he had something to do with the cocaine deal. I was in the room only for a moment before I was asked by Warren to step out. A short time later, the phone conversation ended, I was brought back into the room and was seated before Warren and agents Sakert and Cuthbert. My attorney was not present.

Tom Warren went on to offer me a cooperation deal. He explained that he wanted me to testify at Juan Carlos's trial and then "Do something else" for him. My understanding of "Do something else" was that Warren wanted me to help him build a case against Wayne Newton. If I chose to be a dirty rat I had every reason to get back at Juan. In my eyes, Juan was no good but it wasn't in me to rat him out. I hadn't been the most honest person but what the prosecution was attempting to do to Newton did not sit well with me. What I learned from dealing with the feds was if I was a low-life snake, I could go along with their version of "the truth" and put an innocent man behind bars. I didn't realize that the prosecutor had that much power. The ball was now in my court and I was holding a chance at freedom. I knew the best thing to do was to accept a plea, take it on the chin and move on to prison to do my time.

PLEA AGREEMENT

Robert Kirste came to visit me at MDC on Feb. 9, 1996, plea agreement in hand. I was tired of not knowing the outcome of my sentence and wanted to end the back-and-forth bargaining. I flipped through the pages of the plea agreement and signed it. I was at level 36 for the amount of drugs with a two-point gun enhancement for carrying a firearm in the commission of a drug-related crime. As part of the plea deal, I was offered a three-point reduction for acceptance of responsibility. The three-point reduction brought my sentencing level to 35. The gun charge, which could have cost me five more years, was dropped. Level 35 carried a sentence of 168 to 210 months in prison. I pled guilty on March 6, 1996, before Judge Stotler to conspiracy to possess cocaine with intent to distribute, attempted possession and forfeiture. I then waited to be sentenced. Immediately after pleading guilty before Judge Stotler, I felt that I had made the biggest mistake of my life.

When I called Robert Kirste to find out what the status was on my sentencing, he told me that Juan skipped bail and was on the run. Kirste thought it was an opportunity for me to help myself. The feds wanted to know if I knew Juan's whereabouts. Juan and I had bought a house in Sinaloa, Mexico, but I didn't believe he was there. Juan had told me that the feds took the title to the property when they raided his office but the real story most likely was that Juan sold the house and probably kept the money. I was sure that Juan took the three missing paintings on the run with him. I told my attorney that I didn't know where Juan would be and left it at that.

Many federal inmates were being housed at San Bernardino County Jail and, every week or so, in the middle of the night officers would come to Unit Seven South and call the names of inmates who needed to roll up their property for transport. When an inmate was told to roll up his property he was usually shipped to another institution. The officers who snatched inmates in the middle of the night were given the nickname "Body Snatchers." When the Body Snatchers opened my cell door, I knew I was going to be shipped and I had a good idea where I was going. Inmates who were called by the unit officer were taken to awaiting buses that had "San Bernardino County" logos on their side. The horror stories about inmates being housed at San Bernardino County Jail were known among inmates at MDC. Most federal inmates didn't want to go there.

CHAPTER 5 Life Is In Session

I arrived at San Bernardino County Jail in April 1996. When the bus carrying inmates stopped at a security gate, a sheriff walked around the vehicle with rod and mirror in hand as he checked the undercarriage to make sure no persons were hiding underneath and it was clear of weapons. Once inspection was over, a gate opened and the bus rolled onto the detention center. Sheriffs escorted chained inmates off the bus. We were led down a hallway and placed in holding cells.

A black chair with restraining straps and wheels stood on display in a hallway, to let inmates know that the sheriffs were not ones to mess with. While at MDC L.A., I had heard stories about how the sheriffs had a reputation for laying hands on inmates. I wasn't in the holding cell 10 minutes when two black inmates started to complain and protest being there. When a nurse came by to give inmates who were on medication their pills, the two blacks refused to take them. They thought if they refused to take the medication, they would be shipped back to Los Angeles. In federal facilities, staff members would reason with inmates who refused medication before using force but the sheriffs didn't bother to ask twice. They were known for rushing a cell full of inmates and dragging out the ones who caused trouble.

I could tell the nurse was not in the mood to play games. She gave the two inmates one more chance to take their meds and when they refused she called the goon squad. The uncooperative inmates were told if they refused to take their meds, they would be hogtied, strapped to a chair and force-fed the meds through a tube down their throat. The blacks took one look at the chair that stood before them and decided to take the medicine.

A group of us were escorted to a property room by a female sheriff. We were instructed to remove all of our clothing. While in custody, I had stripped down so many times that I was no longer bothered by it, but being ordered to strip down in front of a female officer was a first for me. A trustee stood by to hand me my San Bernardino-issued jumpsuit, underclothing and bed roll. After I was processed into the jail, I was placed in E range. This tier contained five 10-man cells and every two cells shared one television that was mounted on a wall. There was not much a person could do to entertain himself besides watch television, read books, work out, or play cards and dominoes. Most inmates slept during the day and played cards and dominoes during the night. I chose to spend my time reading books, working out and writing letters.

After a few months at San Bernardino, I was moved to F-tank, which was dorm living. When I arrived at F-tank, I met Jorge Del Rio from Riverside County and a Mexicano named Indio, who I knew from MDC. Jorge's bunk was next to mine and at times I could hear him talk to other inmates in whispers. They discussed inmates who were informing for the feds. How they knew this I had no idea. I also overheard Jorge tell another inmate how his brother was "working" with the feds so Jorge could get time knocked off his sentence. After I heard Jorge's confessions I made sure to keep my distance from him.

A new group of inmates arrived in F-tank; one of them was Javier Acosta. I knew Javier from MDC Los Angeles; he too was from Riverside. When I saw Javier talking to Jorge; I pulled Javier aside and warned him that Jorge was a rat. Javier later told Jorge what I said. As F-unit waited to be released for chow, an angry Jorge approached me yelling, "Did you say I was a rat?" I had to back up my words, so I responded with, "You are a rat." Jorge came at me like a raging bull. He was much bigger than me, and he was overweight and out of shape. I knew Jorge had no endurance and would tire quickly if we were to go at it. I warned Jorge to not get too close to me. Jorge suddenly stopped but he kept talking.

When he inched closer to me, I planted my feet and cracked Jorge on the nose with a solid right fist. Jorge stumbled back against the cell bars and I rushed him, locking both of my hands to the bars as I pinned him against the steel. I kneed Jorge in his bulging stomach, then with combinations I released my hands from the bars to connect punches to Jorge's face. Jorge managed to slip a couple of blows to the back of my head but I continued hitting him with rights, lefts and knees. Javier Rios and another inmate broke us apart but I wasn't finished fighting. I called Jorge upstairs to the dorm where there was more room for us to go at it.

The barred doors to the dorm opened for chow and Jorge walked out with the rest of the inmates, ignoring my invitation. I followed Jorge as he headed to the dining hall. Jorge's mouth was bleeding and his face had swelling but he happened to get through the chow hall without the sheriffs noticing. After chow, I arrived at the dorm ready for round two. I then heard Jorge Del Rio's name called over an intercom instructing him to roll up his property. I was later told by another inmate that Jorge went back to court for some "unknown reason."

WELCOME TO THE HOUSE OF PAIN

Those who have been in San Bernardino for any amount of time know the rules when eating in the chow hall. Those who didn't know the rules received free lessons on chow-hall etiquette. Most lessons were taught by sheriffs when the new inmates arrived at San Bernardino. Class was in session when a group of new arrivals entered the chow hall. One of the white inmates in the group saw someone he knew sitting at a table. The white inmate laughed and waved at his friend. Those in the chow hall stopped to look at the inmate and most knew what would come next. Three sheriffs noticed the happy inmate and escorted him out of the chow hall. Moments later, screams from the inmate and yells from the officers were heard coming from a hallway. The white inmate returned to the chow hall with his head hung low and his hands crossed in front of him. His shirtless body was covered with red welts as if he received a beating. It was clear that the lesson given to the white inmate was a lesson learned.

I usually worked out with one of the Breseno brothers, who were in prison on drug charges. The Bresenos were hired by their boss in

Mexico to cross the border with two trucks loaded with weed, but when the trucks crossed to the U.S., they were pulled over by highway patrol. Police searched the vehicles and found kilos of cocaine instead of weed. The Breseno brothers received 12-year sentences.

I was asked by one of the Bresenos if I would talk to the group of men we were housed with about noise and keeping the dorm clean. When living with 50 or more men in one dorm, it got noisy and unsanitary. Some of the Mexican inmates regularly got together at night to sing *corridos* [ballads] while other inmates tried to sleep. Inmates would piss on the toilet seats and not clean up after themselves. Other inmates would spit on the floor where peopled walked.

I was hesitant to get involved in keeping order in the tank but I was also tired of the unruliness, so I agreed to call a meeting with the entire dorm. A group of inmates came up with a list of rules: There was no singing after 8 p.m., no spiting on the floor, the first two toilets were used to piss and the other two toilets were used for crapping; the televisions were to be shared so each ethnic group had a time slot to watch a show of their liking. All agreed to the rules. A few days later, four sheriffs stormed into the dorm, cuffed me and hauled me off to the SHU. I asked one of the sheriffs why I was being put in Segregated Housing. He asks, "You don't know?" "No," I said. "Fifteen inmates dropped a note on you saying you were running the tank," answered the sheriff.

I was asked to keep order in the tank, something that I didn't want to do, then a note was dropped on me because someone didn't like the rules that were set. That's what I got for trying to help out. After a few months in solitary confinement, I was released and moved to a unit in general population. My first day out, I saw inmates from F-tank walking past me as they entered the chow hall. I stared into the face of each inmate who I suspected dropped a note on me, as I sat eating at a table. I came to the conclusion that the ones who avoided eye contact with me were the ones guilty of dropping the note but I couldn't prove it.

I was called to the visiting room, where Robert Kirste was waiting for me. He informed me that Juan Carlos had been caught in Mexico. Tom Warren was preparing for Juan's trial and wanted me to testify. In exchange for my cooperation the government would file a motion to the court for a reduction in my sentence. I sat staring at Kirste for a moment. Then I responded, "You're fired." Kirste warned me that I was making a big mistake. If it was a mistake, it sure felt good getting rid of him. I had a number of reasons to dislike Juan but I refused to rat him out; karma would visit him eventually.

AT MY DARKEST HOUR

Being housed at San Bernardino was one of the darkest points in my life. Prison was a very lonely place and being locked away tested the spirit of a man. I realized that I had to walk down the road I chose and I had to walk it alone. Prison has made men lose it mentally and morally. Isolation tends to make the mind wonder. I often lay in my cell and thought about where I went wrong in life. I thought about the times I felt abandoned by my parents and about how being in prison was similar to being dead. Life went on in the free world as I sat locked away in a prison cell, forgotten. I was a distant memory to the people who were in my life. So many thoughts rushed through my mind all at once. The noise of dominos slamming at night, and the rowdy people playing cards and yelling at all hours of the day began to fuel my anger. I thought about how I had goals and dreams in life, and I thought about how my dreams were shattered. I thought about how old I would be when and if I walked out of prison. I found myself at times praying to God, asking Him to walk with me and to carry me through my darkest hours.

I was placed in a 10-man cell with Speedy from Venice Beach, a Mexicano named Felix Reyes, a Colombian named Luis Huerta and two white inmates. The Colombian was somewhat arrogant and he had made a rude comment about Felix. Felix overheard the Colombian but did nothing to Luis at the time. A few days later, Luis walked over and removed a magazine from Felix's bed without asking permission. Taking another man's property without asking is a very serious offense under the unwritten prison rules.

When Felix saw Luis take the magazine, he attacked the Colombian. The Mexican and the Colombian wrestled with each other, and ended up on one of the bottom bunks. Felix overpowered the Colombian, and began choking Luis and scratching his face. The rest of us backed up to let them handle their differences. Felix and Luis wrestled to the concrete floor, where Felix gripped the Colombian by his long hair. Felix slammed Luis' head against the hard floor repeatedly. When Luis' head hit the concrete it sounded as if someone were hitting a watermelon with their hand to test for ripeness. Luis' eyes rolled back white. I knew if I didn't stop Felix he would kill the Colombian. I told Speedy that we had to break it up. Speedy and I then grabbed Felix, pulling him off of the Colombian.

When the Colombian got his bearings back, I asked him if he was all right. His face was scratched and swollen with lumps as if he was stung by a swarm of bees. Luis said he would be OK. I gave the Colombian a jar of Noxzema and I told him he needed to put the cream on his face during count time so he could cover the marks on his face. I had other inmates pitch in soups and other food items from commissary so Luis wouldn't have to go to the chow hall and risk being seen by officers. This went on for a few days until I arrived back at the cell from chow to notice that the Colombian was gone. I looked down the hallway and saw Luis sitting on a bench near the infirmary. After a beating like the one he received, most people would need some kind of medical attention. Luis had been complaining of headaches, so I didn't blame him for wanting to get checked out by a doctor.

I knew what was coming next; it was just a matter of time. We all sat waiting in the cell and heard the iron door open. It was the goon squad, all geared up in black paramilitary riot armor. Eight guards, men and women, marched down the tier and stopped in front of our cell. The goons instructed us to lay face down on our bunks and to not lift our head up or look around. One by one, an officer called inmates off their bunk and instructed us to strip down naked in front of female officers. Once we were down to our skin, we were ordered to place our hands against a wall and not to move. The officers stood with taser guns and pepper spray aimed at us. After all the inmates were out of the cell, the goons went through inmates' personal property, tossing it onto the floor.

One of the lieutenants yelled at us, calling us cowards. He wanted to know how we could stand by and watch while another inmate received a beating and had his food taken from him. We figured the Colombian told the lieutenant that someone in our cell beat him and took his food while all of us did nothing to help him. Luis told the sheriffs that the person who took his food left the jail on the last transport out. After hours of standing at the wall, we were released and told to clean up our cell. At least no one was taken to the SHU.

I grew unhappy with my decision to plead guilty. Being housed at San Bernardino for nearly a year took its toll on me. The federal system was designed to break a man's spirits. It was all part of a psychological game they played; everything from the amount of time a person is facing to denying a person bail, from postponed court dates, to threats of indictments on family members. It was a process to get a man to flip. The words from the federal agent who offered me to be "Queen for a Day" continued to ring through my head. I wrote a letter to Judge Stotler, informing her of my decision to withdraw my plea.

KTE

The new Santa Ana jail opened March 1997. When I arrived it was like a breath of fresh air. The lobby looked similar to that of an airport waiting area, with televisions mounted on a wall. The first thing that caught my attention were the attractive and friendly female officers who worked at the jail. As new arrivals sat waiting to be processed, a female officer rolled past with a cart of food to pass out to inmates.

I was housed in Unit C. The unit was spotless, with a modern design. The visiting area was connected to the unit and located on the top tier. During visitation, inmates sat in a booth with a glass window where they could see visitors and two-way phones were used to communicate. When the female officers asked inmates if they wanted to work, I volunteered to do laundry and deliver food to other units.

134

Working got me out of the unit for a few hours, plus it earned me an extra tray of food and gave me access to new clothes from laundry.

If an inmate didn't have a high school diploma, when he arrived at the jail it was mandatory that he signed up for a class to earn a General Education Development. Santa Ana Jail was a holding facility but it offered many classes including parenting, drug awareness and basic computer training. I was eager to earn my diploma, so I locked myself (so to speak) in my cell for two months and studied the GED book. I read the entire book repeatedly and completed all the exercises. When I took the pretest I did well enough that the teacher from the training facility thought I was ready for the real test. I was and, when the scores came back, I had passed. I was excited. Growing up I hadn't done well in school, so passing the GED test was a great achievement for me.

A graduation ceremony was held for the male and female inmates who earned their GED diploma. We were provided cookies, cake and punch as part of the festivities. Graduates were also offered a video of the ceremony so we could send it to family members. After I completed all the classes that Santa Ana had to offer, I began researching drug cases in the law library. I searched for any defense that might be of help in my case. The more I researched, the more I felt that I was entrapped by federal agents. The feds brought 50 kilos of cocaine to an artwork deal and then they charged me for conspiracy to possess with intent to distribute. Those charges did not sit well with me. I did a search for entrapment defenses. I had not heard back from the court, so I had a friend who lived in Las Vegas file a motion requesting to withdraw my plea.

On June 19, 1997, I was called to roll up my property. I was being shipped from Santa Ana. Hours later, I arrived at MDC Los Angeles, where I was housed on the sixth floor, south wing. When I walked into the unit with my bed roll, one of the first persons I saw was Jorge Del Rio, the man I got into a brawl with at San Bernardino. Jorge saw me enter the unit and a worried look came over his face. I headed to my new cell in Jorge's direction and, as I got closer, he called me over to him. I put down my bedroll, ready to go at it again with Jorge, but he had a different attitude.

Jorge apologized for what took place at San Bernardino and realized that he should have kept his mouth shut. "Just keep away from me and there won't be any issues," I said, then walked way. A few days later, I was hauled off to the federal court building in Los Angeles. I sat in a holding tank for close to an hour before DEA agents Jan Sakert and Peter Walker, two of my arresting agents had arrived. "I have nothing to say to you," I told them. The agents ordered me out of the cell and proceeded to handcuff me. I was aggressively escorted down a hall, through secured doors, and into an elevator.

When the elevator stopped, we exited onto the seventh floor. I was taken to Tom Warren's office. My former attorney, Robert Kirste, was present as well. Warren wanted to know why I wrote letters to the judge requesting to withdraw my plea. I told him that there were untruths in the plea agreement. I explained that I had not read the plea in its entirety until recently. I knew that Warren was preparing for Juan's trial and had expectations of me testifying on the government's behalf but I wasn't giving the feds the satisfaction of flipping me. I told Warren that I had been requesting copies of my discovery for months and that Kirste ignored my requests every time. Warren retrieved a copy of my plea agreement and he handed it to me, but he never asked me to name the untruths in it. When I left the federal building, Warren most likely thought that we would work things out but my mind was made up. I was withdrawing my plea.

KTE

In Unit Six South, I often walked past a steel door that had a Plexiglas window. The door led into a hallway and at the end was a second door that led into Unit Six North. From my unit, I saw inmates walk past the door's window at Six North. A familiar face caught my attention; it was Johnny Blanco, a childhood friend. My father disliked Johnny and warned me not to hang around him. The last time I saw Johnny was at the Carson mall in California. He happened to walk by me while I ate at a food court. Johnny told me that he was on the run and asked if I had a place for him to hide out in Las Vegas. I told Johnny that I couldn't help him, especially if he was on the run. I didn't want the heat following me to Vegas. It was strange that I ran into Johnny, because a few months earlier my father had left a message on my beeper warning me to stay away from Johnny. I was told that Johnny ratted out a guy I went to school with named Ed Martinez. When I saw Johnny at the mall I already knew not to associate with him. How my father knew that Johnny was a rat, I have no idea.

When I saw Johnny standing near the door at Sixth North I walked over to the recreation deck, where a second door from Unit Six South connected to a recreation door at Six North. I called one of the inmates through the door and asked him to tell Johnny Blanco that I wanted to talk to him. We talked briefly, then Johnny asked me to put in a request to transfer to his unit. I submitted the request to my unit counselor and it was approved. Johnny and I became cellmates. He told me that he was waiting to be sentenced on his fed case and he had a pending drug case in the state. I could hear the fear in Johnny's voice when he expressed that he did not want to go to the state. Johnny asked me questions about my past criminal activity but I avoided answering him. I didn't trust Johnny and the questions he asked made me suspect that he might indeed be a rat.

Johnny wanted to know why I didn't help him when he was on the run. I told Johnny that I heard he snitched on Ed Martinez. "If I ratted, then why is Ed on the streets and why am I the one locked up," he answered. I wondered the same thing. Before my arrest I saw Ed Martinez at an auto-parts store in Wilmington. I asked Ed if Johnny ratted on him. Ed's answer was, "Yes." All I could base my opinions on were what people on the streets were telling me and on my instincts.

Johnny frequently smoked in the cell we shared. I often grumbled to him about the smoking and Johnny complained that I was always in the mirror flossing my teeth. After bunking with Johnny, I learned that he was just a miserable person. It got to the point where I couldn't stand to be around him. On one occasion I walked into the cell to find Johnny attempting to pick my lock box. Johnny knew where I kept my legal documents and the documents had all the details about my case. I asked Johnny what he was doing with my locker. Johnny said he was just messing with the lock, but I knew better.

After a few months, Johnny went to court, supposedly to get sentenced, but when he returned to MDC his sentencing had been postponed. Johnny told me that he had filed a motion to withdraw his plea and he wanted to know who the prosecutor on my case was. I told Johnny that it was Tom Warren and David Jessner. Johnny then told me that the assistant U.S. attorney on his case was transferred to another state and Warren was now his prosecuting attorney. I didn't believe that Warren becoming Johnny's prosecutor was a coincidence. When I wrote letters in my cell or if I worked on legal documents, Johnny wanted to know what I was doing. I told Johnny on more than one occasion to mind his own business.

The final straw was when Johnny entered the cell in a playful mood. He reached his arm around my neck while I sat writing at a desk and attempted to put me in a choke hold. Instantly, I grabbed Johnny by one arm and leaned my body forward, flipping him over my shoulder. He crashed to the floor, landing on his back. I rushed on top of Johnny, pinning my knee to his throat. "You're lucky I don't break your neck. Never grab me like that again," I warned him. I could see the anger in his eyes as I pressed my knee against his throat. I knew he wanted to do something to me but he couldn't. After I released Johnny, I gathered my property and told the unit officer that I wanted to move to another cell. After I moved, I cut all ties with Johnny.

NEW COUNSEL

During a court hearing, Kirste was released as my counsel. The court informed me that they would appoint me a panel attorney. After the hearing, I was housed at Santa Ana County Jail. When my new attorney, Mike Meza, visited me, I made sure to tell him that there was an entrapment defense that I wanted to pursue. It just didn't seem right for the feds to bring the 50 kilos of cocaine and then indict me for it.

Mike was not like most attorneys. He seemed sincere about doing the best he could for me. Though we went back and forth on a few legal issues, overall I had a feeling that Mike was a fighter. During one of the attorney visits with Mike I asked him if he had a son. "Yes," told me. "Then defend me like you would defend your own son," I said.

138

Mike paused to look at me. He assured me that he would do his best. Mike went on to tell me that he nearly won a sentencing entrapment case that was similar to mine. A client he represented was attempting to trade lithographs for drugs. If it wasn't for his client having a prior drug conviction, the judge said he would have granted in favor of the defendant. When Mike told me this it was music to my ears; it gave me hope.

When Juan Carlos arrived at Santa Ana he was housed in a unit next to mine. At times, I saw Juan through a window when I was in the law library. The library separated Juan's unit from mine. The court had an order to keep Juan and I separated from each other. One of the guards who was friendly with Juan and myself let us meet in the law library alone -- on the condition that we didn't kill each other. As we stood face to face, I wanted to know where the three missing paintings were. Juan told me that I got caught up in something that really had nothing to do with me. He said that the feds had been targeting him for years. Alcohol Tobacco & Firearms had tried to sell him guns in the past. Juan felt that he was being targeted because of a lawsuit he had against the government and because he was part of the Brown Berets, a Chicano Movement during the Sixties and Seventies that sought political empowerment and social inclusion for Mexican-Americans.

Juan said that I was snared in the net that was set for him. He went on to say that he had to sell all his personal belongings. His brother, a retired postal worker, lost the home that he put up for Juan's bail when Juan fled the country. Juan said he first met Lucho and Jorge in court while Juan was an interpreter for an attorney in San Diego on the case of Ezekiel Garcia, a Colombian who got caught with a boatload of cocaine. Lucho and Jorge paid for Ezekiel's attorney, and they were at his court hearing when Juan met them. It was Lucho and Jorge, Ezekiel's own *compadres*, who set him up to get busted by the feds. Juan attempted to win me over by giving me copies of the grand jury transcripts and other court documents that I had never received from my attorney.

I told Juan that I didn't care about the stories he fed me. I wanted to know where the three missing paintings were. Juan said when he was in Mexico on his way to pick up money from someone who owed it to him, he got pulled over by the highway patrol. An officer found one of the paintings in the trunk of his car. Juan was arrested on a federal warrant. Juan said he gave the other two paintings to his brother, the mailman, for safekeeping. As I looked into Juan's eyes I saw a selfish, greedy snake. I wanted to pounce on the guy but I let him walk. I thought to myself, "I'm getting soft or maybe I'm just getting a little wiser."

Juan had scammed people at MDC L.A. Before his arrest Juan had a U.S. citizenship-and-immigration service that he ran in downtown San Diego. Juan claimed he could file deportation papers for illegal immigrants who wanted to be deported back to their country and receive an early out instead of remaining in the U.S. and doing their entire federal sentence ... all for a fee, of course. A few of his prison clients had paid Juan in advance and, when nothing came of it, they wanted their money back. When Juan didn't have their money, he got busted up and tossed in the SHU for his own protection. Karma was catching up with Juan.

MIKE MEZA

My next court date was set for August 22, 1997. At that hearing, the court denied my motion to withdraw my guilty plea. Mike Meza then filed an opposition motion to the court regarding sentencing factors in my case. The motion was heard on October 3, 1997, before Judge Stotler. The following issues were brought before the judge for consideration: Downward departure for post-offense rehabilitation, three-point reduction for acceptance of responsibility, reduction in sentence under sentencing entrapment. According to an Eighth Circuit judge, sentencing entrapment occurs when a defendant "although predisposed to commit a minor or lesser offense, is entrapped in committing a great offense subject to greater punishment." Meza's motions were all denied.

On November 11, 1997, I returned to court. Mike looked bothered as he read a document titled, "Tentative Ruling." After reading the paper, Mike turned to me and said, "Don't say anything to get the judge

140

upset." Mike then handed me the document. "This is how much time the judge plans to sentence you," he said. "It's way too much." When I read "235 to 293 months imprisonment; five years supervised release and $25,000 to $4,000,000 in fines," my heart sank. "We will appeal this," Mike assured me. Everyone in the room was ordered to stand as Judge Stotler entered the courtroom. Meza spoke a few words before the court and then prosecuting attorney Warren made his case.

I was given an opportunity to plead my sentencing issues to the judge. I wanted to present myself to the court as a changed man. I explained to Judge Stotler that I had finished every program that Santa Ana had to offer, including a substance-abuse program, parenting class, life-skills class, computer-skills class and I had obtained my GED. I wanted Judge Stotler to see that I was sincerely working on rehabilitating myself but my words fell on deaf ears. She handed me a sentence of 235 months. The only thing good that came out of it was that she denied the government's request for a two-point enhancement for obstruction of justice, which would have given me more time. I had played with fire and been burned, but I had some satisfaction knowing that the feds couldn't turn me into one of their "Queens for a Day."

Jaime Guzman and I were housed in the same unit at Santa Ana. We were brought before Judge Stotler and sentenced the same day. Jaime's girlfriend Monica was at his sentencing to support him. After Jaime and I were handed our sentence we returned to Santa Ana. When we walked into the unit, inmates were waiting to hear how much time Jaime and I had received. When I told them I received a 235-month sentence, some of the guys looked sicker than I felt. I didn't go to my cell right away. There were volunteers who held a Bible study in the multipurpose room. I sat at a distance but close enough to hear the words being spoken. I needed words of encouragement. The 235-month sentence rocked me to my soul.

When Jaime returned from visiting Monica, he told me that she overheard the two prosecutors talking about me. One of them said that, "Mr. Torres is a lot smarter than he's making himself out to be." He also made a comment about me: "Always in the mirror flossing his teeth." When Jaime told me this, the first person that came to mind was Johnny Blanco. Johnny was so desperate to get out of going to state prison that he began having secret meetings with the feds, feeding them information about me in hopes to get a reduction in his prison sentence. Johnny never got the information that he needed because I moved out of his cell when I suspected he was up to no good.

The night of my sentencing was one of the loneliest nights of my life. I was a 28 year old being sentenced to 19 years and seven months for a first-time offense. I went to my cell to lie on my bunk. I thought about how old I would be when I was released from prison. I felt as if my life was over. I prayed and asked God to carry me through the storm I was going through. I wondered, what my life would have been like if my parents hadn't kicked me out of the house. What if they had been there for me instead of letting the streets raise me? Was I blaming my parents for my actions? I reflected on the promise that I had made to God while I sat in that South Gate substation years earlier, the promise to do right if he got me out of the mess I was in. I had broken that promise.

I didn't want to tell my family or Antoinette how much time I got. I just wanted everyone to forget about me. After a few days in my cell I got my second wind back, so I decided to contact my family to give them the bad news. I began right away to look for a lawyer for my appeal. I had Leanna place Las Vegas attorney David Chesnoff on a three-way conference call. When I spoke to David, he told me that Wayne Newton had recently contacted him for representation on getting his paintings back from the government. David went on to ask me how many kilos I was charged with dealing. Fifty kilos I told him. David said he was willing to drop Wayne Newton as a client and take my case for $150,000. I explained to the attorney that the feds brought the 50 kilos to sell *me*; they didn't catch me selling that kind of weight. David stood firm on his price. "For $150,000 are you guaranteeing me freedom," I asked. "There are never any guarantees," David responded. Many attorneys say those exact words after they receive their retainer.

Going back to San Bernardino was like returning to a nightmare. New Year's Eve 1998 was one of the worst nights of my life. Inmates slammed dominoes in the middle of the night, others yelled like men going mad and there were those drunk on *pruno* (an alcoholic drink made from fruit, milk, syrup, candy and whatever else is on hand). They sang the entire night. It was like being housed in an asylum and I was ready to snap on anyone who gave me reason. I prayed for God to help me and somehow was given the strength to get through the night.

A few days later, I got a letter from Guam. It was from Antoinette. She wrote to let me know that she had met someone else and was moving on with her life. She said that she wanted to be honest with me and we each agreed that there was no holding back secrets. Antoinette went on to say that the guy she met made her happy. She hadn't felt happy in a long time. As much as it hurt, it was only right to let her go. Antoinette deserved to be happy. On February 24, 1998, I was called to roll up my property. I was being transported to federal prison.

CHAPTER 6 Gladiator School

FCI Phoenix Arizona was a medium-high security prison; also known as "Gladiator School" or "Black Canyon." The prison was surrounded by double fences that were equipped with motion sensors and razor wire. Corrections officers in perimeter trucks patrolled the prison grounds 24 hours a day. Black Canyon was used as a disciplinary yard by the Bureau of Prisons for those who violated rules at other institutions. Since 1985, the bureau has used a point system to determine where inmates were sent. The more violence in a criminal's background, the more points he received; age, education and previous record were also factors. It was common to see inmates serving sentences of 20 years to life.

At R&D, inmates were ordered to walk through a metal detector. This was to make sure that no weapons were hidden in any body cavities. Next, each inmate had to see the bureau's Special Investigative Services (SIS), which operated like the FBI inside federal prisons across the nation. Officers questioned every inmate that came into the institution. Some of the questions were. "Did you testify against anyone?" "Do you have enemies?" "Are you a Separate Inmates Management Services case?" "What gang do you run with?" If an inmate didn't let the officer know who he ran with, the feds could put that inmate on a yard where his gang was not allowed to walk. That wrong choice could cost an inmate his life. Once an inmate was on file within the bureau as a known gang member, that status was there for life.

The day I walked into prison and the steel door closed behind me, I knew I stood alone. When a man is in prison and has a problem, there is no one he can run to. He would have to deal with it on his own. In prison, a man is tested by inmates and by guards. Predatory inmates fell upon the weak ones, who became victim to extortion and rape.

Prison has been called "The House of Pain" and I was advised early on to leave my feelings at the Receiving & Discharge Department. Inmates had been known to get stabbed or cracked in the head with a lock in a sock for not paying a gambling or dope debt. Riots have erupted because of disagreements over a television.

I was being housed at Yuma unit, one that housed holdover inmates. Being confined to Yuma was like being in a county jail. It was noisy, and there were drugs and hooch available if an inmate desired. I told myself that if I had to do the rest of my time in that madhouse, I would go crazy myself. I later learned that all inmates at FCI Phoenix were housed in Yuma unit until they were assigned a permanent cell on the yard or were transferred to another prison. A few days later, I was being moved to Pima-A unit. When I walked out onto the main yard I was surprised to see the nicely cut, green grass, trimmed trees and well-kept housing units. FCI Phoenix looked more like a university.

Pima-A was comprised of top and bottom tiers with two-man cells. There were two TV rooms and one TV in the common area, along with tables and chairs. The showers were at the end of each hall. There was a laundry room. Phones lined one of the walls. I walked up the stairs to the second tier, carrying my belongings. I came to a six-by-ten cell with concrete walls and a steel door. The cell contained a bunk bed, metal trash can, two metal lockers, a wooden desk, a steel sink, steel toilet and polished steel that was used for a mirror. A small window gave me a view of a grassy area with barbed-wire fence. Jeff Lopez from San Pedro was my cellmate. He was at least six feet tall and weighed about 300 pounds. Jeff reminded me of a gentle giant. He gave me a short speech on how things were run on the yard. There was a list of unwritten prison rules and prison etiquette that any inmate who had sense followed.

1. Protect yourself at all times.
2. Always respect others.
3. Mind your own business.
4. Don't be a thief.
5. Your word is all you have; don't break it.
6. Don't be a rat.

7. Don't spit in the sink.
8. Don't piss on the toilet seat.
9. Give your cellmate alone time.
10. Know who you associate with.
11. Don't talk about your past sins to any man; it could come back to haunt you in the form of a new indictment.
12. Don't gamble or use drugs if you can't pay your debts.
13. Do not take part in homosexuality.
14. Never fart in front of someone who is eating or cooking; it could cost you your life.
15. No smoking, eating or drinking with any other race but your own.

The Bureau of Prisons had its own rules; just like MDC Los Angeles, every inmate was counted at least five times a day to make sure that no one had escaped. All inmate telephone calls were monitored and inmates were allotted 300 phone minutes a month. The phones shut off every 15 minutes and reset after 30 minutes so inmates could make other calls if needed. During the holidays in November and December, inmates received an extra 100 phone minutes a month.

In the chow hall I learned to sit with my back to a wall, so if something jumped off I wouldn't be caught by surprise. Another pointer I was given was to take one leg out of my pants before sitting on the toilet. If someone was going to attack an inmate it would be during a moment when the attacker had an advantage and an enemy sitting on the toilet would be the best time. If both legs were in the pants, chances were that a person would trip over their own feet if they were surprised by an assault.

On one side of the FCI compound was a women's camp and on another side was a building known as the Cheese Factory. It was a place where the marshals housed inmates who were in custody under the Witness Protection Program. Word from correctional officers who worked the unit was that Salvatore "Sammy the Bull" Gravano was once housed there. It was also known with officers that WPP inmates received special privileges. At times, I saw helicopters land on the prison property. Soon afterward, a white van raced from the Cheese

Factory to the helicopter, dropping inmates off. Then the helicopter would take flight again. Inmates who had been at FCI Phoenix for some time said the helicopter was there to pick up high-profile rats to testify against someone.

WORK DETAIL

The first job I had was working in the kitchen as a dishwasher. My first day was the worst. It was the lunch meal and the garbage disposal was broken so I had to dump the leftover food from each inmate's tray into a trashcan. Inmates were piling trays through the kitchen window faster than I could clean them. Food was splattering all over me; I was so frustrated that I thought if I had to do dishes for 20 years I was going to snap. I asked one of the homies to get me a job in the vegetable-preparation department. A few months later, I was transferred to veg-prep. The base pay for working in the kitchen was $5 a month but an inmate could work his way up to $120 a month. I could have made more money working at McDonald's for two years than I would during my entire prison sentence. But if I wanted food in my locker I had to work.

If an inmate didn't have his GED or high school diploma, it was mandatory that he went to school to earn it. If an inmate refused education, he was hauled off to SHU. I had earned my GED at Santa Ana and was happy that I did. On arriving to Phoenix, I wanted to start programming as soon as possible. I went to the education department and enrolled in a computer class taught through Central Texas College. In addition to going to college, I started writing movie scripts. I was the first of my immediate family to earn my GED or high school diploma and I was the first of my immediate family to attend college … in prison!

I was determined to use my time wisely, so I joined an institutional program called The Insiders. It allowed inmates to share their life stories of bad choices with troubled youths who were heading down the road to prison. I had spoken to one of the inmates who took part in the Insiders program. He told me that I had to be cleared by SIS, by the captain and by the warden in order to participate. I went through all the proper channels and submitted my paperwork requesting to be a member of the Insiders.

A few months later I received notice that I was approved. I became a panel speaker, sharing my story with groups of young kids. It was hard seeing a boy who was 10 years old, the same age as Ray Junior, who was caught selling crack cocaine -- his second offense. I asked the kid where his parents were and what they thought about him being involved in drugs. The kid told me that he got the drugs from his parents, who both smoked crack. That was a hard reality for me. It made me think about the drugs that I sold on the street and how many families may have been destroyed because of my drug dealings. The more I worked with The Insiders the more I felt that it was my calling to help make a change in the lives of kids.

KING OF MY CASTLE

FCI Phoenix was a boiling pot of hotheads. Tension was usually high at the prison and it was known that a riot could start at any time. I came to realize that most people in the feds were king of their own world, the one they controlled before they were arrested, and prisons were filled with these kings who felt that they were deserving of respect. FCI Phoenix housed drug traffickers, killers, white-collar criminals, bank robbers, and rapists, but the worst things a person could be in prison was a rat and a child molester, and there were many in the federal system. If a person was found out to be a rat or a child molester, violence was usually the end result.

The number-one rule in prison was, "Protect yourself at all times." For some inmates that meant carrying a shank (a homemade knife); I didn't want to carry a large piece of steel on my body, because getting caught with one could have brought me more prison time -- but I didn't want to get caught dead without one. I came up with my own weapon, in case I needed it. I bought copy cards from commissary and I sanded one end of the card until it was razor sharp. I kept one in my pants pocket and I kept the other one in the holder behind my ID card, just in case I needed a backup. Not that I was looking to get into a war with someone but it was comforting to know that weapons were available if needed.

Most fights broke out over gambling debts, drug debts and the TV. Sometimes cells were set on fire because either a person wanted an individual off the yard, or because an inmate owed a drug or gambling debt. The debtor would drop a note on himself or set his own bed on fire. Corrections officers would take the debtor off the yard and admit him to the SHU. If a person who owed went to the SHU, he would stay in Segregated Housing to avoid paying his bill and would later be shipped to a different prison.

Most people with long sentences were on the edge, capable of snapping at any time. Inmates doing 10-years-to-life sentences were common at Phoenix. In the feds, there was such a diverse group of people it was wise to know who was who. With the Latinos alone you had the Southsiders, Northerners, Pisas, Border Brothers, Texas Syndicate, Latin Kings, just to name a few. Some groups were rivals and if an inmate belonging to one of the groups was placed on a yard with a rival it could be deadly. Such was the case when a Tejano inmate arrived in Yuma unit. He was on his way to the chow hall. A rival inmate recognized him and decided to attack the Tejano by slicing open his back with a homemade knife and attempting to peel the skin from his body. Inmates were often getting sliced; lockdowns were implemented regularly. Investigations were conducted and shakedowns by officers were constant at Black Canyon.

THE DAY MY POPS DIED

On October 10, 1998, I had just finished doing laundry and was carrying my clothes past Case Manager Rodriguez's office. When Rodriguez saw me he called out my name. He told me that I needed to call home because my father was in the hospital. Immediately I went to the phone to call my mother's house. Debrah answered the phone and when she heard my voice she began to cry. I asked her what was wrong. She told me that my father was in the hospital and that it didn't look like he was going to make it.

149

My father and one of his crew members were loading an air compressor into the back of his truck when an aneurysm erupted in his brain. One of my father's coworkers called my mother and, when she arrived a short time later, my father was sitting in his truck with his face distorted. He continued to lift one of his fists in frustration, as if attempting to speak but was unable. My mother called 911 and my father was taken to a hospital, where he was put on life support. I was told that he passed away not long afterward but the doctors kept him on life support because they were waiting for our family's decision to pull the plug. While my father was on life support, a pastor performed a ceremony and married my parents, something my mother had wished for many years.

I wanted to attend my father's funeral to say goodbye. I put in a request to the warden but was denied. My father and I had begun mending our broken relationship. My sister told me that my father planned a surprise visit to see me and was going to bring my kids with him. The funeral went on without me. I was told there were many family and friends who attended, and many good things were said about my father. At the funeral, we learned that one of my father's coworkers, who was a Christian, had walked my father through the sinner's prayer while they were at work on a rooftop. My father accepted the Lord Jesus as his Savior before he died; hearing that gave me a sense of peace, knowing that I would see my father in Heaven someday.

My father's death didn't hit me until I received a letter from my mother; when I opened it I found four pictures of my father. I was in my cell, alone. I broke down in tears, crying as if I had been holding back the tears for many years. I couldn't believe that my father was gone. He looked at marriage as being just a piece of paper, which was his reason for not marrying my mother. She had always wanted to marry my father and finally got her wish.

My father was an organ donor, so his kidneys and his eyes went to two women in Los Angeles who were in need of transplants. A tree was planted in honor of my father at a park in Los Angeles. The words of my father would ring through my ears at times, "Life is in session. Are you present?" or "Be a leader, don't be a follower." My father was right and I began to take that to heart. My father and I had our ups and downs but one of the things I regret is not telling him that I loved him before he died.

UNICOR, PRISON INDUSTRIES

After being on the waiting list for over a year, I was hired at UNICOR. It was a job sought after by most inmates because it enabled them to earn money for themselves and their families. The feds had factories all over the United States. UNICOR at Phoenix was an electronics factory that made circuit boards, rocket-launcher cables for Apache helicopters, phones for military vehicles and other components. Starting pay was $35 a month but a person could work his way up to $200 or $300. The money was helpful, especially for inmates who didn't have anyone sending them funds. UNICOR also offered apprenticeship programs and provided scholarships toward college. My first job at UNICOR was janitorial. I would clean the bathroom toilets, strip and wax the clean rooms and the hallways.

Inmates had filed a lawsuit against UNICOR for hiring illegals to work in the prison factory. The inmates who filed won the lawsuit, so UNICOR was ordered to layoff all inmates who were being departed to other countries. The layoff of illegal immigrants opened up job opportunities for other inmates who were U.S. citizens; I was hired on as a warehouse clerk. That was where I met Juan "Gonzo" Gonzales, a tall, thin Puerto Rican who wore prescription glasses. Gonzo trained me for warehouse duties. My first impression of Gonzo was of a hot-tempered man. Gonzo had a chip on his shoulder and he took his anger out on other inmates.

When I got to know Gonzo, I learned that he was doing a 125-year sentence. After months of working with him, he began to open up to me. Gonzo had been in the military, stationed in Spain. He was on medical detail and was convicted of murdering a man who dated his female roommate; Gonzo was also having a relationship with her. The victim was found with a punctured heart. Presumably a screwdriver or a crossbow was used in the murder. A crossbow was found at Gonzo's apartment. Also, a pair of latex medical gloves was found at the scene of the crime. Gonzo was tried in a military court and, once he was convicted, he was transferred to the feds.

Gonzo made every effort to train me because he was scheduled to be transferred to a medical facility in Rochester, Minnesota, to have heart surgery in a month. After he left, I took it upon myself to do some housecleaning in the warehouse. I found weapons stashed in numerous places: iron bars, broomsticks, razor blades, metal poles with tape, plastic crafted into shanks. I had a feeling the weapons were being stored for other inmates in case a riot jumped off.

When Gonzo returned to Phoenix about four months later, he shared his experience at Rochester. While in surgery, doctors had Gonzo's chest cut open. As the surgeons were replacing an artery they had taken from one of Gonzo's legs, he flatlined. Doctors attempted to revive him but he was pronounced dead. Gonzo went on to tell me that he was in a body bag when he awoke. He said doctors didn't bother to stitch up his leg where the artery was removed; they just put a butterfly Band-Aid on it.

Gonzo returned to work at UNICOR but at times he seemed winded. I could tell his health was failing. Gonzo had a vacation brochure of Puerto Rico. He always talked about going there someday. At times we would sit in our work area and talk about life, family and the things we looked forward to once we were released. He often told me that he wished he had the 20-year sentence that I had, because at least he would see freedom. Talking to Gonzo helped me realized that I still had a chance to do it right. It wasn't the end of the road for me. Deep inside, I believe Gonzo knew that he would spend the rest of his life in prison but he still held onto hope. Just a little hope is all a man needs to keep him going.

During my time at FCI Phoenix, I ran into Bernard "Bubs" Renfro from San Pedro. The last time I had seen Bubs was on the streets. At the time, he had caught a fed case and was on house arrest, waiting for trial. I happened to drive by his grandmother's home in Wilmington when I saw him standing outside watering the front lawn. I stopped to talk to him. The last words he said to me were, "The feds don't play. Whatever you are doing, stop it." But I didn't listen. I knew I would get caught if I continued in the drug business -- I just didn't think I would get 235 months. When Bubs saw me on the yard he said, "I told you so."

KTE

I got word from an associate that Santi Rivelli, was telling people that I owed him money for the loss of the paintings that were seized by federal agents. When I learned what Santi was saying, I was angered. I got Alex Cardenas, a mutual friend, on his cell. Santi happened to be riding with him in his car. Al handed Santi the phone without telling him who it was on the other end. When Santi heard my voice he sounded surprised. I explained to Santi that I heard he was telling people I owed him money. I reminded him that I was the one sitting in prison doing a nearly 20-year sentence. I also reminded him that he could have easily been in prison with me. By the end of the conversation, Santi's attitude changed. He agreed that all debts were cleared and to never bring it up again.

BLOODBATH

I was warned that at any given day and time a riot could break out. I arrived back at Pima unit from the yard. When I entered the unit there was no one around. I was walking up a flight of stairs to the second tier when I noticed a trail of blood leading down a hallway toward my cell. It looked like the aftermath of a bloody fight. On the ground, in a pool of blood in front of my cell, was a Mexican inmate with long hair. He wasn't moving. At first I thought it was my cellmate, Jeff Lopez. As I stepped closer I saw that it wasn't. I looked into my cell but Jeff was not there. I did not want to stick around, because I knew the goons would be coming soon. I rushed past the unconscious inmate and headed down the stairs.

I saw a Latino inmate dash out of a cell. He grabbed the knocked-out inmate by the hair, attempting to drag him off the second tier. Another inmate intervened by grabbing the unconscious man by the foot to stop the knocked-out inmate from going over the side and falling to the first floor. The two men played tug-of-war with the unconscious inmate's body. I continued down the stairs and onto the first floor in search of Jeff. When I walked past the laundry room, I saw him washing clothes while his headphones bumped rap music. Jeff wasn't aware that a fight had broken out in the unit. Moments later officers rushed into the unit yelling, "Lock it down!" The entire unit was on lockdown and under investigation.

When lockdown is called, all inmates must stop what they are doing and immediately return to their cell. Once all inmates were locked in their cell, pairs of officers opened each cell door and conducted a body-search of all inmates. The officers checked for scratches, bruises or knife wounds. After I was searched, I watched from my cell window as inmates were taken out of their cell three at a time and escorted by officers to rooms used by staff members. Once inmates entered the rooms they remained there about five to 10 minutes before being escorted back to their cell. An officer unlocked my cell door and he instructed me to go to the room where the door was open. When I arrived, present was a white SIS officer with salt-and-pepper-colored hair sitting behind a desk. "Have a seat," he said. "Do you know anything about what happened?" "No, I don't," I responded. I knew better to say anything about the incident. The last thing I wanted was to be labeled a snitch. That could cost a person his life. The SIS officer asked, "If you knew anything would you report it?" "No," I replied. "Why is that?" "Because it's none of my business," I responded. The SIS officer took a long look at me, then went back to filling out paperwork. "OK, you can go," he said. A group of inmates were later shipped to other institutions while the inmates who stayed remained on lockdown for a few weeks.

Just about any type of drug was available if an inmate chose to pay for it. Commissary and stamps were the prison currency. I never fully realized how drugs destroyed people until I came to prison and lived with inmates who had used drugs most of their lives. Many suffered health problems at the cost of drug abuse. Some had hepatitis, rotting teeth, heart conditions, liver conditions, bad kidneys, scarred skin and then some. I was ignorant to the harm drugs hand on people. For me,

154

drug dealing was about survival. I thought that if I didn't sell drugs to those who wanted it, someone else would. Being in prison began to change my way of thinking. Some inmates made hooch, a combination of bread, oranges, water and sugar left in a plastic bag to ferment for days. Drinking hooch has been known to cause blindness and -- if not prepared right -- death. I've seen an inmate have part of his intestines cut out because the bacteria from hooch that ate at his stomach. When I came to prison, I decided to stay away from drugs. I had no desire for them.

I SMELL A RAT

I was told by other inmates to never talk about one's case to anyone and that's a good rule to live by. I met Jack Humphrey when we worked together in the veg-prep department at the prison kitchen. Jack also lived in Pima unit. The first day I met Jack he was talking about how he used to go to Las Vegas and visit this guy named Scott. I asked Jack what Scott's last name was. "Potter," he said. I told Jack that I also knew a Scott "Scotty Rock" Potter from Vegas. Jack then asked if I knew Scott's drug connection. He told me that the last time he saw the connection was at Scott's house, driving a black Slantnose Porsche 911. I did not tell Jack that it was me at Scott's house and that I was his connection. I remembered a white guy named Jack from Phoenix being at Scott's house. Jack said he often bought drugs from Scott.

Jack wanted to know about my business dealings in Las Vegas. Jack suspected that I was Scott's drug connection. He seemed stressed about the 15-year sentence he received. It was his second time in the federal system. His first stint was for bank robbery. Then he caught a fed case for moving large amounts of marijuana. Jack commented how he should have told on his drug connection in Arizona because the guy tried to pick up on his girl after he was sent to prison. Jack had a partner named Neal who was from Las Vegas. Neal and Jack occasionally asked if I wanted to have the guys who ratted on me "taken care of." Neal said that he could have it arranged. I sensed that Jack and Neal were attempting to set me up with a murder-for-hire scheme so they could turn me into the feds and get a lighter sentence.

I told Neal, "I don't wish harm on anyone." I then asked Jack, "Why don't you just tell on me?" Jack responded, "I tried to but the Feds said they already have you." Jack wore a grin on his face, as if he was joking but I knew he was deadly serious; Weeks later my intuitions were confirmed by another inmate. I was sitting in my cell reading when Fabien Tolentino knocked at my door. He told me that he recently came back from a visit with his attorney. When he arrived at the visiting room, a corrections officer stopped him and told him that he had to wait because the feds were talking to someone. After about 20 minutes, Jack Humphrey walked out of the visiting room. Fabien warned me to be careful with Jack. I thanked him for the heads-up.

I decided to pay a visit to Jack. I walked over to his cell, where he was eating a soup. I asked Jack how his visit went with the feds. He was speechless for a moment, then responded with, "What officer told you?" I said to Jack, "It's not important who told me. I better not find out that you are trying to set me up." Jack remained silent. "Do yourself a favor, Jack, and keep my name out of your mouth." Then I exited the cell. During the rest of my stay at Phoenix I would see Jack from time to time but I kept my distance from him.

APPEAL

I was notified by letter that on May 27, 1999, the Ninth Circuit Court of Appeals issued a "Memorandum" in which it affirmed my conviction. When I learned that my appeal was denied it was like the wind was knocked out of me again. I wanted to yell at the top of my lungs. I knew that I had to keep my mind occupied with things that were productive. I refused to let the system break me. Like most inmates, I was hoping that something would change in the laws that would benefit me. There were always rumors of bills that were before Congress. Some were rumors of the feds bringing back parole and others were rumors about the Bureau of Prisons giving out more good-behavior time.

To clear my mind, I would take walks around the yard while I listened to music over my headphones. As I did, I began to think that maybe I was paying for all the things that I thought I got away with. I thought that if I was charged with every wrong I'd done in the past, I would probably be in prison for the rest of my life. I may have gotten away with many things without the law knowing about it but I believed that I didn't get away with anything in the sight of God. As I walked the track I would look at the beautiful sunset. The scenery of the clear, blue Arizona sky could calm any savage beast. Every so often, the promise that I made to God years earlier when I got busted trying to jack cars for Dayton rims in South Gate kept coming back to me. I had promised God that if he got me out of that mess I would do well with my life. God came through for me and I broke my promise. I felt that I was paying for that.

I may have been blaming the government for setting me up to buy the cocaine but deep down inside I knew it wasn't a fight with the government, I was picking my fight against God and knew I would never win. It was clear to me that I had to give in and let God do what he wanted with my life. I soon realized that whatever God had planned for me was much better than any plan I could come up with myself.

PRIVATE INVESTIGATOR

After my appeal was denied I received a letter from a private investigator who claimed to work for Wayne Newton. He said he was hired to recover some paintings involved in my case. He wanted to travel to Arizona to visit with me to discuss recovering missing artwork and other valuables. This was the second time the investigator had attempted to contact me. At first I let him know that I couldn't help him.

Now that I was convicted I had nothing to lose. I wrote back, letting him know that I was willing to hear what he had to offer. I later received a third letter from the investigator, saying that he had set up an appointment through my counselor to visit me.

A few weeks later, I was called over the institutional intercom to report to the visiting room. When I entered, a dark-haired man in his mid-thirties with a medium built was waiting for me. Christian Filipiak introduced himself to me, then we seated ourselves. The P.I. asked me if I wanted anything from the vending machine. I requested an ice cream and a soda. We then sat down and began to discuss why he had come to visit me. He informed me that one of the paintings that was stolen from Newton ended up in New York at Sotheby's auction house. Someone from Mexico City was attempting to sell it. A woman employed at Sotheby's recognized the painting. She was suspicious of the low asking price the seller was requesting. She contacted authorities and police recovered the stolen artwork.

The investigator wanted to know if I could recover other missing items that were stolen from Newton's storage. I explained to Christian that it would be difficult for me to do that from prison. Christian showed me a binder full of photos taken of items that belonged to Newton. He said they were of sentimental value to the entertainer and his wife. I explained to the P.I. that if I was free then I might be of some assistance. Christian's nice-guy attitude changed into a demanding one. He said angrily, "The bottom line is, Mr. Newton wants to know how you got a hold of his property." I stood silent, grinning. Christian then asked, "Did the maid have anything to do with it?" I responded, "No, the maid had nothing to do with it. I'm going to be straight with you. I don't know who you are. For all I know, you are a fed. If Mr. Newton wants to know how I got his property, tell him he can ask me himself." Christian left the visiting room, clearly bothered.

KTE

I began to think about the life I had lived and the people that I had wronged, especially the women that I've hurt. I decided to write letters or call all the people that I could who I had wronged in the past, asking them for forgiveness. One of the calls was to an ex-girlfriend named Linda Menendez. When I contacted her, she told me that she wanted to visit me. I agreed to see Linda so, once the institution approved her for visitation, Linda booked a flight to Phoenix.

When Linda saw me, she stood to give me a big hug and a kiss, then took a seat. She told me that she was soon to be married and had a few unanswered questions. I told Linda to feel free and ask me anything; I would be totally honest with her. Linda wanted to know if I really cared about her when we dated or "Was I just another one of your playthings?" I cared about Linda but, during the time we dated, I was so caught up in myself that I didn't know what I had. I explained to Linda that when a man is a fool he does foolish things. I asked her for forgiveness. Linda assured me that I was forgiven and seemed satisfied with my answer. We talked for hours. When it was time for her to leave, I wished Linda the best in her marriage. It felt good to be honest to Linda and to restore a relationship that I had broken in the past. Linda must have been holding onto that question for nearly six years.

PACK YOUR BAGS

I made it a point to keep up with any changes in BOP policy, hoping there would be something from which I could benefit. A new ruling was in effect about the custody-level point system. The amount of drugs a person was charged with was no longer a public-safety factor, so my points dropped to low-level custody. I brought the change in policy to Case Manager Rodriguez's attention, letting him know that I was requesting a transfer to a low-level institution. He agreed to look into the matter but months went by and I hadn't heard back from him. I followed up on my request but Rodriguez kept putting me off. I decided to go to his supervisor, Mrs. Mitchell. I pled my case to her, explaining that I should be eligible for a transfer to a low-level prison under the new policy. After reviewing my file, she agreed that I was eligible to be transferred. Mrs. Mitchell informed me that she would e-mail Rodriguez to let him know that she approved of my transfer request.

After a few days, I decided to ask Rodriguez about my transfer. He told me with an attitude that he never received an email from Mrs. Mitchell. I decided to see her to let her know that my case manager didn't seem interested in putting me in for transfer. Mrs. Mitchell typed up a letter ordering Rodriguez to expedite my transfer and signed it. I took the letter to Rodriguez and, when he read it, he exploded into a rage, threatening to put me in for a transfer, but to Texas. He said that I knew what those Tejanos did to people from California. On some prison yards in Texas, Southsiders were considered enemies. It was a suicide mission to walk out on a rival

159

Tejano prison yard. I stared at Rodriguez for a moment, thinking that this guy was a real jerk. I then took the letter back and told him to forget about the transfer.

A few months later, Rodriguez was transferred to a different unit and replaced by a case manager who was new in the system. It was perfect timing, because most new case managers were willing to help to some extent. Most of the case managers who had been working in the system for years were desensitized to inmates' needs and I'm sure it was because some inmates pestered for more than they had coming. I put in my request to the new case manager and instantly my transfer was granted. A case manager is not supposed to inform an inmate where he is being shipped but inmates are asked to choose two or three prisons where they would like to transfer. The day I was told to pack my property, I made sure to get Juan "Gonzo" Gonzales' booking number. I told Gonzo that I would keep in contact with him. A few days later, I was called to R&D where I was processed, loaded onto a bus and on my way to a destination unknown.

CHAPTER 7 F.C.I. Safford

I arrived at FCI Safford, Arizona, in March 2001. When I walked into R&D, two SIS officers were waiting for me. They informed me that I was in their gang files. The officers warned me that they would not tolerate any trouble on their yard and that they would be keeping a close eye on me. I was then instructed to strip down to my boxers. One of the officers took a series of photos documenting my tattoos. I don't know where the officers got the idea, but causing trouble was far from my mind. I was just happy to be away from Black Canyon and at a low-level facility.

After processing was completed, an officer escorted us to Saguaro housing unit. The unit had one long tier and four shorter, connecting tiers. The longest tier was where the bathrooms, showers, eating tables and additional bunks were located. The other four shorter tiers were A, B, C and D. I arrived at C Range, which housed about 150 inmates. C Range was made up of dorm living with eight-to-10-man cubicles. Like other prisons, there was a chow hall, a UNICOR, a handball court, basketball court, baseball field, chapel, visiting room, education department and a recreation building that contained three walls with mounted TVs. There were also cabanas throughout the prison with mounted televisions. The prison had a band room and a bocce court, a horseshoe pit, a laundry room and a study hall, along with a law and leisure library.

As soon as I was settled in, I went to the education department to see what programs were available. Education offered courses through Eastern Arizona College. Teachers came into the prison to educate inmates. I signed up for classes in short-story writing and Introduction to Drama. A group of inmates who had a passion for acting would go out on the yard and practice dialogue and character development from our favorite scripts. A popular one amongst inmates happened to be *Scarface*.

I have always felt a tug on my heart to work in the movie industry, so I had to make a decision to either continue taking college classes to earn a degree in general studies that I might never use or to follow my dreams and continue to write my movie scripts. I decided to take only college classes that would improve my writing and had to do with moviemaking.

There was less tension at FCI Safford compared to FCI Phoenix, but there were still riots. Some of the rivalry carried over from other prisons onto the Safford yard. One of the riots broke out when a black inmate who arrived on the yard was assigned a bunk with Demon, a Southsider who was in his early twenties. Demon told the black inmate that he couldn't bunk with him and ordered him to find another place to sleep. The black man refused to bunk elsewhere so Demon gathered a few homies and gave the man a beating. Word got back to other blacks on the yard and, after the 8:45 p.m. count was cleared, the black inmates attacked the few Southsiders who were on the yard, catching them by surprise. The blacks and the Southsiders battled with homemade weapons made out of mop handles, trashcans, pieces of Plexiglas and whatever they could get their hands on.

A Southsider named Big Happy walked out of his unit, right into the middle of the riot and didn't have a clue to what was going on. Happy happened onto three blacks beating and kicking a Southsider named Benny, who was curled up on the concrete. Happy grabbed a mop stick from one of the other homies and began swinging it at the blacks, backing them away from Benny. Big Happy grabbed Benny by one of his arms, dragging him to safety. The Special Operations Response Team (SORT) rushed the yard in black paramilitary gear. SORT ordered all inmates to lie face-down on the ground. Some inmates complied and others rushed back to their unit before the officers could lock them outside. The blacks and the Latinos who were caught on the yard were contained and separated in gated areas on the prison compound. During riot sweeps there were always inmates caught who had nothing to do with the riot, casualties of war, and there were inmates who were part of the riot who got away.

SIS reviewed surveillance tapes to identify those who were involved in the riot. Big Happy was one of the persons caught on tape. Happy was finishing up his prison sentence and was months from going home to his wife and kids. Demon didn't follow protocol and let the rest of the Southsiders know about his plan to attack a black inmate, nor did he tell Southsiders in other units about it so they would be ready in case the blacks were to retaliate. Demon took matters into his own hands without getting approval from one of the shot-callers who ran the yard for the Southsiders.

Months later, I got word that Big Happy was offered a plea deal for five more years or the BOP would push to give him 10 years for inciting a riot if he went to trial. Big Happy wasn't too happy that Demon got him caught up in more time. Demon was disciplined by his own people for what he had done. When it came to warring with another race, the decision to riot was usually voted on. Demon violated rules because the bunk issue could have been resolved without an incident. When inmates from two different races don't want to bunk together, it's usually handled by their shot-caller. The shot-caller finds another bunk for his own people, especially a new arrival, end of story.

KTE

After being on the waiting list for six months, I was hired at UNICOR, working in the factory warehouse. Safford UNICOR was a textile plant that manufactured everything from leather gloves to sweatshirts and sweatpants, jacket liners, mail bags, and neck gaiters. Most of the items were produced for General Services Administration and sold to the military, and to other state and government agencies.

On September 11, 2001, it was about 6:30 a.m., Arizona time when I walked out of the chow hall and over to one of the cabanas to watch television. The news was reporting that a plane had crashed into one of the World Trade Center towers. After watching the news I headed to UNICOR, so I wouldn't be late for the 7 a.m. work call.

Inmates and guards listened to the news over the factory radio. It reported a second plane hitting World Trade Center tower two. The news was that it was a terrorist attack and rumors started spreading quickly within the prison yard. Inmates were worried about being executed under martial law. Others said that the government would or could execute all inmates if martial law went into effect, because inmates would be considered enemies of the state. Inmates that were suspected to have ties with terrorist groups were hauled off the yard and placed in SHU. After a few months, the yard was back to normal and, thank God, the talk of executing inmates under martial law was only gossip.

KTE

Antoinette and I hadn't spoken since I was at FCI Phoenix. She was scheduled to visit me in Phoenix but never showed. When I called home, Debrah told me that Antoinette sent her a Christmas card and asked how I was doing. Antoinette had gotten married to a man she met in Guam but divorced him after she caught him cheating. Antoinette would ask my sister about me every so often. I felt that Antoinette still had hopes for me coming home sooner. Deep down inside I had that same hope.

I called home and learned that a close friend of mine named Todd Davis had passed away. Todd was the kind of person who drank on a regular basis. He used drugs and was a married womanizer. Todd died at the age of 30; alcohol poisoning was the cause of death. After the funeral, I called a friend who attended the service. The friend told me that the funeral service was so sad. He said when the priest asked if anyone had any good words to say about Todd at the eulogy, not a single person got up to say a thing. I could imagine how his family must have felt -- especially his wife and children.

I began to think about how many people had died since I'd been away. I thought to myself that coming to prison may have saved my life. I was living the fast life, just like Todd. He and I were identical in many ways. I asked myself, "How do I want to be remembered when I die?" I did not want to be remembered as the Ray I used to be: the drug dealer, cheater, criminal, liar and thief. I didn't want to be remembered for my crimes or for my past. I wanted to be remembered as a good father, a good son, a giving person and a trusted friend. I wanted to be remembered as a good and godly man.

LETTER FROM JUAN CARLOS

I met Jose Castro when I arrived at Safford; we happened to share the same cubicle. When Jose and I began to talk I found out that he was from La Jolla and knew Juan Carlos. The two had been keeping in contact while in prison. Jose Castro told me that he was going to send a letter to Juan, who was doing time at Lompoc, to let him know that we are in Safford together.

A few weeks later, I received a letter from Juan and a copy of a motion that he filed with the court. In the letter, Juan asked if he could borrow money from me for an attorney who would be able to help both of us get out of prison before our release date. Juan Carlos never stopped trying. He got over on me once but it would never happen again. The motion Juan filed was for a hearing, stating that there was newly discovered evidence that could have changed the outcome of his trial. The so-called evidence was that I was the one who made the drug deal with the Colombians without Juan's knowledge. So Juan was now shifting the blame onto me.

In the motion it was also stated that there was a conspiracy to silence Juan Carlos by the U.S. government. Juan claimed that he had a letter that was sent to J. Edgar Hoover before Hoover died. It suggested that Juan needed to be silenced because he was causing trouble. He was part of the Brown Berets movement that took place in the 1970s. The Brown Berets served as the paramilitary arm of the Chicano Power movement in Barrio Logan, San Diego during the 1960s and 1970s. Juan said that the government had been targeting him since the Seventies. The first thing I thought when I read the letter was that Juan Carlos had finally lost what was left of his mind. I didn't bother to respond. I figured Juan Carlos would get the hint when I didn't write back.

A few months later, Jose told me that he was being transferred to FCI Lompoc, the same prison where Juan Carlos was being housed. The morning that he was scheduled to leave Safford, he asked me if there was anything I wanted him to tell Juan. I told Jose that I had nothing to say. I wished Jose good luck, we said our goodbyes and he went on his way.

Twice a year, inmates were scheduled for team meetings where they sat before a counselor, a case manager and other members of the prison departments to evaluate how they were progressing in education, financial goals, mental health and physical health. I informed my case manager, Mr. Keller that I was under my 10-year sentence and was eligible for camp. He looked through my file and agreed. Keller asked me to give him the names of two camps as part of my transfer request. Federal Prison Camp Nellis was my first choice and Camp Lompoc my second. Keller informed me that he would send a transfer request to the Western Regional office. It usually took a month or so before an inmate was transferred once a request was submitted and approved. UNICOR had a lot of work, so I continued to do overtime. I wanted to save as much money as possible before I was transferred.

I hadn't heard anything from Keller in over a month, so I decided to find out what the status was with my transfer request. When I approached my case manager, he told me that the BOP had recently lowered the length of time from 10 years or less to seven years or less when an inmate would be eligible to transfer to a minimum security. My heart nearly dropped out of my chest when I heard the news. That meant I had to wait another three years until I would be eligible for camp.

Disappointments were something that regularly came with being in prison. I decided to bury myself in overtime at work. I continued to put in as many hours as possible, even on my days off. I worked all month and was able to earn close to $475 each paycheck. When I got paid, I took turns sending money to my kids once a month. Ray Junior would get money one month, Alexis the next and Serina received money the following month. I tried to do as much as I could for my kids despite

166

being locked away. Months went by and I continued my routine of studying, writing movie scripts, and working UNICOR to keep my mind occupied and to further my education.

After a long day's work, I decided to call Serina, who was 10 years old at the time. When we spoke on the phone, she asked me when I was coming home. I didn't want to lie to my daughter nor did I want to get her hopes up and make her believe that I was coming home sooner. I wanted to be honest. I told Serina that I had about nine years left on my sentence. Immediately I could tell she was bothered. The tone of Serina's voice saddened. I attempted to cheer her up before the phone call ended, but my 15 minutes were gone. It was eating me up inside that Ray Jr, Alexis and Serina had to go through life without me. The choices I made not only affected me but my entire family, especially my children. The guilt was something I would have to live with.

The next day on my lunch break, I called Serina to see how she was doing. Leanna answered the phone. She wanted to know what I said to Serina when I called her the day before. Leanna told me that when she arrived home from work, Serina was in her room lying on her bed in tears. I explained to Leanna that Serina had asked me when I was coming home and I told her the truth. Leanna yelled at me, asking me why I would do such a thing. She went on to say that Serina was very upset. Leanna was right, it wasn't something I should have told a 10-year old. I just didn't want to lie to her. Leanna handed Serina the phone, so we could talk. I tried to cheer Serina up but I could tell that she was still hurt. As I walked back to work I began to pray, asking God to help comfort my brokenhearted daughter. I asked God to allow me to see Serina so I could hold her in my arms and let her know how much her daddy loved her.

Before I finished praying, a coworker named Lester Lewis yelled out across the yard for me. I stopped praying and I walked over to Lester, who had a big grin on his face. "You're going to camp!" he said. Lester said that he read an article in a Families Against Mandatory Minimums publication stating that the BOP reinstated the 10-years-or-less eligibility for camp. Lester asked the prison warden if it was true. The warden assured him that it wasn't a rumor. My heart jumped for joy at the news but I still had my doubts. I thanked Lester for the good news and headed to work.

After work, I rushed over to see my case manager. Keller also confirmed to me that the 10-years-or-less eligibility was reinstated. I then requested that he resubmit my transfer to camp. He asked if I was sure that I wanted to go to a camp. He said most inmates at camps had not been to a higher-level institution and were whiners, willing to tell on each other for any reason. Keller wanted to make sure I was OK around that type of environment. I explained to him that my goal was to be closer to my family and whatever other inmates did would not be an issue for me. Keller seemed to be satisfied with my attitude and he agreed to resubmit my paperwork for a camp transfer. I also requested a Private Owned Vehicle furlough transfer. A POV transfer was one where an inmate's family transported him from one low-custody-level prison to a minimum-custody-level camp on their own dime. Mr. Keller agreed to add the POV request.

At the end of the day, I laid on my bunk thinking about how God answered my prayer, making a way for me to see my family and especially my brokenhearted daughter.

FURLOUGH TRANSFER

When I was called into the unit secretary's office to go over my transfer itinerary I was told that a POV furlough to U.S.P. Atwater Camp had been granted. The secretary was a very nice Latina in her mid-thirties. She explained to me it was about 14 hours' drive to Atwater, California, including time to stop and eat. With a wink of the eye, the secretary said she gave me 15-and-a-half hours to get there, but if I knew of any other way to get their sooner, it was up to me. She finished with, "You didn't hear that from me." I knew exactly what the secretary was saying: I could take an airplane flight to get to Atwater quicker. That way it would give me extra time to do as I pleased.

After leaving her office, I made a phone call to my sister, instructing her to book two one-way tickets from Safford to Las Vegas, one for me and the other for Alex Cardenas. I was excited that I would be

168

walking out of prison a free man for 15 and a half hours. I couldn't believe the feds allowed inmates who had 10 years or less in their sentence to travel unsupervised, trusted that they would turn themselves in to the prison.

I arrived at R&D at 7 a.m. with all my prison possessions. An officer called my name about 30 minutes later. He packed my property into two boxes which were then sealed for shipping to U.S.P. Atwater Prison Camp.

In the lobby, Alex was waiting for me with a change of clothes. I then entered a bathroom where I changed into the new wardrobe. What a great feeling it was to get out of those khaki prison uniforms.

As Alex and I walked out the front door of FCI Safford and toward the rental car, I said, "Don't look back, and drive quickly but calmly out of the parking lot." Alex looked concerned; he then asked what was going on. As we entered the rental car, I tried to keep a straight face as I told him the guards were paid to let me go. Alex looked worried as he drove off in the car. I couldn't hold it in any longer; I finally cracked a grin and showed Alex my transfer itinerary. Alex seemed relieved after I explained to him what a POV furlough transfer was.

When we arrived at Tucson International Airport, we found a coffee shop and grabbed a bite to eat, since we had time to spare before our departing flight. The coffee shop had so many different cakes, cookies, fruits and bagels that it was hard for me to decide what I wanted. I settled with a croissant and coffee. Alex and I sat and people-watched. It felt great just being free for the day. My senses were so heightened that I could smell the shampoo on a woman who walked past me about 10 feet away.

After Alex and I ate, we headed toward the check-in line. People were already boarding. Before Alex left Vegas, I told him to bring my driver's license, which had expired; also the photo on the license looked nothing like me. In the photo, I had a full set of hair, weighed over 200 pounds and was sporting a thick Fu Manchu mustache.

My transfer took place after the 9/11 attacks on the World Trade Center and I thought for sure that I would be questioned about my expired license but nothing came of it. Just being on the plane was enjoyable. I took in my time of freedom. I wondered if it was really happening or was it one of the many dreams I'd had in prison about being free. When the plane took to the air I looked out the window, enjoying the Tucson scenery. About an hour later, the plane arrived over Las Vegas. It was another beautiful sight. I was so close to being home but yet still so many years away.

Alex took me for a ride down the Strip in his truck. Vegas was a sight for sore eyes; parts of it looked the same, others had new hotels and casinos. Before we arrived at Alex and Deb's house, I gave her a call on Alex's cell phone. Deb wanted me to let her know when we were pulling up in the driveway so she could give a reason for Ray Junior, Alexis, Serina, and my nephews Rob and George to come outside. My sister told the kids that Alex needed help outside with the groceries. None knew that I would be arriving.

Alex and I had stopped at a flower shop to get some roses for my daughters. As I stood at the front door of my sister's home, I hid my face behind the bouquets of flowers. I rang the doorbell, waiting excitedly. When Deb opened the door, all the kids were standing there. I removed the flowers from my face. My nephews and my kids looked surprised. Ray Junior yelled out, "My Dad's home!" After greeting friends and family, I sat my three kids down and explained that I was only visiting for a few hours. I told them that I was on a transfer through Las Vegas to another prison but was permitted to stop off at home to spend time with them. They seemed to understand.

My mother and my stepfather Ricardo Guerra, who I was meeting for the first time, were there as well. My mom and sister had prepared a traditional Mexican meal with *ceviche con carne asada* tacos. After everyone ate, my sister brought out birthday gifts and a birthday cake for all the years that I missed while I was in prison. It brought tears of joy to my eyes to see how much love my family and friends had for me. The tears were something that I needed to release. I had kept my feelings bottled up inside of me for so many years that it was a relief to cry. Serina stayed by my side, holding my arm during most of the time we shared together.

The quality time with my family was more than I expected: It was a true answered prayer. After spending about four hours with friends and family, it was time to head out. I had about eight hours left to get to Atwater, California. Deb, Alex, my three kids, and my two nephews loaded up a rented van and our road trip began. Before leaving Las Vegas, we stopped by my little brother Marcus's job at Game World. I wanted to see him even if it was for only 15 minutes. Marcus and I gave each other a hug; he then showed me around the store. After the quick visit, we all hopped back into the van and headed on to Atwater.

When we arrived in Merced, California, I had about an hour and a half to spare before I was to turn myself in to the prison. We decided to stop at Marie Callender's. I ordered a plate of salmon with shrimp and brown rice. I knew that it would be awhile before I had a chance to eat food from the streets again.

CHAPTER 8 U.S.P. Camp Atwater

As the van drove down a dark road leading to the penitentiary, I could see the prison's bright floodlights at a distance. When we arrived at the compound, there were three security vehicles that blocked the entrance. Our van stopped before three prison guards who wore black, bullet-resistant vests and carried firearms at their side. One instructed us to follow him onto the grounds, because the institution was on high alert. The perimeter truck led us to the entrance of the penitentiary. I knew I would be leaving my family in a matter of minutes, so I wanted to keep the mood a positive one for my kids. When the van pulled up at the penitentiary entrance, we all got out and took pictures together. I gave everyone hugs and we said our goodbyes. It seemed as if the kids were in a cheerful mood when I left, so I felt somewhat at ease.

When I checked in, waiting in another cell was Steve Banner, an inmate who left Safford the same day I did, also on a POV furlough transfer. Steve and I were escorted out a security gate where an officer walked us next door to the camp. When Steve and I arrived at the camp we were met by a Latina woman in her late forties who said she was the camp administrator and knew who we were. "I read your files. I don't want any trouble in my camp," she said. "I am the one who approved you to be here and I will be the one who sends you back if you mess up. Am I clear on that?" I nodded a yes and, like a light switch, her attitude changed into someone more hospitable. She showed Steve and me around the camp as she conducted an inspection of the unit. She looked under bunks and on top of lockers, inspected beds and checked floors.

We were able to settle in quickly but we still had to wait for our property to arrive through the mail and, once it arrived, it usually sat in R&D for another few weeks. The night I arrived, some of the

Southsiders were cooking, so they offered me a bowl of coconut shrimp. I didn't ask where the shrimp came from but I was sure the institution didn't sell it in commissary. The coconut shrimp was even better than the meal I had at Marie Callender's. At Atwater, there were many ways one could get the same luxuries that were offered in the free world.

WORK DETAIL

When an inmate arrives at an institution, he has a certain number of days to find a job or a counselor will find one for him. I hadn't heard back from commissary or UNICOR about jobs that I applied for, so I was placed in the landscape department. The duties included cutting grass and weeds, cleaning the gun range, watering plants, cleaning the parking lot and training center, as well as other odd jobs. Inmates were provided vehicles called Gators. The Gators were four-wheelers and green, with two seats plus a small bed in the back for hauling tools and materials. The first time I was approved to drive a Gator, I felt like a kid at an amusement park; I drove it all around the compound with no supervision. The simple things in life that I had taken for granted were now pleasures.

It didn't take long for me to get into UNICOR, since I had prior experience. My first position was tearing down. The tear-down area contained tables where inmates disassembled computers and separated components by motherboard, hard drive, memory sticks, fans, and so on. Anthony Borages was one of the supervisors at UNICOR. He had no problem badmouthing inmates. When I started working at UNICOR, I told myself that I better stay away from this walking time bomb. Sure enough, I was unloading a truck of computers along with other inmates when Borages came out of his office screaming, "Get the heck out of that truck, you rats!"

I was one of the inmates to whom Borages had directed his comment. When I heard those words my blood began to boil. I walked out of the truck and headed to the housing unit, where I went into my locker to grab my Judgment & Commitment Order, which detailed the crime I was convicted for and the sentence I received. It also states if an inmates received a reduction for ratting. I walked back to UNICOR, directly into Borage's office, where I slapped my paperwork onto the desk where he was sitting. I told him, "There's my paperwork, read it." Borages picked up the document and glanced through it. I knew that the administration had Borages at the camp UNICOR for a reason. Borages knew very well that he wouldn't be talking the way he did to inmates if he was behind the fence. "Before you call someone a rat, know what you are saying," I told him.

From that day forward, I never had an issue with Borages. In fact, he promoted me to laptop refurbishing. I was unofficially allowed to build my own laptop and write my movie scripts when there was not much work in the factory. An inmate having his own personal laptop was against UNICOR regulations but Borages would turn a blind eye when he saw me doing my work.

RATS

When Julio Franco walked onto the yard it was as clear as day that he was scared and that he had never been schooled on prison etiquette. After being on the yard for a few months, he began to get comfortable and cocky. He would openly tell people in the camp that he had ratted out his cousin. Why he would do that I had no idea. I made every effort to avoid Julio.

While I was reading a book on my bunk Julio walked over to me and he asked if we could talk. I was hesitant but agreed. Julio told me that people on the yard were calling him a rat. He went on to ask if I thought it was wrong to tell on someone. "It depends," I replied. "Doesn't God want people to tell the truth," Julio asked. I looked into Julio's eyes then told him, "Yes, God wants man to be truthful but I don't believe God wants a man to tell on someone because that man wants to get out of the legal mess he got himself into; that would be ratting." "Telling the truth or ratting, what's the difference," Julio asked.

I explained to Julio that most people who use the word rat really don't understand what it means. When I hear an inmate say that the

174

correctional officer "is a rat" or when a mother tells her son to "stop ratting" on his little brother, it makes me wonder how they associate speaking the truth about an event or situation with ratting.

Plain and simple, a rat is someone who puts another man in prison because he doesn't want to do the time for his own crime. Julio walked away after our talk but hopefully he understood why people were calling him a rat. A few weeks later, Julio got into a confrontation with another inmate and was beaten with a lock in a sock. He was then removed from the yard and transferred to an unknown location.

On September 26, 2003, I called home to learn from Debrah that my mother had a heart attack. My sister told me that she received a "missed call" from my mother, and when Debrah called her back my mother was complaining of chest pains and was having trouble breathing. My mother told Debrah that she just wanted to lie down and rest because she was feeling tired. Debrah made my mother stay on the phone with her to keep her talking. She then asked my mom where she was. My mother didn't know. Debrah remembered that mom said earlier in the day that she was going to clean the home of Dr. Tourney. She told my mom that she would call her back after she phoned for help.

After Debrah hung up the phone, she called Dr. Tourney's son Rob to tell him that mom was having medical issues but she did not know the address to my mother's location. Rob immediately called 911. The ambulance arrived and my mother was rushed to a hospital. The doctors told my family that it was a miracle that my mother survived a heart attack so major. She had to undergo an angioplasty to clear out the clogged arteries.

Immediately I put in a request to be transferred to Camp Nellis in Las Vegas so I could be closer to my mother. A month or so later, my case manager informed me that my transfer request was denied by the Regional Director's Office, which oversees designations for inmates being housed and transferred to institutions in the Western Region. I then wrote letters to Senators Barbara Boxer and Dianne Feinstein, explaining my mother's situation and requesting a transfer to FCP

Nellis under hardship grounds. The senators' office wrote back informing me that they had contacted the Regional Director's Office, which told them that transfers were not granted under hardships. I prayed about my mother's situation and about my transfer request, then left it in God's hands.

I continued with my programing, attempting to keep my mind occupied. I was now volunteering my time as a panel speaker for a youth impact program called VISION, or Values Integrity & Self-Respect in Our Neighborhoods. Officer Jesse Valero was program coordinator for VISION. It was made up of corrections officers, wardens, camp administrators, SIS officers and inmates who shared life stories with the youth in hopes of steering them down the right path in life. At times, Warden Paul Schultz would show up to give his support. Warden Schultz was present during one of the meetings and when he heard inmates share their stories, he called us all together at the end of the meeting and thanked us. He informed the inmates that the VISION program was one of his pet projects and went on to say that he was glad that we were participating in changing the lives of our youth. The warden also told us that if there was anything he could do for us within reason, to let him know.

When the warden made the offer, an idea crossed my mind. As soon as he finished with his pep talk, I approached him requesting a transfer to Camp Nellis. I mentioned my mother's heart condition. Schultz asked me how long I had been incarcerated. I told him that I had been in for eight and a half years. The warden wrote down my name and booking number. He then said he would see what he could do. Less than a month later, my case manager called me into her office. She was familiar with my previous camp transfer requests being denied. She told me that she didn't know what strings I pulled but my transfer to Nellis was now approved. The news brought joy to my soul. I told her there were no stings pulled: It was definitely an answered prayer. When I left my case manager's office I stopped for a moment to thank God for always coming through for me. I've learned that God does not always work on my time but He is always on time.

I was granted another POV transfer and given eight hours to get to Las Vegas by car. Victor Mercado and Alex Cardenas were waiting for me when I walked out the front gate of Atwater Prison Camp. We drove to Merced Municipal Airport, where we boarded a small plane heading to North Las Vegas Airport.

CHAPTER 9 F.P.C. Nellis AFB

From the North Las Vegas Airport, Alex drove us to his and my sister's home. I spent a few hours with Ray Junior, Alexis, and Serina, along with my two nephews, Rob and George, and Marcus. Then it was time to turn myself back into the BOP. Debrah drove me to Nellis Air Force Base. After I checked in with an airman, a corrections officer driving a perimeter truck arrived about 15 minutes later. The officer's last name happened to be Torres. As Officer Torres drove me to the camp, he asked me what I was in prison for. I told him for trading stolen artwork belonging to Wayne Newton for 50 kilos of cocaine. Torres told me that Newton performed for the airmen at the base from time to time. I thought to myself, "What a small world."

I noticed that there were no gun towers and nothing to keep inmates confined to a closed area within the camp. But there were fences surrounding the Air Force base and there were military police patrolling the grounds along with corrections officers in perimeter trucks. One of the things that really surprised me was seeing airmen carrying M16-rifles over their shoulder while walking directly past inmates.

CLUB FED

At Nellis Federal Prison Camp there were judges, former cops, Border Patrol agents and people from all social statuses. Some of the guests who stayed at Club Fed were Harry Shuster, a Beverly Hills entrepreneur whose ventures included animal safaris and cigar clubs. He had been convicted of securities fraud and other charges. Gregory Hutchinson, *aka* Cold 187um, had made his name as one third of the Los Angeles rap group Above the Law. He was serving 105 weeks on charges of conspiracy to traffic 1,000 pounds of marijuana. Peter

Bacanovic, the Merrill Lynch broker who spent five months in prison as part of the Martha Stewart insider-trading scandal was also a resident of Nellis, just to name a few.

The camp was also called Cub Fed because it was known for luxuries such as an indoor gym with basketball court, numerous workout stations and a movie theater. The inmate work details also had many perks. Duties included, janitorial services such as cleaning floors, cleaning restrooms and emptying trash from office buildings around the base.

When I settled in at Nellis, I applied for a job in the warehouse and in the commissary. Those departments were not hiring, so I was placed on the Nellis AFB work program. I was assigned to the 99 Supply building. Working on the base was like being in the free world. Airwomen roamed freely and most people on the base were respectful.

After working on the detail for a few months, airmen and civilians seemed to take a liking to me. On every Thursday, one of the airmen sold chips, hotdogs and sodas for some type of fundraiser, and on every Thursday a plate of hot dogs, chips, and a soda were left for me on my desk in my work area. During Christmas, I was offered food from some of the officers who attended parties at the offices and you better believe I took it. One of the women who worked in an office that I cleaned would ask me to take out her trash and, with a wink of the eye, would inform me that she brought me something. I would look in the trash can and there would be a bag of burgers and fries from a local fast-food restaurant.

Other times when staff needed inmates at the officers' club I would volunteer for the detail. After our duties were complete, we were offered whatever was on the menu: chicken, shrimp gumbo, salads and pies; it was like no other prison that I had been to and I enjoyed the perks.

JOB BENEFITS

There was so much contraband coming into the camp that the goon squad raided it every other week. When drugs were found on an inmate or when one was caught wearing shoes that weren't sold in commissary that's when officers conducted shakedowns of the camp.

The biggest shakedown happened when one of the inmates who worked maintenance got busted with drugs by an officer. This inmate was the one who built secret compartments in the units for other inmates to store their contraband. He decided to tell the officers where all the stash spots were in the units. Every inmate was evacuated from their housing area. We stood on the yard watching as officers cleared out contraband and property from the units by the cartful. The good thing for me was I was in charge of laundry in the warehouse, so when all the bins of contraband came to me I was the one who sorted everything. It was clear that officers snatched any property belonging to inmates and tossed them into the laundry carts for whatever reason.

When I was sorting through the property, I found watches, $200 sneakers, street clothes, gold chains, radios, money, cigarettes, chewing tobacco and just about anything an inmate could smuggle into the camp. I put the goods aside for inmates who did not go to the SHU, with the intention of return their property to them. I kept the items in the warehouse until I confirmed that inmates were not returning to the yard. The inmates being shipped out would not be able to receive any property confiscated by officers, because the property was considered contraband. I gave some of the items taken from inmates to others who were less fortunate and had my guy Shorty sell the rest of the goods at a markdown price, giving him 40 percent while keeping 60 percent of all sales.

KTE

While I was at a visit with friend Drake Perez, a second group of visitors showed up: Camille, Ray Junior and Alexis. We all sat around a table while Drake told stores of the past. Drake was talking to my son about life and the consequences of bad choices. Drake jokingly

180

told Ray Junior that his brother Jordan Perez called me "The Hugh Hefner of the Crazy Horse Too." He bragged that I had women, money and fancy cars. I just couldn't believe that he was saying this in front of my ex-wife. Drake told Ray Junior that "People flocked around your father mostly because of what he had to offer them. Very few people stick by a man's side when he is down. When your Dad went to prison, there was another Ray standing in line to take his place."

The words Drake spoke were literally true. I met the other Ray, who happened to be doing time at Camp Nellis at the same time I was. Ray Santos, of Filipino descent, was also into illegal business. Santos and I happened to be talking with each other when he told me that he used to hang out at The Crazy Horse Too in 1995. He told me that some of the girls who worked at the Horse would ask if he was the Ray that used to date Antoinette Woods, the *Hustler* Magazine centerfold model. When I met Ray Santos, it really made me think about what Drake had said to Ray Junior. It is true that most people may love you when you are on top of the world but when you fall they forget about you and move on to the next man standing at the top.

KTE

During one of my visits from Alex Cardenas, I was told that on December 10, 2004, the California Supreme Court upheld Jesse Morrison's death sentence for the murder of Alex's brother Cesar. Jesse was now awaiting his execution and the day he would stand before God to answer for his past sins. Michael Berry was serving a life sentence, and Nathan and Shawn had been freed. I still wanted revenge but one thing I had learned through life's lessons was that God's revenge was sweeter than any I could come up with and who was I to interfere with God?

There were rumors going around that Camp Nellis was closing; then the official notice came. Inmates were being transferred to institutions all over the U.S. The prison camp had opened in 1989 to provide laborers for the Air Force base, but after 9/11 security at Nellis was beefed up considerably. The government did not want federal prisoners and their visitors in such a sensitive area, so the prison was scheduled to close.

My case manager asked me to choose three prisons where I would like to be transferred. The camp life was good but I still wanted to stay as close as possible to Las Vegas. My case manager asked me if I was interested in transferring to Terminal Island; she said she would recommend that I be placed in the Coast Guard Program. It was similar to the work-furlough program at Nellis; inmates did what the Coast Guard instructed them to do, for minimal pay. I submitted my three choices: Camp Lompoc, California; Camp Sheridan, Oregon; and FCI Terminal Island, California. Seven months after I arrived at Nellis, I was transferred. On the early morning of July 6, 2004, inmates were loaded into two vans, destination unknown. After traveling some distance down the I-15 freeway toward Los Angeles, I had a good idea where we were headed.

CHAPTER 10 F.C.I. Terminal Island

This medium/high-security federal prison for men was located on the Los Angeles Harbor near San Pedro and Long Beach. FCI Terminal Island consists of three cell blocks built around a central quadrangle. The concrete island also has gun towers, concrete buildings and palm trees. The average daily population is approximately 1,100 inmates. Terminal Island was home to some of the most infamous inmates including Rosario Gambino, a New York crime boss serving 45 years for his part in the "Pizza Connection," heroin ring. Al Capone was a prisoner at FCI Terminal Island from 1939 to 1940.

In July 2005, I arrived at Terminal Island in a two-vehicle caravan filled with unshackled inmates. When the vans pulled up to the prison, two perimeter trucks rolled out to meet us. Ms. Salazar, a female guard who looked like an ex-*chola* [Latina gangster] walked out of the prison to meet the camp officers. When she saw that the arriving inmates were not secured in handcuffs and leg irons, she started snapping at the camp officers. She demanded to know why we were not shackled. One of the camp officers who brought us explained that we were coming from Camp Nellis. All the inmates were then escorted into the prison and placed in holding cells at the R&D department.

As usual, we were strip-searched and processed into the prison. Ms. Salazar kept staring at me as if she knew me from somewhere. Then she asked me where I was from. When I told her that I was from Wilmington, her face lit up with a smile and she replied, "So you're from the HA?" I answered back, "From where?" "The HA!" she repeated. "The Harbor Area." She then handed me a clipboard and instructed me to fill out the paperwork.

We received a bed roll and were escorted onto the yard. Moments later, I heard someone call out my name. It was Victor Hernandez, who I did time with when I was at MDC Los Angeles in 1995. Arriving at TI was like being at a high school reunion, but instead of classmates they were men I'd done time with at other prisons. Whites, blacks, Mexicans, Southsiders, Asians ... I knew someone from just about every race. I was housed in K Unit when I arrived. K Unit was where the new arrivals were placed until they were assigned a permanent bunk.

SIS Officer Guerrero stood by, searching inmates as they exited the chow hall. When I walked out, Guerrero asked if I was a new arrival. I told him that I was and Guerrero then asked me to stop by the SIS office. Anyone who was from the Harbor Area was forbidden to go to the SIS office without bringing a Southsider with them to verify that they were there for legitimate reasons. It did not look good for an inmate to be at the SIS office alone; inmates had no reason to be there unless they were ordered by an SIS officer.

When I arrived at the SIS office, Officer Guerrero asked Angel Garcia, the homie who went along with me, to wait outside. Guerrero didn't waste any time asking me about my gang affiliation. I was asked to write on a piece of paper any tattoos that I had. I was ordered to strip down to my boxers while photos were snapped of all my tattoos. I was then instructed to sign a statement confirming that I was from the West Side Wilmas gang. I refused to sign anything saying that I was a gang member or even that I was affiliated with any gangs. I wasn't going to give SIS evidence to use against me if there was an issue in the future.

Every SIS officer must have had an all-points bulletin out on me. SIS Officer Steve Marroquin spotted me walking toward him as he stood talking in front of my assigned housing unit with SIS Officer Bronco, who reminded me of a Mexican Lurch from the *Addams Family*. I noticed that both officers turned to look at me, so I stopped to talk to an inmate who I knew. Marroquin called out, "Hey you!" I ignored him. The officer called out a few more times, but I continued to ignore him. Bronco then yelled, "Hey, Poindexter!" I knew he was calling me because I was the only one wearing glasses. My back was to Bronco, so I continued to ignore him. The inmate I was talking to must have gotten spooked, because the next thing he told me was that he had to go.

I had to walk past the two officers to get to my unit. As I approached Officer Bronco, he asked, "Didn't you hear me calling you?" I replied by telling him, "No, I didn't hear you calling me. I heard you calling someone by the name, 'Hey You,' but I didn't hear you calling me." Bronco stared at me, annoyed. Then Officer Marroquin asked me who I ran with on the yard. I told Marroquin that I came to prison alone and I walked the yard alone. Marroquin replied, "I know who you run with. You run with the Harbor Area." "Then why would you ask me who I run with if you say you already know," I asked. Bronco and Marroquin both looked lost for words.

FOOD SERVICE

My first job was in the kitchen, where most new arrivals were assigned. My duties were to mop the floors, scrub the walls and do trash runs. Base pay was $5 a month and as high as $175 a month. When I arrived at TI, I immediately requested to be placed on the UNICOR waiting list. Being at TI was like being in a small community; most inmates wanted the highest-paying jobs. I went to UNICOR's factory with my resume and was given an interview with the quality-assurance manager right on the spot. The manager, Pete Marin, liked that I had experience in UNICOR and with the SAP software used by the factory. After my interview, Pete told me he wanted me to work for him. So now I had to wait for approval by my case manager, the warden, my counselor and by the factory manager. It took me about four months to get hired.

I was later moved to D Unit on the north yard. D Unit was dorm living with top and bottom bunks; my bunkie was Petey Zacharias, who happened to be from Wilmington. Petey was a big Mexican who could be mistaken for a Samoan. We knew many of the same people from the neighborhood, so we connected with each other from the start. After I was hired at UNICOR, I signed up for the Quality Control apprenticeship program. I figured if I had to work, I might as well get

185

an education and learn a trade that could be used once I was released from prison.

I was later moved from D Unit on the north yard to G Unit on the south yard. The south yard was made up of palm trees, green lawn, an ocean view, a softball field, a football field and basketball courts. The south yard was for inmates who were programming. Inmates on the south yard had easy access to the weight pile, the law and leisure libraries, and the education department. Some of the guards would call G Unit "the baller's unit," because most inmates who lived there were working UNICOR, a high-paying prison job and other non-UNICOR inmates who were housed at G Unit seemed to be well off financially.

During times that I would walk the track on the south yard, I would see a tour boat called the *Fiesta* cruise near Terminal Island with a guide naming a list of infamous prisoners who were once housed at TI. If a man had to do time at TI, the south yard is where he wanted to be.

FATHER'S DAY

It was Father's Day and usually someone from my family came to visit me. The day was getting late and no one had shown. I was sure that I wasn't getting a visit. The latest a visitor could check in at visiting was 2 p.m. and it was already 1:30. I decided to lie on my bunk to take a nap so I could clear my mind. My bunkie at the time was Fernando "Speedy" Garcia from San Diego. We often talked about our families and our kids. It must have been obvious that I had the blues because Speedy looked down from the top bunk and told me, "Don't worry, they will show." I decided to close my eyes and mumbled in a sarcastic tone, "Wake me when they show." It seemed as if I was sleeping for about 30 minutes when the unit officer knocked at my cell door to tell me that I had a visit. Speedy grinned and said, "I told you they would be here."

I hurried to get dressed, then raced over to my visit. I had to go through the usual body pat-down before being allowed into the visiting room. When I entered the room I immediately saw Ray Junior, Alexis and Serina waiting for me at a visiting table. We all hugged each other.

Then I asked where Debrah was. I figured that Debrah had brought them from Vegas and must have picked up Serina from Victorville on the way. Alexis told me that she and Ray Junior took a bus from Las Vegas and arranged to meet Serina on the way to Los Angeles. When they arrived in L.A., her uncle Romy Guimary picked them up at the bus station and brought them to Wilmington, then her other uncle, Robert Guimary, brought them to TI. I was moved that they went through all that to come and see me. It was definitely the best Father's Day that I had while behind bars.

DRAMA TEAM

I was called into Chaplain Richards' office and I was asked if I would be interested in starting a drama team for the prison. The chaplain told me that he heard I put on plays when I was at Safford FCI. He went on to say that he wanted to uplift the morale of inmates during their stay at Terminal Island, especially during the holiday seasons. Chaplain Richards even gave Terminal Island a new name. He wanted men to have hope that came to the island, so he called it "Hope Island." At first I was hesitant about taking on more tasks. I was already working UNICOR, taking classes through Harbor College, writing my movie scripts and was a volunteer speaker in a youth-impact program called Positive Choices. I had no time to start a drama team but I told the chaplain to give me some time to think it over. On Sundays, I would attend church services and every Sunday the chaplain would be there, staring at me as if waiting for me to commit. Maybe he was right. Maybe God wanted to use me to reach out to a lost or hurting soul and I was putting my own selfish desires first.

I went to Chaplain Richards' office to let him know that I was on board. The chaplain was thrilled. Besides, I figured that by directing a drama team it would polish my skills for my own future movie projects.

Once I committed myself, I put my all into the drama team. Chaplain Richards wanted plays done every few months and especially for Christmas. I had the chaplain search for plays online. My first was

"The God Who Fights for You," taken from the Bible story in Exodus 17:11.

I took a break from working on my personal projects and I began putting together a Christmas play. I was looking through my files and found a poem titled "Footprints" that Debrah had sent me when I was at one of the darkest points of my prison sentence.

I wanted to put a play together that inmates could relate to so I wrote one that was inspired by the poem "Footprints" and the book *Twice Pardoned* by Harold Morris. I titled it, "Pardoned." It was a story about a man who was to be executed for a murder he did not do. He was angry at God for the death of his brother and would not accept God's grace. God had visited the condemned man in a dream; it was then that the inmate asked God a number of questions and God had an answer for each one. When the condemned man awoke only days from being executed, he received three visitors. God used the three visitors to speak words of wisdom to the condemned man and they peeled off layers of the inmate's hardened heart. The condemned man's attorney arrived at the last hour with an order to halt the execution. The real murderer had confessed to the killing and the wrongly accused inmate received a pardon from the governor. The former death-row inmate knew that God had answered his prayer. At the end, the newly freed man surrendered his life to God.

Many inmates got involved: building the sets and, making costumes and making music to enhance the play. Quite a few South Side homies took part in the production also. The fellas were not the only ones who helped. So did other races, as did staff members. The great thing was that many of the volunteers didn't usually attend church but they offered to help anyway. When the production was nearly complete, Chaplain Richards announced that he was being transferred to MDC L.A. He was not able to see the play, for his last day at TI was a few weeks before the drama team was to perform but we continued with Father Kirkness supervising the production.

When casting the lead role, I knew that I needed someone who could play a man who was filled with rage. Just the man caught my attention

-- Kevin Walker. Kevin and I had worked together during the production of previous plays that I directed. He was in charge of the music ministry at Terminal Island. Kevin was a cheerful person who got along with everyone but, getting to know Kevin better, I learned that he had caught Valley Fever while doing time at Taft Correctional Institution, a federal prison in Western Kern County, California. Kevin nearly died from the disease. Valley Fever is a fungal disease that is endemic in certain parts of the Southwest and Mexico. Infected individuals experience fever, chest pain, coughing and other symptoms.

Once Kevin Walker was diagnosed with Valley Fever, doctors put him on an antifungal drug but it caused his kidneys and liver to begin failing. He was switched to another antifungal drug but the disease continued to spread throughout his body, even into his bone marrow; boils, then holes, developed on his spinal column and clavicle. The disease damaged Kevin's bones to the point where he required a walker to help him get around.

Hearing Kevin's story, I knew he had been through pain and frustration. It didn't take much to persuade him to play the lead role but I had to work on bringing Kevin out of his shell. During one of the rehearsals, I could tell that Kevin was holding back. I stopped him and said, "All the pain and frustration that you have inside, the pain that Kevin Walker carries, that is what I want you to pour into this character; release your demons during your performance." Kevin took heed to my words and every time we rehearsed his role he was so convincing that he brought tears to my eyes. The pain in his voice, his body movements and the tears in his eyes proved that Kevin was made for the lead role. Kevin was passionate about the role he was playing. Word got out on the prison yard about the Christmas play and a large number of inmates wanted to see the production. The night of the play the chapel was packed with every race of inmates, South Siders, Islanders, blacks, whites, believers and nonbelievers. At the end, the play was a success. Kevin did such a great performance that there were very few dry eyes in the building, mine included.

GONZO

I promised Juan "Gonzo" Gonzalez that I would keep in touch with him after I left FCI Phoenix. I wrote letters to him when I arrived at Safford and other prisons that I had transferred to; a man only has his word in life and if a man's word is no good then he has nothing. Gonzo had written back and our correspondence continued from time to time. When I arrived at Terminal Island, I sent Gonzo a letter, but months had passed and I still had not heard from Gonzo. I sent another letter and still nothing. I later got word that Gonzo passed way. I was not sad for Gonzo. I was happy that he was no longer locked in that cage.

KTE

Years had passed since I had heard anything about the members of Mi Gente, until I ran into a person I will call Weasel. We knew some of the same people from the Mi Gente organization. Weasel told me that Martin "Shadow" Pasqual got life in prison for robbing drug dealers and for murder. Carlitos Bustamante nearly overdosed on drugs; he later became a Christian. Henry "Pops" Ortega was said to have cut ties with Mi Gente and become a drug counselor. Eddie "Sleepy" Parrilla had done something that was in violation of Mi Gente rules and was stabbed while in prison. The Messenger who visited me in Las Vegas from time to time received 25 years to life in California for robberies. I guess God was not only working in my life but in the lives of those men who I clashed with back in the day. I had to stop to take a look at myself and, when I did, I concluded that I was no better than the members of Mi Gente who I was fighting. God showed me that he has mercy on whomever He chooses and who am I to argue with that?

KTE

Terminal Island was being converted into a level-three medical facility. At these facilities, inmates are considered fragile outpatients with conditions that require frequent clinical contacts. The inmates arriving at TI had a variety of problems, including diabetes, HIV, mental illness, psychotic disorders and/or cognitive impairment. Many of the inmates were highly medicated and some walked the yard looking like zombies. The Angel of Death seemed to have followed when the medical inmates arrived at TI, because inmates were dying more frequently. It made me realize that I did not want to die an old man in prison. There were many men on the yard who had abused drugs, and who had contracted hepatitis and AIDS. It wasn't unusual to see an inmate who had liver damage from drug abuse defecate his pants or in his bed while sleeping. Seeing inmates in such conditions was a harsh reality of what drug abuse does to those who use it. It made me think about the drugs that I may have sold to someone on the streets and how I was part of the problem.

ANTOINETTE'S FATE

Every so often I would call Joe Murrin, a friend who lived in Las Vegas. When I spoke with Joe on the phone he told me that Jason Arsenic was there with him. Jason was a mutual friend of Joe's and mine. Joe handed Jason the phone so we could talk.

It had been years since I had spoken to Jason. We shared small talk. Then he asked me if I heard about Antoinette Woods. He said, "She is gone." I thought Jason was saying that Antoinette had moved out of Las Vegas and responded, "Yeah, she moved to Guam." Jason said, "No Ray, she's gone. She committed suicide." My heart nearly dropped out of my chest when I heard those words. I began to feel sick to my stomach.

As I lay on my bunk, I thought about the things that Antoinette and I had gone through, the way I had treated her. I wondered if I had anything to do with her wanting to take her own life. I didn't want to believe that Antoinette had committed suicide. I had so many unanswered questions. Why would someone want to end their life? I called Debrah and told her what I had heard about Antoinette. I asked her to call some of her old friends and ask if it was true. A few days later, I called Debrah again and she confirmed that Antoinette had died of an overdose of pills. I was heartbroken but, being in prison, I couldn't cry to release the pain. Crying was a sign of weakness and nobody wanted to be seen as weak, especially in prison. I had to hold it all in. The guilt of how I treated Antoinette in the past was heavy on my heart.

Art Castro was an inmate who had battled addiction in the past and was doing time at Terminal Island on drug charges. It seemed that he had turned his life around. He frequently worked out and participated in the Bureau of Prisons' 500-hour Residential Drug Abuse Treatment Program, which gave him the possibility of reducing his prison time by up to 18 months. After completing R-DAP, for reasons unknown, Art was told that he did not qualify for any time off his sentence. Art's family hired an attorney to fight for the 18-month reduction for completing R-DAP. After months of battling with the court, Art prevailed. He was scheduled to be released within a few months of receiving the news.

I had borrowed the latest *Muscle & Fitness* magazine from Art earlier that day. Before I finished reading the magazine, I saw Art walk past my cell as if he was in a hurry. I paid no attention. When I was finished reading the magazine, I walked over to Art's cell and I noticed a white inmate standing at his cell door. The guy looked nervous; he kept glancing down the hall as if he was a look out for whatever was going on inside the cell. As I looked into the cell, I could see that Art was sitting on a chair and another white inmate was standing over him. He looked to be slapping Art in the face while yelling, "Get up!" I could only see the bottom half of Art's body because, from where I stood, the bunk bed was blocking my view.

At first I thought, "What kind of game are these Woods playing?" When I bent down to look at Art I noticed that his face was purple from lack of oxygen; right away I knew something was wrong. I yelled at the inmate standing at the door to call the corrections officer for help. He hesitated. "Go get help! He's dying," I yelled. The inmate ran down the hall and he returned a short time later with inmate Chris Davis. Chris attempted to revive Art. A short time later, an officer arrived and called over the radio for a medic. When medics failed to revive Art, he was rushed away on a gurney and the rumor around the prison was that he died of a heroin overdose.

It was confirmed that Art had passed away when Case Manager Rebecca Eaton called a town hall meeting. She was clearly emotional during her speech. Ms. Eaton thanked the inmates who attempted to save Art's life but she was also upset at the people who were responsible for not getting Art the help he needed. According to Ms. Eaton, inmates involved with Art attempted to cover up the drug overdose instead of trying to save his life. She was so upset that she was in tears. Rebecca said that there were inmates that seemed to think that the case manager's job was to make inmates fail and there was some conspiracy to keep them in prison. "I don't know where you guys get this information," she said. "We are here to help you. When you are doing good, that means we are doing our job. You think that we don't care about you. Well, you are wrong! Art had a young daughter who was waiting for him to come home in a matter of weeks. I had to call his family to give them the news that Art had died. It was one of the hardest things I had to do." said Ms. Eaton.

Her words were damning. At the memorial service, Chaplain Kirkness shared stories about Art and how he would use the chaplain's phone to call his daughter, how Art's daughter would tell her dad that she was going to keep him at home so he wouldn't ever go away again. The question I had was why a man would use heroin when he was close to going home to his daughter? I had no answer.

KTE

In the federal system there are many inmates who use being in prison as an opportunity to sharpen their criminal skills and to make contacts for future illegal business. I've met inmates that were doing 20 and 30 years who, once released, planned to get back into the drug game. Rudy Vega was one of them. He was doing nearly 30 years on drug charges and his sister Mary was a federal judge. I did time with Rudy at other federal prisons and we would talk occasionally. Rudy offered to deliver me as much cocaine as I wanted and anywhere I wanted, even while I was in prison. Rudy told me that he had connections that were able to move that kind of weight. Every time Rudy asked me, I declined. I wanted nothing to do with drugs. I asked Rudy why he would want to get back into the drug business when he knew if he were caught he could spend the rest of his life in prison. Rudy told me that he was too old to work. He felt that no one was going to hire a man with no education, especially at his age. The drug business was all he knew and, once he was released from prison, his plans were to go at it full force.

Alfonso Perez was another drug trafficker in his mid-twenties from Tijuana who was recruiting soldiers for his drug organization. Alfonso approached me, asking me to be a part of his organization. The kid was young and cocky, and he was only doing five years on drug charges. After listening to Alfonso's proposal I told the kid that either he was trying to set me up or he wasn't a very bright person, especially if he was willing to recruit anyone. Alfonso defended himself by saying that he had asked around about me and that he knew I was doing a 235-month sentence for drugs. I looked at Alfonso and chuckled. I explained to the kid that just because a man gets 235 months in prison means nothing. I left him with words of advice: "Do yourself a favor and quit the drug business while you're ahead."

BROKEN ARROW

There were ducks, seagulls, pigeons, sparrows, cockatiels and other birds on Terminal Island. In the morning, on the way to work, I would feed birds peanuts or pieces of tortillas. The birds would land on my arms and would eat out of my hands. Some of the birds would follow me to work until I got to the metal detector, then they would stop. After an eight-hour shift at work I headed to my housing unit; as I walked down the breezeway; I noticed a flock of seagulls circling overhead. They were making screeching sounds as if calling out for help. I knew what was going on. I've seen it many times. As I walked onto the south yard I noticed that a seagull was caught in barbed wire by one of its wings. The seagull was between the two perimeter fences.

Most birds caught on the barbed wire lasted for a few days until they died, or until the raccoons or opossums got a hold of them. The next morning I headed to work and was surprised to see that the bird was still alive, as it hung from the fence. It looked as if it barely had any life left in it. I figured the seagull would be dead by the time I got off work. After I ended my shift at UNICOR, I headed back to the south yard.

When I arrived at the fence where the bird was hanging, it was no longer there. I wondered if an animal got to him. I asked one of the other inmates if he saw what happened to the bird. He told me that the maintenance supervisor and his crew cut the bird down when they walked through to clean trash between the perimeter fences. The inmate went on to say that the bird was released onto the yard somewhere. When I found the injured seagull, I gave him water and a pack of mackerel that I bought from the commissary. The bird ate the fish up as if he hadn't eaten in days. His right wing looked broken and it dragged when he walked. I figured the bird would die eventually or he would be confined to the prison yard for the rest of his life.

On weekends, I would walk laps around the track or watch the seagull as I sat on one of the south yard benches. I grabbed the bird to get a good look at his wing. It was clear that the wing was broken, and not only the wing; the bird seemed to have a broken spirit. I wanted to give the bird a name; it seemed to be a male bird, so I started calling him Broken Arrow. After a few weeks, Broken Arrow routinely wobbled across the football field attempting to flap his wings. I stood wondering what he was doing. The bird would also run back and forth across the field, and when he did he looked winded, like an out-of-shape athlete.

As the weeks went on, I noticed that Broken Arrow persisted. He ran across the soccer field every day, attempting to flap his broken wing. I also noticed a group of seagulls that seemed to be watching him from a distance as he ran across the field. Some of the gulls cocked their heads back as they squawked, cawed and screeched, as if mocking Broken Arrow for his effort to fly. After a few months, Broken Arrow seemed to be improving. Every day, he would run back and forth across the football field flapping his wings but he couldn't get airborne.

One day, I watched Broken Arrow running across the football field and he got off the ground for a slight moment. At that moment, I knew if he didn't give up, someday Broken Arrow would make it to the other side of the barbed wire fence a free bird. The other seagulls seemed to watch him, but now with a different look. They seemed to be as one giving it a second thought that Broken Arrow possibly could fly again.

Broken Arrow's day came on a weekend when I was walking laps around the track, enjoying the music playing over my headphones. I watched Broken Arrow make a few practice runs, then suddenly he took to the air and was headed straight for the fence.

My heart skipped a beat when it looked as if Broken Arrow was going to hit the barbed-wire fence. He seemed to be flapping his wings with all he had and was still not high enough to clear the fence. Broken Arrow reached the razor-sharp fence, barely clearing it by inches. I watched as he glided to freedom and onto the rocks near the water, where he landed. He was now free. Witnessing Broken Arrow's triumph was like a message for me to keep going and not give up hope.

Good news came for me when a notice was put out to the inmate population about changes in the Residential Drug Abuse Program. After years of fighting to be eligible for time off in R-DAP, I was finally granted my wish. Under R-DAP guidelines, if an inmate was given a 2D1.1 gun enhancement, he was not eligible for the "up to a year off." *Arlington v. U.S.* changed all that, allowing an inmate who was charged with a 2D1.1 gun enhancement to receive up to a year off for completing R-DAP. Once I received a letter of confirmation stating that I was now eligible for up to a year off my sentence, I put in a request to be transferred to a camp that offered the R-DAP program. Terminal Island was offering the program but the waiting list was so long that inmates were only getting six to eight months off by the time they graduated. I decided to take my chances at a different institution.

A GENTLEMENS' QUARREL

Just about everybody on the yard knew that I was waiting to be transferred to camp. An inmate named Johnny Cruz used to run with the South Siders. He was not from a gang but he was associated with gang members. He claimed that he was busted for pistol-whipping a federal agent, but at the same time Johnny was allowed to be out on bail and he later surrendered at Terminal Island. Johnny was housed in the same unit as I was and lived a few cells away from mine. He often shared farfetched stories with me about his violent criminal past, as if he had something to prove. He was a bully to some of the younger inmates who were from his city. Johnny made up stories and talked so much that he began to get on my nerves. I finally told Johnny that he didn't have to be in killer mode when he was around me. I told him that it was OK to be a nice guy. I reminded Johnny that I'd been around killers most of my sentence.

Johnny knew I would be leaving for camp soon and commented that he would hide heroin in my cell so officers could find it; that way I wouldn't be going to camp. I took those words seriously. I began to distance myself from Johnny but he was the type of person that knew how to push a man's buttons. He got me to the point where I called him into my cell so we could handle any differences that we had, but when it was showtime he began to backpedal, saying, "I knew I could get you. I was only joking." No one had ever pushed my buttons and then acted like he was only joking. I had a talk with Johnny, letting him know that I wasn't a kid to be playing games and we left it at that.

Johnny was surely missing a few screws. It was like he had short-term memory. He had forgotten everything I had told him about joking with grown men to the point where it was disrespectful. I was over my head with Johnny. I called him every name in the book in front of all who could hear. I now *wanted* to push Johnny's buttons. I wanted him to jump first. When I called him into my cell I told his younger homeboy Joey Anderson to keep watch and to make sure none of the officers walked up on us. While in the cell, I yelled and cussed at Johnny. He wanted me to lower my voice, because I'm sure he didn't want anyone hearing some of the words that I was calling him.

It took a while but I finally got him to jump. As soon as Johnny made his move toward me we went at it like two charging rams. The next thing I knew, Johnny was down on the floor between the bunk bed and the locker. Johnny attempted to get up but I rushed over to hit him with a right to the face, knocking him back down. Every time he tried to get up, I kicked him, forcing him back to the floor. I was so enraged that I attempted to hit him over the head with a thick piece of tabletop that I used as a desk, but the cell was so small that I couldn't get the tabletop between the bunk bed and the locker to crack him in the head. I tossed the tabletop to the side and grabbed a trash can.

I was about to hit Johnny in the head when the cell door swung open. It was Joey, the youngster from Johnny's neighborhood. I rushed up on Joey, not sure if he was there to jump in and help Johnny. I stepped out of the cell, backing Joey up and away from the door. The kid seemed startled. I grabbed him by the throat and told him, "Don't you ever walk up on me like that. I almost did something to you." "I just came in to try to break it up. I wasn't going to do anything," Joey said. "How do I know that," I asked him.

I released the kid, then told Johnny to come out of the cell and into the hallway so we could have more room to finish what we were doing. For some reason, Johnny didn't want to step out of the cell. After I saw the unit officer walking down a hallway, my clear thinking kicked in. I realized that I might have just messed up my chances for camp. Now I just wanted Johnny out of my cell. I walked up to him and told him that our beef was over. My cellmate Speedy arrived to see the cell a mess, so he began to clean things up.

Johnny finally stepped out of the cell and he headed down the hall. The officer never came down our range. I went to the restroom so I could look in the mirror to see if I had any marks on my body. On the left side of my neck was a four-inch nail scratch and there was a small scratch on my forehead. I was wondering how I was going to cover them up without any of the officers seeing it. If an officer notices any bruises, scratches or cuts on an inmate and the inmate had not reported it, it's off to the SHU. Johnny also walked into the restroom area to look in the mirror. He had a knot under his left eye, a busted lip and one of his ears was bruising.

After I got cleaned up and returned to my cell, Johnny came to me, offering to cook for me. I'm guessing it was his way of bringing the peace but I refused to eat after laying hands on him. How would I know he didn't put anything in the food? Johnny's bunkie Teco was from my neighborhood, so Johnny must have felt some fear that Teco was going to do something to him while he was sleeping. After the incident, Johnny seemed jumpy. In my eyes it was a gentleman's quarrel. Two men got their differences off their chest and, after all was settled, they were able to go about their business. That doesn't mean I cared for the guy nor did I want to be around him. It just meant that we were able to live amongst each other without killing one another.

The next day I went to work at UNICOR. I wore a towel around my neck so my supervisor wouldn't see the scratch. Supervisor Raul Arceo came into the Q.A. area where I worked. He stopped to ask me a question. Raul began to look at me closely. He must have seen the scratch on my neck. Raul then asked me what happened. I told him that I got scratched playing basketball. Raul asked if I had reported the injury to any of the officers. I told Raul that I did not. He then asked, "Why not?" "Because I didn't want anyone to overreact like you are doing," I said. Raul gave me his word that he would not say anything and then asked, "What really happened?" I responded with, "I already told you. I was playing basketball and I got scratched. That's what happened." "All right, don't worry about it," Raul said and walked away.

About 15 minutes later, I walked outside the warehouse to see four guards coming in my direction. One guard saw me and called out, "Torres! Come here!" I already knew what was up. The goons arrived and escorted me to the factory business office. I was then instructed to take off my shirt and my pants. One of the officers conducted a body search for any visible marks. He looked at my knuckles and noticed that my right hand was slightly swollen. The officer instructed me to get dressed. Then I was escorted out of the business office, where Officer Guerrero and his goons met me and the other officers. Officer

Guerrero asked me to get against a nearby wall so he could pat me down. Then he placed handcuffs on me as he told me that I was under arrest.

Guerrero asked me what happened. I told him I got scratched playing basketball. Guerrero responded, "Oh, you're gonna go out like a real gangster, huh, Torres?" I chuckled, then was taken to Medical, where a physician's assistant documented my wounds. After visiting Medical, I was taken to Segregated Housing. Mrs. Perez, one of the SIS officers in SHU, approached me when I arrived. The first thing she said when she saw me is, "Damn! Who scratched you? I didn't know we had bitches on this yard." Mrs. Perez took a close look at my neck, then she snapped a few photos. Captain Smith then walked into the SHU with a no-nonsense look on his face. He asked one of the officers a question, then approached me. The captain asked me to hold out my hands so he could see my knuckles. I held my hands open, hoping my swollen knuckles wouldn't show. Captain Smith asked me what happened. I told him, it was a rough game of basketball. The captain responded, "Yeah, I've been hearing that one a lot lately." I was then given a copy of my detention order by one of the SIS officers. I was being put in the SHU pending investigation.

I was placed in a cell that contained a bunk bed, a combination sink and toilet, and a small window. I spent most of my time working out but a man could only work out so much in a day. I had been locked up for so many years that I stopped dreaming about people and things in the free world. Those who were in my dreams were now people that I came across in the prison system, female guards, staff members and other inmates. It is said that being isolated from people can make a man go mad. My body remained in solitary confinement but I was determined to keep my mind free. I requested reading and writing material, so one of the officers rolled my property to the cell I was housed in. From my door window, the officer allowed me to pick out the books that I wanted. I requested my Bible and a few of the movie scripts that I was writing. Most of the officers working the SHU were ones who had worked G Unit where I was housed. Many asked me what I was doing in the SHU. They knew I wasn't a troublemaker. I stuck to my "Rough game of basketball story."

When it was shower time I had to back up to my cell door so the officers could place handcuffs on me through the feeder slot. Once the handcuffs were secured, the officer opened the cell door and another waved a handheld metal detector over the parts of my body where weapons could be hidden. I was then escorted to a shower where I was locked in a steel cage. I had to back up to the barred door so the officer could remove the handcuffs. When I was ready to shower, I called out to the officer and he turned the water on. I couldn't shave my head in the shower, because the type of razor blades given to me got dull after 10 strokes or so. Once I was finished, I let the officer know. He then shut off the water. I was handcuffed again and taken back to my cell.

I was allowed to go to recreation every other day to exercise. There were approximately 10 caged areas on the SHU yard. Some of the cages had pull-up bars. I spent my time getting sun, walking laps around the cage and doing pushups. Once my time was up, I was taken back to my cell where I took a bird bath in the sink. A bird bath consisted of clogging up the sink with a towel then filling the sink with water. I would then strip down to my boxers and use a wash cloth and soap to lather my body. After I was covered in soap, I would rinse off the soap with cups of clean water and dry off with a towel, bird bath complete.

During the day, new inmates would arrive at the SHU and other inmates would be released. When a new group of inmates came in, one of the officers knocked at my cell door asking me if it was OK for this white inmate to bunk up with me. I told the officer that I had no problem as long as he wasn't ratting on someone and wasn't a child molester or a rapist. I made it clear to the officer that if I found out otherwise there would be trouble. The officer moved the white guy down the hall and placed him in another cell. I'm guessing the guy had issues.

Part of my SHU routine was to go over my movie scripts. I would practice the roles of characters to make sure the dialogue sounded real. Officers would come by my cell and hear me getting into character. They would knock on my cell door asking me if I had gone crazy. It was a great time for me to get into character without any interruptions.

Anytime I wanted to get out of the cell I would submit a request to go to the law library. The library was a cell with a computer, law books, and a copy machine. I would sit in the library and read other people's cases. During one of the times while I was at the library, Officers Smotherman and Juarez approached the cell; Smotherman told me that my library time was up. Smotherman instructed me to turn around so he could place handcuffs on me.

As Officer Smotherman placed the cuffs on me, he commented, "I just want to know one thing. Who won the fight, you or Johnny?" "What are you talking about," I asked. "The word on the yard is that you and Johnny were going at it in the TV room for about an hour," he told me. "See, it's people like you who get those nasty rumors started," I said. I knew he was fishing for information because the fight with Johnny and I did not take place in the TV room. Smotherman looked bothered but he didn't say another word as he and Juarez escorted me back to my cell.

A few days later, I was called out of my cell and I was taken to a visiting room in the SHU. SIS Officer Steve Marroquin entered the room a few minutes later, along with an officer in training. The first thing Marroquin told me is, "You lied; you were not seen on the cameras playing basketball." "All I know is that I was on the court playing basketball. I don't know what else to say," I told the officer. Marroquin wanted to know if I had gotten into it with any other race or any other gang. I answered, "If I got into it with another race or another gang, don't you think the yard would be rocking and rolling right now?"

Marroquin continued to pry for information, "If it was personal with your own people, I don't have a problem with that. I just want to make sure that nothing is going to jump off on my yard." I assured him that the incident was nothing for him to worry about. He advised me to sit quietly until the investigation is over and not to bug any of the lieutenants about getting out of the SHU. Marroquin went on to tell me that if there were no safety concerns I would be let back on the yard.

BAD NEWS

When my case manager did a walk-through in the SHU, I had a chance to ask her about the status of my transfer to camp. She told me that my transfer was terminated. She explained that when a person goes to the SHU, all transfers stop. It wasn't her doing; it was done by the Western Regional Office. The news had me in rage and I began plotting what I would do to Johnny if I lost my chance for getting the year off for taking the drug program, but I knew dwelling on the issue was dangerous for me. I knew that I needed to cool off and to think things through with a clear mind. As I lay in the cell I had plenty of time to do just that.

I requested to use the phone on the day Alexis was scheduled to give birth. Nahlina Giselle Gonzalez was born August 14, 2009, and it was a bittersweet moment for me. When my granddaughter was born it made me realize how long I had been out of my children's lives. Alexis was only four years old when I went away; now she was a mother.

A week or so later, an officer came to my cell instructing me to gather my property; I was being released back into general population. While I was being processed out of the SHU, my case manager happened to be there. She told me that she was going to resubmit my transfer to camp. I thanked her then was let out onto the main yard. I hadn't cut my hair the entire time I was in the SHU. When I walked onto the yard, there were a few Southsiders near the chow hall. One of them recognized me and yelled across the yard, "Is that you Ray Ray?" I laughed. He went on to say, "Damn! I didn't know you could grow hair." A female guard also commented as she walked by, "You look better with a shaved head." As soon as I arrived at my new assigned housing, I grabbed my electric clippers and a razor blade and I gave myself a clean-shaven head.

My new bunkie was Allen Madrid, a Latino from Southern California. Allen told me, "The word on the yard is that you touched up Johnny pretty good. Now I don't want any trouble, Ray." I could tell Allen was joking. I let Allen know that he had nothing to worry about and I assured him that I was the nicest guy on the yard. Allen laughed, then said, "Johnny's attitude has changed since you laid hands on him; he is much quieter now." "I don't know what you're taking about, Allen." I replied. Allen caught on and left the issue alone.

When I arrived on the south yard I was greeted by fellas from the Harbor Area. Teco from East Side Wilmas was one of them. When he saw me, he told me *a la Goodfellas*, "Hey, you popped your cherry. You kept your mouth shut. You did good kid." I laughed and reminded Teco that it wasn't my first rodeo in the SHU. As the fellas and I walked the south yard track we saw Johnny returning from work. When Johnny saw me with homies from the Harbor Area, he began to look concerned. He had nothing to worry about; I was on my way to camp so the issue between Johnny and I was over. For precaution, I kept Johnny at a distance because I knew if he said the wrong words to me there would be trouble.

I went back to work at UNICOR. I was placed in the assembly department, where I worked my last days. I was at my work station when I heard a phone ring at a foreman's desk. The officer on duty answered the phone. I knew it was the call I was waiting for. I said my goodbyes to the fellas, and strolled across the yard and into R&D, headed for a new destination.

CHAPTER 11 In Transit

After I was shackled with leg irons, waist chain and handcuffs, I was walked out of Terminal Island prison along with a group of other inmates and loaded into a waiting bus. I took in the view of the Vincent Thomas Bridge as the bus headed out of Terminal Island. I enjoyed seeing the large ships at the docks, the cranes unloading containers off of vessels, and the small boats that cruise the port.

When the bus arrived at George Air Force Base in Victorville, California, I figured those who were designated to Sheridan, Oregon, would be flying out on Con Air. The bus pulled up near a parked 727 jetliner. Other buses and vans were waiting nearby when we arrived. A team of shotgun-carrying BOP guards stood positioned around one of the planes. A marshal came on board the bus and called out the names of inmates who would be boarding one of the planes. When my name wasn't called, I began to wonder where I was going. After about an hour of sitting on the bus with other inmates, we drove away. Before long we arrived at United States Penitentiary, Victorville.

USP Victorville is located approximately 85 miles northeast of Los Angeles on I-15. As the bus approached the prison, I noticed the massive, V-shaped buildings and the six gun towers that lined the prison. At the central yard there was another gun tower. The facility was surrounded by a lethal, electrical double fence, about eight feet high, and a brick wall was on its northern side. The entire prison was on lockdown because an inmate had recently been stabbed to death.

I remained in Victorville for three days and, on the third day, an officer called me out of my cell instructing me to roll up my property. We arrived back at George AFB, where Con Air was waiting for us along with a small army of U.S. marshals. When custody changes hands between BOP officers and U.S. marshals, inmates are searched. After I was searched, I was chained to two other inmates; the three of us were then escorted onto the plane. The special-needs inmates or disruptive inmates wore a "Black Box," which is a plastic casing over the chain linking the handcuffs, to prevent any movement.

When the plane took to the air, the marshals were positioned throughout the cabin, keeping a close watch on each passenger. They would signal each other every 15 minutes, as they continued eyeing their prisoners' every move. The marshals only carried Taser guns and handcuffs. When an inmate had to use the restroom, a guard went along, watching the inmate with the door remaining open. Cuffs were not allowed to be taken off during flight, and for our meal we were fed bologna and cheese sandwiches, cookies, and water. I asked one of the marshals if the plane was going to Sheridan. He shook his head and said, "Nope, it's going in the opposite direction." I was now wondering where I was going.

At first it looked like I would be put up in the Federal Transfer Center (FTC), Oklahoma City, a prison facility for male and female inmates. It houses holdover offenders and parole violators who have yet to be assigned to a permanent prison facility. FTC Oklahoma City serves as the main hub of the Justice Prisoner & Alien Transportation System. However, after four days there I was ordered to pack up for another move. Roach, Huero, and I were from California, and we made sure we stood near each other so we would be chained together and seated next to each other on the plane.

I sat at a window seat staring out at the sky and it made me think about the time I flew home from that vacation in Guam. It reminded me of the mass of ocean and the curve of the earth seen from the altitude of the plane. So many thoughts had gone through my mind during that flight home from Guam. Now that I was flying Con Air, I was a changed man. The women in my life were gone, all my worldly possessions were stripped from me, there were no more vacations and my freedom had been taken. But I had gained a new appreciation for life.

The plane landed at McCord Air Force Base in Washington State. Another team of shotgun-carrying BOP officers and marshals stood guard around the plane as groups of inmates were unloaded. Roach went on his way to SeaTac Federal Detention Center. Huero and I were loaded onto one of the buses to Sheridan. Besides the two-dozen prisoners on board, there were three guards. One shotgun-armed guard sat in a steel cage at the rear of the bus while another guard stood with a shotgun at the front of the bus, in a similar cage that separated the guards from the inmates. A third guard drove the bus and was packing a handgun at his side. Despite it all, the scenery from Washington State to Sheridan was an enjoyable sight for me.

CHAPTER 12 F.C.I. Sheridan

I arrived at FCI Sheridan on September 22, 2009. That day also happened to be my birthday. FCI Sheridan is in northwestern Oregon, 90 minutes south of Portland. I was processed in at the detention center before I could be transferred to the nearby camp. As part of the processing, officers and case management ask inmates a series of questions to ensure that inmates are housed in the proper unit. After questioning, I was given a yellow jumpsuit and a bed roll. I had one more phase of processing to go through with an SIS officer and a counselor. I was called into an office where an SIS officer was looking through my prison history file. The officer took a look at me and asked how come I didn't tell him I was from Southern California. "You didn't ask," I answered. The SIS officer warned me that such a mistake could have cost me my life. He then asked, "What if I would have put you in the yellow tank with the Northerners?" What could I say? I just shrugged it off.

Once I changed into an orange jumpsuit I was escorted with other inmates to a unit where we would be housed. Some inmates were housed in the unit because they were still going to court to fight their case. Others were holdovers designated to the medium-level prison on the same compound and still other inmates were waiting to go to camp. Anytime I arrived at a new facility I would make it a rule to find out if there was any tension on the yard with other races. The homie, Dino, who was running the unit told me that a few weeks back there was friction between the Pisas and the Southsiders over a TV issue, but all was now quashed. I was housed at the detention center for less than two days then I was called to pack out.

CAMP CUPCAKE

All new arrivals were then taken to the camp visiting room for orientation. When Counselor Tracy Moss arrived, she greeted us with "Welcome to Camp Cupcake." The counselor went on to warn the new inmates that there were many people at the camp who wouldn't hesitate to tell on someone. She made it clear that the camp was full of rats and that staff members knew everything that went on at Sheridan. Counselor Tracy offered any inmate who didn't want to be at the camp to let her know and she would ship them back to where they came from.

It was explained to the new arrivals that we were moving into a community and that all inmates participating in the drug program were obligated to live by the community rules. All the R-DAP participants lived in the same unit and were instructed to police each other.

Once orientation was over, we followed the officer toward the housing units. Many inmates that I was locked up with at other institutions were now at Sheridan. As I approached my unit I heard someone call out, "You are the reason why I'm in prison!" I turned around to see Ruben Alvarez, someone I grew up with in Wilmington. I snapped back defensively, asking him, "What did you say?" Ruben continued, "I looked up to you when we were kids. I wanted to be a drug dealer just like you. When you came to Wilmington in the red Corvette, I wanted one too." I laughed at Ruben. "You should have gotten the message when you found out that I was sentenced to 235 months. That should have changed your mind about wanting to be like me." Angel Montes, another inmate I grew up with in Wilmington, was also at Sheridan. Ruben, Angel, and I were all at Sheridan to complete the drug program, get time knocked off and go home.

According to the BOP, R-DAP is its most intensive treatment program. It follows the Cognitive Behavioral Therapy model of treatment wrapped into a modified therapeutic-community model in which inmates learn what it is like living in a pro-social community. Inmates live in a unit separate from general population; participate in half a day of programming and half a day of work, school or vocational activities. R-DAP is typically a nine-month program.

As I walked into the R-DAP unit, the first thing I noticed were the following words painted on a wall: "Today as I come to treatment, I am reaffirming my commitment to change. I will continue to build a foundation for a life of sobriety, integrity and purpose. I will think rationally, form healthy relationships and learn to live a balanced life. I will be responsible, honest, willing, open-minded, caring, objective, and display humility and gratitude. I will strive to rehabilitate myself to become a productive member of my community. Today will lead me to a better tomorrow." Those words gave me something to think about. Being in the R-DAP program was like being in boot camp and there were a long list of rules that participants had to follow.

When I arrived at Sheridan I submitted a copout to UNICOR requesting a Quality Assurance Inspector position at the camp warehouse. I was hired not too long after. Sheridan was setting up a plant where inmates would produce solar panels, so my task was to set up the Quality Assurance Department in the camp warehouse so we could receive and inspect all the raw materials for the solar plant.

During winter I would often stare out the unit window at the blanket of white snow that covered the yard. It reminded me of a picture on a Christmas card. The deer that roamed the camp added a tranquil touch to the beautiful scenery. During those days, I would sit back and think about how blessed I was to be at a desk, working on my movie scripts and enjoying the beautiful scenery. I thought about how pleasant it was to wake up sober, in my right mind and how fulfilling is was to work towards something purposeful in life. I had a lot to be thankful for. I was given a second chance at freedom and to do it right.

TWELVE BROKEN MEN

During R-DAP meetings, 12 broken men sat in a room sharing their past mistakes, their regrets and their hurts while R-DAP Counselor Antonson listened. All were required to participate and give feedback. Every few months we would change counselors, and with the new counselor there was always something new to learn in group discussions. We discussed telling, ratting, snitching, doing the right thing or whatever you want to call it.

I gave my opinion that I didn't feel it was right for a man to tell on his codefendants just because he wanted to get out of the legal mess that he got himself into. Counselor Antonson then commented, "So you rather turn your back on your children and betray your family than your so-called friends or crime partners who really didn't care about you?" I hadn't looked at my situation as betraying my family. I guess in a sense I did. My children depended on me to be there for them, to provide for them, to guide them, to give them moral support, to give them encouragement and to love them.

The topic of the day made me think about my past choices. I concluded that the counselor was right. I betrayed my family over some street codes that I no longer lived by. Most people who live by the street code say that a real man would stand strong and do his time, but years later I didn't feel like a real man, knowing that my three children had to grow up without a father. I didn't feel like a real man knowing that my kids had to suffer for the bad decisions that I made. The ripple effect of the choices I made touched all those who were close to me. I couldn't take back all the wrong choices that I made. I had to let time take its course and do my part to help mend those past wounds that I caused on my family.

I thought about what the judge had said to me during my sentencing, about shifting the blame on the government for my actions. I came to realize that I needed to stop blaming others for my own actions. I still believe I was entrapped but not by federal agents. I was entrapped by my own criminal desires. A Biblical scripture helped me understand this. James 1: 14 says, "But we are tempted when we are drawn away and trapped by our own evil desires. 15 Then our evil desires conceive and give birth to sin; and sin, when it is full-grown, gives birth to death."

I had three months, 11 days, and a wakeup until my release date. As the days got closer to my release, it seemed the more irritated I got.

My case manager at Safford was right about the camp. There was a whole different breed of inmates at Camp Cupcake. One of the most irritating things I heard an inmate say while at camp was, "I don't know why people talk about how much time they got. Twenty years or three years, it's all the same." When I heard the inmate make that comment I almost lost it. I wanted to smack that man right in his mouth. He was the one doing three years for distributing ice. If he was doing 20, 30 or 40 years, I'm sure he would have had a different outlook. The guy had never been anywhere else but a camp and he was a self-surrender. I just bit my tongue and reminded myself that my prison time was almost over. If there is one thing I learned out of R-DAP it was that I couldn't control what happened to me in life but I could control how I reacted to situations I came across.

Every so often I would have nightmares about getting out of prison only to get into a vehicle with a friend and later find out that the car had drugs in it, or I would show up to a friend's house when a drug transaction was taking place. In my dreams I would be doing all I could to get away from the situation. What a relief it was when I would wake up from my nightmare to find myself in my cell. Some inmates get used to being behind bars and mentally make it their home. They become institutionalized. Prison was never my home. My body may have been locked up but my mind was always free.

I caught my case in California and, in the federal system, an inmate being released from prison is usually released to the state where he was arrested. I notified my case manager that I would be releasing to Las Vegas, where I lived at the time of my arrest. Case Manager Meezner informed me that she was going to request to have my case transferred to Las Vegas. Weeks later Ms. Meezner called me into her office, telling me that someone in Vegas was trying real hard to keep me from coming back. My probation officer had denied my transfer to Las Vegas. Ms. Meezner told me that she couldn't understand why this probation officer had it in for me but she was going resubmit my transfer papers.

A few weeks later, Ms. Meezner called me back into her office to tell me that my transfer to Las Vegas was approved. She went on to tell me that she had to get the unit manager involved. The unit manager had to contact the head of the Las Vegas Probation Department to bypass the officer who kept denying my transfer. On February 18, 2011, I sat looking at my calendar, reflecting back to when I first was arrested. When I was at MDC Los Angeles, I would cross off days on my calendar with a pencil. When I had reached three months of incarceration, it seemed as if I had been there a lifetime. Now, 16 calendars later, I had less than three months until my release.

GRADUATION

Graduation day was here. All inmates in R-DAP gathered for the graduation ceremony in the visiting room. Inmates graduating were called up to the lectern, giving speeches and words of encouragement to those still in the program. After my time at the lectern, I was congratulated by staff members and handed a certificate of completion. Refreshments, cookies and cake were provided for the graduates. After spending nearly 19 months at Sheridan, I was on my way to freedom. I was initially told by my unit team that I was scheduled to be released on April 1, 2011, which was a Friday. I was later informed that the halfway house in Las Vegas did not accept inmates on Fridays nor on Mondays, so my date of release changed to the following Tuesday, April 5.

I guess it was a real April Fool's joke, leading me to believe I would be released on April 1. I couldn't sleep the night before my release. I woke up at 5 a.m. and began to shave. It had been 15 years, 10 months and 12 days since my arrest. I had spent approximately 5,795 days behind bars. Now the day had finally come when it was time to be released. I arrived at the detention center's R&D department, where I was processed out. A corrections officer placed a box on the floor where he opened it to inspect. He then slid the box to me. It contained new pants, a shirt, belt and boots. I took the new clothes to the restroom, where I switched out with my prison rags. After I dressed, I was given my itinerary, flight ticket and the $200 cash that was in my prison account.

Stewart, an inmate whose job was to convey inmates to their release destination, drove me to Portland Airport in a Chrysler PT Cruiser issued to him by the BOP. It was my last field trip with the BOP. It was finally over. I had been told that there was light at the end of the long, dark, lonely tunnel and on this day that light was shining bright as the sun. It was the first day of a new beginning. I was going to be with my family and there were not going to be any more prison walls to separate us. I was excited to get my new life started. I stopped for a moment to wonder if this was another one of those many dreams I had of coming home. Was my mind playing tricks on me? Was I going to wake up in the middle of my sleep only to realize that I was still locked up in a cell? I asked Stewart to pinch me to make sure I wasn't dreaming. Stewart laughed and assured me that I wasn't dreaming.

At Portland International Airport, Stewart and I said our goodbyes. I had to stop for a moment to thank God for getting me through the nearly 16 years of prison. When I was finished thanking Him, I stopped to inhale a breath of fresh, free air. As I walked through the airport, I saw a coffee shop and that's where I headed. I ordered an orange juice and a croissant. It was the best croissant that I had tasted in a long time. I later boarded my plane. I sat in my seat, enjoying my freedom. The pilot's voice then came over the loudspeaker instructing all passengers to fasten their seat belts because the plane was about to taxi. The flight attendants gave their safety demonstration as the plane taxied down the runway. Suddenly the engines revved up and the plane raced down the runway at high speed and took to the air. Like Broken Arrow, I was airborne.

CHAPTER 13 Return to Las Vegas

It was April 5, 2011, as the plane flew over Las Vegas. I was amazed on how much Vegas had changed since 1995, the year I was arrested. There were so many more homes, built all the way to the mountains' edge, and many new hotels and casinos had been erected. I arrived at McCarran International Airport and, as I walked through the airport, I was excited to be free, to be back in Vegas, but most of all to see my family. Waiting for me were Alexis, Ray Junior and my nephew Rob. Reuniting with the family was one of the happiest moments of my life.

I arrived at GEO Care, transitional housing located on Industrial Road behind Circus Circus. During processing, I requested to be housed in a quiet area, because I knew I was easily irritated by unnecessary, loud noise. My assigned sleeping area was a four-man cubicle. The capacity of the halfway house was around 124. I was still under the authority of the BOP and actively serving a federal prison sentence until my supervised release date kicked in.

New arrivals were subject to a highly structured environment. Security measures included 24-hour supervision and frequent census counts. Cameras also monitored the residence and urine-analysis rooms had voice recorders. Residents were required to electronically sign in and out of the facility. The halfway house was set up to provide transitional services under the supervision of staff members. It was structured to assist offenders become employed and law-abiding citizens in the communities. I was assigned to Case Manager William Steele (the brother of famous boxing referee Richard Steele), who was responsible for assisting with reestablishing community and family ties.

I was allowed to leave the halfway house for approved activities such as seeking employment, working, counseling, visiting or recreation. Staff continued to monitor inmates by visiting the approved locations (home or work) and/or making random phone contacts at different times during the day. Staff also administered random drug and alcohol tests for those inmates returning to the halfway house from an approved activity, and conducted random and scheduled in-house counts throughout the day.

The first week home, I had many visitors stop by to see me at the halfway house. Leanna brought Serina to see me. It was so nice hugging my daughter and knowing that I would be in her life physically instead of from behind a fence, or through letters and a phone call. When I was approved for my day passes, I had my mother, my nephew Rob, along with other friends and family members drive me around town so I could get my driver's license, a vehicle, car insurance, and to comply with Nevada's laws and register with Metro Police as a drug trafficker. I was also given passes so I could attend church services.

My daughter Alexis invited me to her church. When we arrived at Central Christian the music was blasting, I felt as if I was at a concert, and there were people of every color and social status, some with tattoos and others with body piercings. After learning how much the church did for the community, for those in prison, for the youth and for the lost, I knew I wanted to help. And Pastor Jud Wilhite's messages were pretty good. I decided to make Central Christian my church. I knew it was the church for me when I heard Pastor Jon Bodin say that Central "Is the place where it's OK to not be OK."

Another friend of mine, Bryan "KoJack" Oneal would take me to run errands. I asked Bryan to drive down the Strip and, when he did, I noticed that parts of Vegas looked like a ghost town. It didn't seem like the same Las Vegas as in the 1990s, when money was flowing through the city. My old hangout, the Crazy Horse Too was closed and some of the people from back in the day had passed away. Scott Potter was gone. Moe from the Crazy Horse Too was gone and Antoinette was gone. So many people had passed but life continued.

Residents at the halfway house were expected to be employed 40 hours a week within 15 days after their arrival at GEO Care. I was thankful to have a job waiting for me as an office manager at a glass company owned and operated by Joey Murrin. Alex Cardenas offered to lend me a truck so I could get around town. I received approval from the halfway house to drive once they verified that I had a driver's license and insurance. It felt great being able to drive again.

Once I had employment, I was told that I was required to pay 25 percent of my gross income to help defray the cost of confinement. I wondered how I was supposed to save for an apartment and get ahead by giving up 25 percent of my earnings. I did some research and I learned that I could file for a Subsistence Waiver and that's exactly what I did. On July 27, 2011, my Subsistence Waiver was granted. I no longer had to pay the 25 percent of my gross income. The halfway house allowed residents to keep a laptop and a cell phone as part of their property. I asked Alex to drop off a prepaid cell phone; I requested a phone with a key pad until I got used to using the newer technology. The last phone I had owned before my arrest was a gray Motorola flip phone with the slim battery. I used to call it a "Doctor Spock" phone from the Star Trek movies. Alexis brought me her laptop so I could get familiar with the Internet and search for other job opportunities and schools that I wanted to attend that were associated with movie production.

HOME CONFINEMENT

On April 16, 2011, William Steele called me into his office to tell me that the Bureau of Prisons wanted me out of the halfway house right away. When Mr. Steele gave me the news, I was overwhelmed with joy. Nineteen days after I arrived at the halfway house I was granted home detention. Under home detention, a resident is required to remain at home during non-working hours. I was ordered to serve the remaining five months of my sentence at home under strict schedules and curfew requirements. I had no problem because it was one more step to freedom. While living at my mom's I slept in the living room, on a couch in her mobile home. It was a small trailer but it was home and I was free. Spending time with mom was great. She wanted to cook for me all the time. She did my laundry and pressed my work clothes. Boy, was I getting spoiled.

The first time I went grocery shopping was so enjoyable. I loved walking down each aisle and looking at all the different foods. I appreciated my freedom and things that most people took for granted. I didn't feel there would be an issue with me adjusting to society, but I lived in a world for so many years where respect was demanded. Disrespecting someone could get a person stabbed, beaten or even killed. Now I was in the free world. I knew I had to change my way of thinking. I wasn't in prison anymore, yet I would feel disrespected at times by people doing some of the smallest things, like cutting in line at a market or cutting me off while driving down the road. The crazy thing about it was that they probably didn't even realize what they were doing. I had to tell myself constantly to let it go. I came this far and was now free; it wasn't worth it to make an issue out of it.

The day I went to visit my father's grave site, I took Alexis and Nahlina with me. The headstone read: "Bob Torres, July 1st, 1942 to October 10th, 1998, A roofer with Integrity, Champ." On the headstone, there were withered flowers that my mother had brought. While visiting my father's grave I didn't feel sad at all. I sat at his grave talking to him, letting him know that I loved him and that I would see him again someday in Heaven. Nahlina was playing near her great grandfather's headstone when she walked into a small hole that was covered by grass. She yelled, "Mom! Help me!" Alexis started laughing. She told Nahlina that grandpa was trying to pull her foot. I began to laugh, too. We left the cemetery in a somewhat cheerful mood.

KTE

While visiting Alex Cardenas he asked me if I was interested in a job as a chauffeur. Phil Mascione, a mutual friend, had talked to Alex, offering me a position at a prestigious luxury-transportation company. Things weren't working out at the glass company, so I accepted the offer. Phil had arranged a pre-hire interview with General Manager Angelo Giancola. When I arrived at the meeting, one of the first things

Angelo asked me is if I had a good driving record. I told Angelo that I hadn't had a ticket in over 16 years. Angelo caught onto my joke and laughed. Phil had explained my past incarceration to Angelo. He seemed more interested in the saga of the stolen Wayne Newton artwork.

At the end of the meeting, Angelo seemed happy with me, and told me to fill out an application and obtain the required documents. One of the documents that I needed was a SCOPE from the police department. A SCOPE (Shared Computer Operations for Protection & Enforcement) is an online system that provides information relating to a person's criminal history in Nevada. It is the same as a rap sheet. When I looked over the SCOPE document, I noticed that my federal conviction was not listed. I'm guessing the reason was because I was arrested in California and not in Las Vegas. For whatever reason, it was to my benefit. I also obtained my Department of Transportation physical, my Department of Motor Vehicles printout and submitted to a drug test. When my drug test came back negative, I was given a date to show up for orientation and told to arrive wearing a company-approved black suit and tie.

The company started me off driving a Lincoln Towncar. I caught on to the industry quickly, and began to network with old and new contacts. I was released from home confinement on September 27, 2011, and placed on probation. Probation Officer Rebecca Capstick informed me that she would be inspecting my place of residence. I would still be subject to drug testing once a week but I didn't mind; I was one more step closer to freedom.

Being released from home confinement was perfect timing. I was no longer on a strict schedule and I could work long hours without violating halfway-house rules. I was offered a detail driving one of the premium cars, a Mercedes S 550, for a VIP at the National Business Aviation Association 64th Annual Meeting & Convention. It was almost four months to the day that I started working for the transportation company when the detail was offered. I really enjoyed my job as a chauffeur. Who wouldn't want to get dressed up in polished leather shoes and a nicely pressed suit for work? And on top of that, I was given an opportunity to drive luxury vehicles. Every day that I got up for work I looked forward to it.

After speaking to a supervisor, he commented that I had the right personality to be a VIP chauffeur; he mentioned that I was a people person and that was a good trait to have in the industry. The comment brought me back to when I was a youth and Mr. Bill, my next-door neighbor, told me, "Ray, you are going to be successful in life. I know this because you have a gift. You associate well with people and that's going to open doors for you in life that others could never go through."

The office must have been satisfied with my work performance from the NBAA detail, because I was asked by the company if I wanted to be a VIP chauffeur permanently. That meant I would be driving some of the top clients, anyone from actors, to singers, CEOs of billion dollar companies to big time gamblers. How could I say no to that? So began my career as a VIP chauffeur.

SOMEBODY'S WATCHING ME

While at work, I was covering one of the properties on the Strip. I had been parked in the staging area for about an hour. Usually, when a hotel guest needs a vehicle they approach the doorman, then the doorman calls the next car up for the guest. Two men who were clean-cut and wearing sports coats stood at the hotel entrance. It seemed as if they were looking at me. Suddenly the men walked past the doorman and in my direction. They approached my vehicle and asked me if I could take them to the Palms Hotel & Casino. I told the men that I was available and when they got in, one of the men asked if I could score some nose candy. I chuckled, then let the man know that he was asking the wrong person. The other man then asked if I could get some weed or girls for them. "Sorry, I'm not into that type of business," I told them.

I soon pulled up at the Palms and, when the passengers stepped out I got a feeling that they are law enforcement. I looked into one of the man's eyes; they were not the eyes of someone who got high. It is said that, "The eyes are the windows to the soul." This soul was definitely law enforcement. One of the gentlemen asked me how much he owed. I told him $45. The man paid me and he added a $20 dollar tip. I looked to my side as the two men stood in front of the casino entrance, watching me as I drove off. My senses were on point. I felt good knowing that I wasn't involved in that old business from back in the days. I didn't have to look over my shoulder worrying that someday the police were going to kick down my door to arrest me. I was in the free world and wanted to remain free.

During my regular work detail I decided to stop off at the Venetian Hotel for a coffee break. When I came out the main door, I stopped for a few minutes to chat with the property starter. We were standing next to the Mercedes when I noticed SIS Officer Steve Marroquin walk out of the Venetian. He was looking directly at me. I approached Marroquin and asked, "Where do I know you from?" He looked surprised to see me and responded, "Terminal Island." I was dressed in my pressed suit and polished leather shoes. He gave me a look over and said, "I see you are doing well with yourself." "I'm doing OK," I told him as I handed him my business card. Marroquin told me that he was in Vegas with a group of coworkers from the prison. He mentioned that they might need a stretch limo later that night and would call me to confirm. I chuckled and said, "OK." I knew he wasn't going to call and whatever reason he was in Vegas wasn't my business.

KTE

I had mentioned to Stephanie Parry, a friend of mine, about my passion for the movie industry, so when the Vegas Independent Film Festival was in town, Stephanie asked me if I wanted to attend. I told Stephanie that I would love to. The festival also happened to be viewing Wayne Newton's movie *40 West*. Stephanie hooked me up with a red-carpet VIP pass. When I got off work, I drove to The Orleans Hotel & Casino, where the festival was held. I arrived alone and immediately I noticed photographers and members of the media taking pictures of cast members, producers and directors of the movies that were showing at the festival. I walked down the red carpet and stopped to pose for a few photos with showgirls.

As I walked off the carpet, I saw Wayne Newton enter the room. Metro police officers escorted Newton into the festival. He looked in my direction, just as of curiosity I'm sure. I don't think he knew who I was. He definitely knew my name but he couldn't pick me out of a crowd if he had to. I looked like a totally different person today than I did in 1995 when I was arrested. Besides that, I had never seen Wayne Newton personally until the film festival.

I was probably the only one at the event who looked like a Secret Service agent. They were my work clothes but I felt slightly overdressed. After Newton posed for photos for the media, he headed toward the movie theater. The films showing at the festival were soon to start, so all attending were being seated. When I arrived in the theater I sat in one of the front rows. Newton and his entourage sat a few rows behind me. The movie didn't impress me much but I was inspired by the film festival. I had a new fueled desire to get the movie scripts that I wrote while in prison produced.

KTE

May 1, 2012, investigator Sam Galvan, working with John Brown & Associates, contacted me by e-mail stating that he would like to speak to me about an event that happened more than 15 years ago pertaining to Juan Carlos. Three days later, Galvan called me to ask if I would be willing to help Juan in his fight to reduce his prison sentence. Immediately I responded by telling him that I wanted nothing to do with Juan. I know I am called to forgive others but that didn't mean I had to go out of my way for them. I declined to assist Juan with his legal issues. I told Galvan that I was sorry that I couldn't be of help.

ROAD TO REDEMPTION

In September 2012, I received a phone call from a woman who introduced herself as Sheree Corniel from the U.S. Probation Department. Sheree told me that I was referred to her by Probation Officer Capstick. She went on to say that she had read my criminal file and felt that I would be a good candidate for a youth-impact program that she was putting together. Without thinking twice, I told her I would be more than willing to be a part of her program.

Our first meeting was November 2012 at the halfway house on Industrial Road. When other former federal offenders arrived, we all introduced ourselves, then sat at a table to listen to what Sheree had to say. She informed us that she read all our files and had handpicked every one of us. Sheree pointed out that we had a story to share. The program would be made up of former and present federal offenders who were dedicated to changing the lives of youth. The program's mission was to assist our next generation with achieving its hopes and dreams, to help build character, and to help them reach their full potential as responsible citizens and future leaders of tomorrow. The program would not just be about federal offenders sharing their stories with the youth but also about providing resources for the youth to follow their dreams in life. After the first meeting, I made sure that I was committed to the program. So Real Talk, Youth Impact Program was born.

KTE

On Sunday, October 30, 2011, I arrived at Central Christian Church with Alex Cardenas. Earlier, when I told him that I was going to service, he said that he wanted to come along. About halfway through the service, Alex told me that there was a lady in the row behind us who kept glancing over at me and smiling. I took a look over at her and she was wearing a big grin on her face. I thought nothing of it.

On the following Sunday I was running a few minutes late when I entered the church. Music was playing and the lights were dim. I walked down the aisle looking for somewhere to sit. I noticed an empty seat next to an elderly man. I asked him if the seat was taken. The man said yes, he was waiting for his wife. I looked past him and there was the same woman who had been sitting directly behind me at service the week before. She was now waving me over, letting me know that there was an empty seat next to her.

I excused myself as I worked my way past the man and toward the woman. I took the empty seat next to the woman and we greeted each other. She had caramel skin and her eyes looked exotic. I thought she might be Puerto Rican, or Creole mixed with Asian. Toward the end of the service the pastor told the congregation to introduce themselves to the person next to them and maybe invite someone to lunch. Before I could say anything, the exotic-looking woman sitting next to me introduced herself as Kelley. I told Kelley my name, then I felt the need to be honest with her. After all, I was at church. No more than 10 minutes after meeting Kelley, I let her know that I was recently released from federal prison. Kelley grinned, then she told me that she had been a Los Angeles Police officer for 10 years.

I laughed. What are the chances of me becoming acquaintance with an ex-LAPD officer I thought? I asked Kelley where she was from. San Pedro, she told me. "What a small world. I'm from Wilmington," I replied. (San Pedro is the neighboring city to Wilmington.) It turned out that Kelley and I knew some of the same people.

As Kelley and I exited the church, I gave her my business card, telling her if she still wanted to call me to feel free to do so. About 20 minutes later, I got a call from Kelley. We started dating. When one of my friends learned that I was dating an ex-cop, he thought the feds sent Kelley to see if they could find out some previously unknown information about me. I laughed at my friend's paranoia. My response was, "If I am not doing anything wrong then I don't have anything to worry about." Plus, if she was a federal agent, she wasn't a bad-looking one.

One blessing came after another. I bought a newer Honda Accord and, not too long after that, I moved out of mom's trailer and got an apartment. Oh, how nice it was to sleep on a new memory-foam mattress and pillow. The first night on my new bed felt like I was in heaven.

Kelley and I continued to date. On Sunday, September 30th, 2012, Kelley invited me to go with her to a Grassroots event with President Barack Obama at Desert Pines High School in North Las Vegas. There

224

were so many people there to see the President, many of them Latinos. After passing security, Kelley and I walked through the event. Secret Service men were posted up on the schools' roof. There was high security all around. The event started with a few speeches, then the rock band Mana from Mexico put on a concert. When they played "Mariposa Traicionera" the crowd went crazy. Then President Obama took the stage. I thought to myself, "Wow, I came from a cold, lonely, steel-and-concrete cell to standing before the President of the United States of America." It was definitely a great experience for me.

ANOTHER SETUP?

In the back of my mind I've always had a feeling that the feds would send someone to me to see if I was into any criminal activity. I was in my right mind and I could smell a setup a mile away. Out of the blue sky, my cousin Mando Marquez called me, saying he wanted to talk. He asked if we could meet somewhere. I was not sure what Mando wanted but I invited him over to my mother's home so he could visit her also. Mando told me that he'd rather meet where we could talk alone. I now suspected that he wanted to talk about something of which I wanted no part.

Mando and I met at a school near my mother's place. I pulled into the parking lot at Judge Myron E. Leavitt Middle School, off of Lone Mountain Road. I hadn't seen my cousin in nearly 20 years nor did I ever mention my past drug business with him. I got out of my Honda Accord and walked over to the Mercedes that Mando was driving. Mando immediately asked me if I could provide him with 100 to 200 pounds of weed. I stared at my cousin, thinking that if he wasn't family I would pop him in the mouth for asking me such a thing. I was offended. I asked Mando, "Don't you know where I've been for the past 16 years? I would be a fool to get involved in any type of drug dealings. Do you even know how much time I would get if I was to get caught in another drug case? I would get a 10-year enhancement for just having a prior drug conviction on top of the time for the new charges."

Mando attempted to persuade me by telling me that I didn't have to get involved, I could just introduce him to a drug connection who could supply him with the weed he needed. I told Mando, "You must not know how the feds work. Just introducing you to a drug connection is getting involved. It's called conspiracy and you don't have to be caught with the drugs in your possession to be arrested. If two or more witnesses say you are involved, then you will be charged in the drug deal if somebody in your drug circle is arrested." I told him to save himself a lot of trouble and get out of the drug game. I let Mando know that if he got busted by the feds he would be looking at 5 to 10 years minimum for marijuana and that's only if it was his first offense.

Mando told me that he couldn't get out of the business. His monthly expenses are about $10,000, he had to support his girlfriend's kids and he owed connections $200,000 for loads of weed that were lost. When I heard this, I thought to myself that he was unstable. Even if I was in the drug business I wouldn't cosign for him. Sitting there listening to Mando, I concluded he was a wreck waiting to happen. It was clear that no matter what I said, Mando's mind was made up. He accepted that he would go to prison for a long time if he were caught and he was cool with that.

As I told Mando that I couldn't help him, a desperate look crossed his face. We said our goodbyes and I returned to my car. As I drove out of the school parking lot I noticed two cars, one parked on one end of the parking lot and another on the street. Both cars had what looked like a surveillance team in the front seat. Were they local police or were they feds? Maybe I was being paranoid, but I refused to open the door when that old lifestyle came knocking. I was no longer that old drug trafficker. My freedom and my family were more important to me than making any amount of illegal money.

Back at work, I was offered a position as a house car for one of the most -- if not the most -- prestigious hotel in Las Vegas and accepted the offer. The clients kept calling and the big details kept coming. A VIP booked me for the 2012 NASCAR races at the Las Vegas Motor Speedway. One of the benefits for chauffeur clients at NASCAR was being right in the middle of all the action. I was given access to the inner circle of the track, where I parked to watch the race and the best part was that I got paid for doing it.

KTE

I was on a detail chauffeuring Louis Carr, president of Media Sales at Black Entertainment Television, who attended the Soul Train Awards. The morning I was to start the second day of the detail, I received a call from my stepfather Ricardo telling me that my mother had a heart attack; she was at Mountain View Hospital. I told Ricardo that I would get there as soon as I could. Carr and I arrived at the Palazzo Hotel for his dinner reservation and, as I dropped him off at the hotel, I asked if I could take a break to see how my mother was doing. I explained to Carr that I had received a phone call saying that my mother was in the hospital. Carr was kind enough to let me visit my mother at the hospital. I thanked him and assured him that I would return before he finished his dinner.

I arrived at Mountain View Hospital. When I entered my mother's hospital room, other family members were present. Mom was bedridden with tubes coming out of her arms and nose. A doctor told me that my mother would pull through. Mom later recovered fully from the heart attack but test results found that she had breast cancer, so she had to undergo chemotherapy. It was a wakeup call for me. I've been known to be a workaholic and my mother's situation reminded me that I had to adjust my priorities. Spending time with family and loved ones needed to be my priority. Happily, Mom fully recovered from the breast cancer.

RUSSIAN DIPLOMATS

A supervisor for my company informed me that a security team requested the profiles of the top five chauffeurs from the company. One of the five chauffeurs would be picked to transport a family of Russian diplomats that would be visiting Las Vegas. I was honored that I was a part of the five-man profile. After the profiles were submitted to the Russian diplomat's security team, I was told that my coworker J.B. was given the detail. J.B. had been with the company a number of years before I started in the industry and was well respected by staff and management. J.B. was also a good chauffeur. I later received a call from J.B. informing me that the Russian family needed a second vehicle to take the wife, teenage daughter, nanny and young son shopping. They also needed a chauffeur who was familiar with security matters. J.B. requested that I be the chauffeur and bodyguard on the detail.

I arrived at the Encore Tower Suites in a Cadillac Escalade. My instructions were to take the family shopping at Fashion Show Mall. I was told by the security team that, "Today you are first a bodyguard, second you are their chauffeur." I was to keep contact with other security members by radio. Security would be out of sight, following the family at a distance. After arriving at the mall, I was told by the Russian wife to keep very close attention to her young son, who must have been no more than six years old.

I stood my distance as the mother and daughter did their shopping. The nanny was with the boy as he wandered around Neiman Marcus, not too far from his mother. As the mother walked into the makeup department just about every sales person attempted to get her attention, as though they knew she was a big spender. I learned that one of the clothes stores at Crystals mall had shipped in their high-end clothes from Los Angeles and closed the store to the public so the family could shop privately. The store had even set up a video game so the son could play while the ladies did their shopping. The wife spent over half a million dollars just on clothes and the husband did about the same. The Russian woman loved to shop; she bought suitcases, makeup and racks of clothes. Money was not an issue. This was a glimpse into the lives of the filthy rich who visit the city of Las Vegas.

PACQUIAO VS. MARQUEZ

I received a call that I would be driving Michael Lombardo, one of HBO's executives to the Pacquiao vs. Marquez IV fight at the MGM Grand. The chauffeurs on the detail were on location at Atlantic Aviation to pick up their assigned HBO executive. When the HBO plane landed, I led the caravan of two Mercedes S550s and four

Cadillac Escalades onto the tarmac and right up to the plane. The VIPs were quickly escorted to the waiting vehicles. Once all passengers were loaded, I led the caravan off the tarmac and out of the gate on the way to the MGM Grand. The HBO security team was waiting as the caravan pulled up at the main entrance; security whisked the executives from the vehicles and into the casino.

I then led the caravan to a designated staging area. During my downtime, I sat in the Mercedes and received round-by-round texts from friends and family who were watching the fight. I was told that Pacquiao had got dropped once but was dominating the fight. Then, toward the end of the sixth round, Pacquiao was knocked out cold. Before the fight ended, the six vehicles were called to stage at the designated pickup location. Moments after the fight finished, the HBO executives were escorted to the waiting vehicles and the caravan sped off to Atlantic Aviation.

One of the executives in the vehicle mentioned that he was shocked how Pacquiao got knocked out. It was said that after Marquez connected the blow, Pacquiao fell face first to the canvas and was laid out for what seemed like 10 minutes. When I arrived at Atlantic Aviation I was escorted onto the tarmac, where I dropped the executives off at the plane. After the drop, the caravan of vehicles parked at the limo staging area. We waited for wheels-up and, once I received the call that the jet had departed, we were all released from the detail.

In February 2013, *American Idol* was to visit Las Vegas. I was notified by the office that I would be one of the chauffeurs on the detail. I often watched *American Idol* while I was in prison. Watching it took my mind away from the reality of being locked up. Being in the free world and chauffeuring Mariah Carey and Nicki Minaj, along with *American Idol* host Ryan Seacrest made me stop to think about how far God had brought me is such a short time. I went from having pictures of Mariah Carey hanging in my prison cell locker to having Mariah Carey sitting in the back seat of the SUV I drove.

My daughter Serina was in town for her twentieth birthday so I surprised her with tickets of the taping of *American Idol*. Her seat was not too far from the judges. When Alex, Seacrest's assistant, offered to send Serina an autographed photo of Seacrest, I gladly accepted. Serina called me when she received the signed photo. It was written, "To Serina, you are my Idol," signed by Ryan Seacrest. He was a genuine person, and his assistant Alex and his security Ralph Diaz were just as great to work with.

2013 BILLBOARD MUSIC AWARDS

I arrived at Signature Flight Support to pick up rapper Birdman, who would be attending the Billboard Music Awards. After staging the vehicles at the pickup point I stood outside my SUV waiting for the clients to arrive. A few moments later, Wayne Newton, his wife Kathleen and his daughter Lauren walked out the main entrance of Signature and in my direction. Newton stopped and looked directly at me as I stood next to the Escalade, wearing a black pressed suit, black leather gloves and dark shaded Prada glasses.

Newton nodded as if to say hello as he walked past me. He surely had no clue that I was the man who'd just done hard time for trying to sell his stolen artwork. When my clients came walking out of the main exit at Signature, I asked one of the bodyguards if he saw Big Wayne Newton. The fellas in the entourage laughed, then one of them commented, "Yeah, that was Big Wayne." Rapper Lil Wayne is one of the artists signed to Cash Money Records. Newton was to attend the Billboard Music Awards along with artists from Cash Money Records. I thought to myself, "What are the chances of running into Wayne Newton for the second time?"

Chauffeuring the filthy rich in Las Vegas can be rewarding at times. Millionaires and billionaires from such places as Russia, Hong Kong and Dubai have been known to give their chauffeurs envelopes stuffed with hundreds, even thousands of dollars. Some chauffeurs have received Rolex watches and gone on shopping sprees with their clients paying the bill. VIPs have been known to take a liking to their chauffeur so much that the client hires the chauffeur as their personal driver.

I am grateful to have chauffeured some of the most prestigious guests who have frequented Las Vegas, including Holly Madison, Elton John, Jennifer Lopez, Mariah Carey, Nicki Minaj, Ryan Seacrest, Chris Tucker, Andrea Bocelli, David Copperfield, Lady Gaga, Neil Diamond, Warren Buffett, One Direction, Dwayne "The Rock" Johnson, Brad Pitt, Jerry Bruckheimer, Kelly Clarkson, Sir Richard Branson, Nicolas Cage, Sean "Puff Daddy" Combs and Will Smith.

KTE

On June 18, 2013, at the Pearson Community Center in Las Vegas, I was scheduled to speak to a group of youth at the Change One Meeting. It was my first speaking engagement with youth since I was released for prison. I wanted to roll all my experiences up in a speech and deliver it to the youth in hopes that it would save at least one life: everything I've learned on the streets as far as criminal activity, life's lessons, bad choices and the reward of good deeds. After I was introduced by the emcee, I began by talking about statistics. "The number of high school students who drop out each day in the United States are estimated at 8,300." (High School Students who drop-out, 1,1 2014) "The FBI estimates, on an average 15, 500 people die each year in the U.S. from gang violence." (FBI) "Drug overdose is now the leading cause of accidental death in the United States, accounting for more deaths than traffic fatalities or gun homicides and suicides." (Overdosing) "Suicide is the third-leading cause of death for 15-to-24-year-olds; it's also thought that at least 25 attempts are made for every completed teen suicide." (Suicide) "Roughly one in three U.S. youths will be arrested by age 23." (Rubin, 2011) "... Real Talk is here today, because we want to change these numbers to zero."

I shared stories about growing up as a troubled youth, my experience in prison, and about my choices in life, bad and good. I let the youth know that when I changed my old ways of thinking to something positive it brought positive results. It was rewarding for me to be able to give back something to the community that I so selfishly took from in my younger days. It was clear to me that God allowed me to go through all the hard times in my life to prepare me for a life of working with at-risk-youth. The bad choices in life that I went through seemed worth it if my story could be used to change a life for the better. Sharing my stories with the youth gave me a sense of purpose in life, something that I didn't have as a youth.

VERY IMPORTANT PEOPLE

My biggest VIPs are Ray Junior, Alexis and Serina, and my five granddaughters, Nahlina, Raelanie, Jayla, Zelaya, and Maelana. My family and friends, those who have been by my side through my trials, are my VIPs. My children and I have our differences at times but God has continued working in our lives and I am greatly thankful. I was told by my good friend Rico Sandoval that my life's story reminds him of the Bible's story of Joseph in the book of Genesis, Chapters 37-49. Joseph was released from prison and found favor with man and God. Joseph became the second-in-command to oversee Pharaoh's kingdom. It seems that God uses the same stories in Biblical days as he does the present; he just uses different characters. I'm not overseeing any kingdom, but I recognize where my blessings come from. God has definitely shown me favor.

Serina was in Vegas for her birthday so I decided to take her to dinner at Kabuki in Town Square, a posh local mall. Sandra, an old friend from California, was also in town at the time. I invited her to have dinner with my daughters, Debrah and a few other friends. Before Sandra arrived, she called to ask me if it was OK to invite her daughter Susanna and Sandra's ex, Antonio Marcos, along with his wife to the dinner. It was the same Antonio Marcos who wanted me dead in our younger days. I thought about it for a moment. I had no problem with Antonio being there. We had our issues in the past but that was over 20 years ago. I've learned to forgive others and have become meek over the years. Some people might mistake meekness for weakness but I define meekness as "knowing within one's self what you are capable of doing but choosing to remain quiet, gentle, tame and non-retaliating."

While we were at the restaurant with family and friends, Sandra and her daughter Susanna, Antonio -- along with his wife -- arrived at the table and we all greeted each other. Antonio and I sat near each other so we could converse. He told me how his life has changed over the years: He had become an airman and later a firefighter, but had an early retirement for health reasons. Antonio's life was different from the days we ran the streets, but then so was mine. I didn't hold any grudges, even though I knew he had attempted to put a hit on me back in the day. I knew that no one could bring harm to me unless God allowed it. I needed to forgive others but, more importantly, I needed forgiveness myself for all the wrong I've done in the past.

KTE

Through a friend I learned that the court can grant early termination of supervised release anytime after the expiration of one year. After I had been on supervised release for over a year and a half, I contacted the Federal Public Defender's office in Las Vegas, requesting to file a motion for early termination of supervised release. I was asked by a member of the public defender's office to fill out a financial affidavit. Once I completed the affidavit and turned it in, I was contacted by Assistant Federal Public Defender Heidi Ojeda. She confirmed that I was eligible to file for early termination but suggested that I wait until I completed at least two years so I had a better chance of getting the request granted. I agreed to wait and, a few weeks before my two-year anniversary, Heidi called to confirm about filing the motion.

In part, it read: "Mr. Torres is a model example of someone who has turned a bad situation around. From his time in prison to his release, he has volunteered and dedicated his time to working to prevent other individuals from following in his same footsteps. Mr. Torres has a stable job that he loves, and he is currently saving up for a down payment on his first home here in Las Vegas. Mr. Torres' probation officer, Casey Anderson, represented to the undersigned that Mr. Torres is in full compliance with his conditions of supervised release, volunteering with at-risk youth and attempting to purchase his first home. Probation's reluctance to support this motion has nothing to do with Mr. Torres post-release conduct. Rather, the office of probation will not support this request based solely upon the circumstances of his underlying offense. The determination of whether early termination should be granted however is and should be based primarily on the offender's post-release conduct."

The government's lengthy response concluded, "Defendant was sentenced to a five year term of supervised release. The Defendant has been compliant and his participation in certain programs while on release is commendable. It does not, however, warrant termination his supervision which is less than fifty percent complete.

"Defendant was initially charged with two serious felony offenses and possessed a weapon during the commission of those offenses. Continued supervision by the Court is reasonable, necessary, and rationally related to deterring criminal conduct and protecting the public. There is no indication that supervision is in some way detrimental to defendant's continued success. Defendant should be commended for the strides he has made on probation thus far, but due to the lack of any special or exceptional circumstances, the Government opposes early termination."

After United States District Judge James C. Mahan heard the arguments from the public defender's office and from the U.S. government he ordered the following:

"In the instant petition, defendant moves to terminate his supervised release three years early. In support of the motion, defendant argues that he has been in complete compliance with all of the conditions of supervised release, has maintained stable employment, participates in programs targeting at-risk youth, and is devoted to becoming a productive member of society. Additionally, defendant argues his supervised release is detrimental to his ability to take short-term job opportunities to chauffeur and provide security service to high-profile individuals, which require travel out of the state on short notice ..."

"The court agrees that compliance with the conditions of supervised release is expected and, alone, is not reason for early termination. However, the defendant has gone beyond mere compliance; he has maintained steady employment, is active in the community, and has dedicated himself to becoming a productive member of society. After consideration of the aforementioned ... factors, the court finds that early termination is warranted at this time."

On October 22, 2013, I was at work when I received a call. "Mr. Torres?" the voice said on phone. "This is Heidi Ojeda from the Federal Public Defender's office. Congratulations, you are a free man. Your termination of supervision was granted." When I heard the news my heart skipped a beat; I couldn't believe it. I thanked Heidi and, after I hung up the phone, I pulled my car to the side of the road. Tears of joy filled my eyes. After nearly 18 years, I was a free man.

I later received a text from my probation officer, Casey Anderson. It read: "Congratulations, you are a free man. I will email you the official letter from the court. Oh, and you get your voting rights back and you can now apply for a passport."

Me: "Thank you very much. Tears of joy are flowing from my eyes."

Casey: "Don't cry. LOL. Good luck, Ray. I just ask one thing of you. Keep working with those kids."

Me: "Working with those kids is a part of my life. I will, Casey. Thanks for all you've done."

Afterword

This book came about after sharing my life's stories with at-risk-youth behind the walls of prison. The "thank you" letters and the letters of commendation I received from youth counselors, prison staff members and members of the community made me ask the question, "How can I share my story with others who are not only in the prison system but also those who are all over the world?" I wanted to write this book so I could publicly apologize to those who I have wronged in the past. In addition, I wanted to clear Wayne Newton's name of any involvement in the artwork-for-cocaine transaction that put me in prison. I hope my stories of bad choices will deter those who are engaged in a criminal lifestyle and prevent them from making the same mistakes that caused me and my loved ones many hardships.

I am a true believer that, though a person starts off in life making wrong choices, God is able to turn that life around and use it for His good. I believe God spared my life from drowning in that pool as a child, He protected me from the mean streets of Los Angeles and He was there with me through my years in prison. I believe God allowed me to go through hardships so I can share my experiences with the youth who may be headed down that destructive path that I once walked. I truly believe that if a person who wants to change their life is presented with the right opportunity, it can have an impact on that person's entire life and the lives with whom he or she comes into contact. Prison can make a man bitter or better. I chose to become better.

God has brought me a long way in such a short amount of time. Two years and eight months after my release from prison, I was blessed to buy my own home and God has restored the years that were lost. God is able to bring a man who has become a mess and turn him into a man of success. I have been given a second chance at life and I want to live it with purpose. I am thankful for all the hard times that I went through because they helped mold me into a man; they directed me to living a law-abiding and purpose-filled life. God is the true author of my life's story. I am forever grateful of His forgiveness and His mighty works.

Acknowledgements

I would like to thank those who have been supportive in giving me a second chance in life. I thank all those who were by my side through the years I spent in prison. A big thank-you to Mr. and Mrs. Jimmerson who gave me a chance to prove myself as a professional chauffeur in the industry.

SOURCES

High school students who drop-out (Education Week, Children Trends Database: Research Date 1, 1, 2014)

Ga n g V i o l e n c e www.fbi.gov/about-us/cjis/ucr/crime-in-the-u.s/2011/crime-in-the-u.s.-2011/tables/table-1

Overdosing - (Centers for Disease Control and Prevention)

Suicide is the third-leading cause of death (Centers for Disease Control and Prevention (CDC)." SOURCES: Brame, R. Pediatrics, study received ahead of print.Robert Brame, PhD, professor of criminal justice and criminology, University of North Carolina, Charlotte.Robert Sege, MD, PhD, professor of pediatrics, Boston University. Journal Pediatrics

Study: Nearly 1 in 3 U.S. youths will be arrested by age 23, December 19, 2011, By Rita Rubin, CBSNEWS

For speaking engagement/bookings go to: TheChauffeurbook.com

To Cristen,

God is good
you be too

Phil: 4:13

Made in the USA
San Bernardino, CA
28 August 2017